THE VICTIM AND
ITS MASKS

ABDELLAH HAMMOUDI

The Victim and Its Masks

AN ESSAY ON SACRIFICE AND MASQUERADE IN THE MAGHREB

Translated by Paula Wissing

The University of Chicago Press
Chicago and London

Abdellah Hammoudi is professor of anthropology and Near Eastern studies at Princeton University.

The University of Chicago Press, Chicago 60637
The University of Chicago Press, Ltd., London
© 1993 by The University of Chicago
All rights reserved. Published 1993
Printed in the United States of America
02 01 00 99 98 97 96 95 94 93   5 4 3 2 1

ISBN (cloth): 0–226–31525–8
ISBN (paper): 0–226–31526–6

Originally published as *La Victime et ses masques:
Essai sur le sacrifice et la mascarade au Maghreb,*
© Éditions du Seuil, November 1988

Library of Congress Cataloging-in-Publication Data

Hammoudi, Abdellah.
    [Victime et ses masques. English]
    The victim and its masks : an essay on sacrifice and masquerade in the Maghreb / Abdellah Hammoudi : translated by Paula Wissing.
        p.   cm.
    Includes index.
    ISBN 0-226-31525-8. —ISBN 0-226-31526-6 (pbk.)
    1. Berbers—Morocco—Middle Atlas Mountains—Rites and ceremonies.   2. Middle atlas Mountains (Morocco)—Religious life and customs.   3. Islam—Morocco—Middle Atlas Mountains.   4. Morocco—Social life and customs.   I. Title.
DT328.M53.H3613   1993
394.2'68297'0964—dc20   93-44672
                                                                                                        CIP

This book is printed on acid-free paper.

Contents

Preface to the English Edition

This book discusses the Sunni Muslim feast of sacrifice as it is locally practiced among North African Berbers and the masquerade which follows that sacrifice and closes the ritual cycle.

Previous anthropological works described the sacrifice as "orthodox" and the masquerade as a pagan "survival." It was taken for granted that these shared no common ground, and the separate accounts given of each denied implicitly or explicitly that a relation between the two obtained. Thus, anthropologists, paradoxically and perhaps unwittingly, lent support to one of the recurrent claims of Muslim militants who have a vested interest in presenting the masquerade as a dangerous accretion that threatens the purity of true religion.

Presented here, in contrast, is a "thick description" that considers as a single, nondivisible ritual process the masquerade that parodies and contests central values and institutions which sacrifice purports to sanctify and legitimize. Working with the metaphors of stage and play, the study shows how each part of the ceremony produces discourses that censor rival ones, but to no avail, because there is always an "other scene" in which occulted discourses strike back. All of the scenes in this theater of regulated improvisation articulate contradictory sets of statements and witness to their irreconcilable character. They attest to both the necessity of ideals and norms, and the impossibility, even the danger, of abiding by rules governing cherished values in religion, community, marriage, and so on.

Ritual appears here as a prepared, indeed rehearsed, course of action, yet it also stages an ad hoc interpretation of a common script constantly rewritten by the actors. These enactment-discourses work against closure. If emotion is generated, it is within this creative display of tacic consensus. Sacrifice and masquerade meet and collide—at the turn of each passing year—as a rite of passage that obviously brings diachrony and synchrony together. The rite puts exemplary figures of past times on a present-day stage. Yet a purely structural analysis would miss the main point: the stage does not bridge the gap between then and now; on the contrary, the gap is brought vividly to the fore in poetic commentaries on particular misfits of this particular society.

The untenable distinction between sacrifice and masquerade contested in this account was a mainstay of colonial assumptions. The dichotomy mir-

rored the division between Arabs and Berbers and their ultimate separation
as subjects of the French republic with different customs, beliefs, and identities. Fragmentation produced two separate entities considered irreconcilable. The postcolonial period simply transposes the dichotomy to a principle of exclusion. For islamist discourses, there is no social fragmentation;
only a body of Muslims that needs to be brought back to the purity of its
faith. By positing the latter as an entity from which reality diverges, it sub-
sumes the colonial concept of fragmentation. When one realizes that colonial discourse also construed an "orthodox" Islam (identified with the Arabs) from which Berber practice diverged, one can only be struck by the fact
that these two "enemy" discourses—colonial and postcolonial—"recognize" each other.

Our enduring dichotomy presents irresolvable dilemmas to this investi-
gator. How can I, a male Moroccan anthropologist, whose mother tongue is
Arabic, whose culture and language are deeply fashioned by the encounter
between a brand of Arabic and Berber, and whose training and writing are
mostly in French, approach sacrifice and masquerade in a postcolonial era
still dominated by colonial universalisms?

I thought I could do so by contemplating the old historical gap between
myself as an other and as the Arabic-speaking actor who was a cultural
Arabo-Berber; and the new gap between myself and that self created by colonial and postcolonial changes: the French-educated old and new Arabo-
Berber. There is no stable and unchanging I, assured that he is meeting
an Other who can be clearly identified with a clear message to grasp and
write down for others to read. Although this book employs structuring notions such as sacrifice/*tfaska,* play/*la'b,* mask/*ujah,* Bilmawn/animal-man-
woman, Abraham/Bilmawn, stage/*la'b,* etc., these notions, I insist, do not
translate into each other completely. Rather they grab and cling to each
other by virtue of something I feel as my will and my choice, even though
their working within the text implies the disappearance of myself as a
subject-writer.

In this fluid and often confused situation, an unbridgeable distance divides and undermines the anthropologist's ever-conflicting and dialogical
I's. And that distance resonates with the fragmenting, conflicting, and dialogical modes of being of the sacrifice-masquerade. The anthropologist is
then an actor among others playing on that scene. The group put on stage
regards itself through that distancing device. Similarly, the anthropologist
both looks and is looked at: the ritual process literally reveals him as distanced from what he thought was his culture. Like the sofa of the psycho-

analyst, the ritual reads him as the old Other (Arabo-Berber) and the new Other (Arabo-Berber, French, anthropologist, comparativist) distanced now—by borrowings from Europe—from the society he would interpret.

This engagement might produce a conversation between the anthropologist (plus his colleagues) and the observed society if the anthropologist and the society to which he belongs were not at each other's throats. Indeed, he is part of it, but alienated from many of its segments and central values. At this point, knowledge and social project emerge: the text, called *The Victim and Its Masks,* comes into being by recognizing otherness as within, as the defining condition of what we are today. Sacrifice-masquerade become in these pages something no one asked them to be before; something the villagers who enact them do not take them to be. But, if sacrifice-masquerade are to mean anything at all in the near future, they require transformation into a founding source for a new interpretive urge, testifying to our very remoteness from them. Anthropology as it is practiced here may mark a beginning for other responses to the entanglement between a new generation of writers and that which they can only take to be *their* customs and traditions with considerable *suspicion.*

Preface

My initial plans to work among the Ait Mizane accorded scant attention to the masquerade. It won its present place by stealth. It is difficult to explain that I set out to examine the relationship between a local society and its production techniques and found myself drawn instead into its ritual.

It is undoubtedly easier to record something that, like this open-air theater, appears to be offered directly, instead of doggedly searching for grudging answers about the organization of labor or the geographical origins of tools. For the first time, something akin to the very life of this society revealed itself to me. I was immediately captivated. The attraction these scenes held for me arises from the fascination that inheres in any deliberate imitation that is cognizant of the distance between itself and that which it represents.

My curiosity, piqued by an initial conversation, was fueled by my interlocutors' conflicting desires to speak and to keep silent. My cultural identity did the rest. Indeed, like the Ait Mizane, my collaborators and I confront issues raised by the coexistence of norms and the transgressions of these norms. The matter is urgent because of the consistency between ethics and behavior that is normally demanded—and equally pressing because of the status of change and mutation in this society.

Under what conditions does one become something other than oneself? Is such a transmutation even possible? As imaginary, utopian, or even "antinatural" as they may seem, the behaviors resulting from a creative metamorphosis do not cease to surprise and serve as a kind of rehearsal prior to the transformation of the real. Hence my wholehearted motivation not to miss any scenes of the dramatic spectacle that is presented in these pages. Particularly since the metamorphosis brought about by the masquerade overturns an initial situation consecrated by a rite operating at the very heart of the culture of my own society: Muslim sacrifice and its founding patterns.

My interest grew as the psychological and cultural stakes emerged and the outlines of the problem became more clear. Inescapably, the question came to be posed in these terms: How and under what conditions can one manifest this other that is oneself?

If there is no way to minimize the perils of such a dilemma, might it be possible to lay them out in a tangible way? Ait Mizane society is endowed with a particular energy, which makes it possible for some groups, with poetic elan, to make these risks visible. And on that point I would like to set myself apart from all of those who would insist on seeing in the masquerade nothing but obscenities, shame, and paganism which must be eradicated. I am not among those who believe that people are drawn into the masquerade because of this other who slumbers within them—this other who makes them do it—and that the masquerade must be confined to the intimacy of the village or quarter, far from the eyes of others, even if they too are part of the community.

The power of the Ait Mizane to project an image of themselves onstage, then, is admirable. Especially since in this look at themselves, and offered to themselves and others, there sparkles an irony and satire that have nothing to do with moralizing. Perhaps this is the living wellspring of a cultural creation based solely on humanity's effort to represent and evaluate itself.

First and foremost, this book is intended to be a recreation of this effort and an homage to those who make it possible—first and foremost to those Ait Mizane who granted me the privilege of attending their festival.

My thanks go as well to Mohamed Mahdi, who assisted with field surveys, and to Hamid Bennani, whose friendship sustained my first investigations. I am also indebted to him for the term "street theater," which he suggested after his initial contacts with the masquerade.

A preliminary version of this work was written in 1985 at the Institute for Advanced Studies in Princeton, New Jersey. I am grateful to this institution for the help and hospitality it extended to me and wish to express my gratitude to Clifford Geertz for his encouragement as well as for the frequent intellectual exchanges that have influenced this study.

Among colleagues and friends who offered their help and comments, I owe a special debt to Lucette Valensi, to whom I express all my gratitude, for her unstinting efforts in making it possible for this book to see the light of day in its present form. In addition, my warmest thanks to Abdelwahab Meddeb for his close reading of the manuscript and judicious comments on the economy of the whole.

In its present form this book is the product of revisions made in 1986 at the Wissenschaftskolleg zu Berlin. I particularly appreciated the criticisms and suggestions offered by some of my colleagues during this stay in Germany. The remarks that P. Von Sivers, C. Poni, and L. Zagari had the kindness to make were of particular help in the revision of the manuscript. I am indebted to J. Heilbron for his pertinent comments on the relationships between the French North African school and the founders of sociology in the metropole, as well as for his meticulous reading of the interpretive chapters.

B. Johansen, of the Freie Universität zu Berlin, was generous with his profound thoughts concerning Muslim law and rites and his methodological sense. His immense erudition was indispensable to my reading of ancient Arabic texts on sacrifice and Abrahamic traditions. I would like to express my profound gratitude and friendship to J. Heilbron and B. Johansen.

These friendly contacts were possible thanks to the situation provided by the Wissenschaftskolleg and the obliging hospitality of then-rector Pr. Wapnewski. Dr. J. Nettlbeck's comments and amicable support helped me organize the work and ready it for publication. His assistance was invaluable, and I warmly thank him for it.

At various points the observations of friends and colleagues I. and M. Bennouna, A. Felk, M. Grosser, R. Leveau, H. Rachik, P. Sanfacon, and A. Udovitch were precisely what was needed; I am most grateful to them. I am thankful to F. de Jong for his generous assistance on the matter of Egyptian popular festivals. Last, I wish to thank Jean-Luc Giribone, whose exacting critical comments helped me bring this work to its final form.

Mme Suzanne Sinton was kind enough to type the manuscript. My warmest thanks to her for her friendly collaboration, as well as to Mme Hélène Allaoui, who was gracious enough to read the proofs.

If despite all these friendly counsels, errors or poorly founded data persist in the present work, only my obstinacy is to blame. Like all else, they are my responsibility alone.

Note on Transcription

’   (*hamza,* glottal catch), found in the middle of the exclamation "uh-oh"

‘   (voiced pharyngeal), ex., *‘Ashura*

gh   pronounced like the French "r"; ex., *lghabt*

h   (aspirated laryngeal), ex., *Herrma*

ḥ   (pharyngeal); ex., *lḥurriyet, aḥwash*

kh   pronounced like German "ch," ex., *takhurbisht*

d   (voiced dental occlusive); ex., *Lafdur*

dh   (voiced interdental), like "th" in "the"; *dhu Lḥịjja*

q   (velar occlusive); ex., *Qaṣaṣ*

r   pronounced like a rolled "r"; ex., *‘Ara’is, takhurbisht*

s   (unvoiced aspirated dental); ex., *taffullust, fasiqin*

sh   English "sh'; ex., *aḥwash*

ṣ   emphatic; ex., *’aṣida*

ṭ   emphatic; ex., *ṭajine*

t   (unvoiced dental occlusive); ex., *talmqsurt*

ḍ   emphatic; ex., *ṣadaqa*

Proper nouns have been given in their English equivalents: Mohammed, Qadi, Ait Mizane, Shilha, etc.

Introduction

Goethe's remark about the Roman carnival could easily apply to the festival that I describe and interpret in this book. The festival is not something bestowed upon the villagers who take part in it; rather, it is they who create it for themselves.[1] And certainly the data used to support this statement could also be used to challenge it. In a sense, two festivals figure in what is described in these pages as a single celebration. And although, by an accepted signal, the second of these opens a period of gaiety and licentiousness far removed from the tone of the official and national celebrations, the first, indicated by words and gestures by the entire Muslim community and performed by ordinary believers and their leaders, is exemplified by the annual pilgrimage to Mecca.

This particular pairing of opposites occurs in the Maghreb and comprises the feast of the sacrifice (the 'id-Lekbir) and the masquerades that often follow it.[2] The long rite of the pilgrimage, one of the canonical obligations that every Muslim, if he has the means, owes it to himself to accomplish, culminates with the immolation of an animal victim. And even though no strictly canonical duty requires it, every believer in his own home simultaneously imitates the actions of those who sacrifice in the holy places of Islam.

Indeed, the blood sacrifice inaugurates a ritual cycle that will end some thirty days later with the ceremonies of the 'Ashura, a festival for the dead in which the participants give alms, eat dried fruit, and buy toys that the children of the community waste no time in appropriating. The sacrifice and the 'Ashura mark the passage of time; the first brings the old year to a close and the second opens the new year.

As many observers have noted, other festivities dominated by pranks and playful uproar frequently accompany these two solemn rites of the Muslim calendar. Depending on the location, either the sacrifice or the 'Ashura is surrounded by disguises, processions, and street theater in which the actors will not rest until they have violated the very norms that sacrifice and 'Ashura serve to establish. When these festivities occur after the sacrifice, as in the case that I describe below (chaps. 4–6), they are organized around a central character called Bujlud, Herrma, Bilmawn, or Bu-Islikhen, to mention only the most widespread names.[3] Wearing the very skins of the sacral-

1

ized, sacrificed animals, this obscene biped brings in his wake a varying
number of noisy and sacrilegious masked characters who seem bent on
obeying only their own inclinations.

The ritual of the blood sacrifice performed each year by Muslim families
extends far beyond the localized settings of the masquerades, processions,
and theater that follow it. Examples of these activities can be found elsewhere, notably in Algeria and Tunisia. But unlike the sacrifice, the diffusion
of their themes and forms does not coincide with the limits of the Islamic
world, and such practices are far from universal. Their resemblances to European and Euro-Mediterranean carnival themes, however, are striking.

Is it possible to maintain with some semblance of accuracy that the first
festival, the sacrifice, is something that has been granted to the participants?
Given the difficulty of directing it from above, the answer must be no. In
1954, when Morocco was in the throes of its struggle for independence,
only a few families sympathetic to French rule in North Africa performed
sacrifices. All Muslim practices, it will be noted, have put down local, popular roots, which makes the shift from badge of conformity to sign of rebellion an easy one. Consequently, it is not difficult to understand why the
government vigilantly controls all religious sites.

In any event, both celebrations are examined here as two parts of a single
whole, and that is the first point this study attempts to illustrate. Anthropologists have long been familiar with the ceremonies that I describe here,
and great scholars have produced works on the subject that cannot be ignored. Edmond Doutté, Emile Laoust, and Edward Westermarck, to mention only the most famous, have made lengthy contributions, often noted
for their precise detail and the breadth of theoretical imagination that they
display. Only Westermarck somewhat integrates the Muslim sacrifice into
his interpretation of the masquerade following it. None of them could depict what was kept hidden, and their accounts are spotty, marked by gaps in
the descriptions. What they did see is noted with precision. But their narratives seem to unfold as if they never sought to discover what went on
behind the scenes, nor even to observe systematically what took place before their eyes, in the street. They seem to act like a stroller who encounters
a band of jugglers and follows them down a lane, only to leave them, once
they turn a corner, without ever wondering if the troupe is going to repeat
the same act or start something new.

In fact, their neglect of Muslim sacrifice is the result of a view that sets it
in an urban, elite context associated with the Arab-Muslim state—in short,
for them it belonged to the world of "high culture." This leads to a disjunc-

tion that implies that elsewhere, especially in the mountainous country of the Berbers, the surviving festivals are of local peasant origin. Westermarck explicitly contrasts these celebrations with the Muslim rite and makes them into a ritual departure from the sacred; the French investigators stress that the two are totally separate and focus on the games and masquerades, which they see as pagan and pre-Islamic. Subtending all these developments is the hypothesis, so tied to the colonial situation, of a quasi-religion competing with Islam and vigorously alive under the mantle of superficial Islamicization. When method is subject to ideology in this way, part of the festival remains invisible; I would like to bring it to light in its full totality. And this restoration plays a decisive role in my interpretation of the whole. Undoubtedly, the scenes that the masked figures enjoy playing before their audience owe nothing to Islamic doctrine; and in the villages there are good Muslims who forcefully condemn them. However, in practice the scenes are, as we shall see, associated with an orthodox rite. One of the main lines of my argument is that the details of the masquerade cannot be made fully intelligible unless their connection with Muslim sacrifice is made clear.

This intelligibility is also closely tied to what I will call, for want of a better expression, the systematicity of the ethnographic account. It entails following the whole process, which for methodological purposes I consider to be a drama. This outlook postulates not only that the dramatic action begins with the Muslim ritual and ends with the spectacle, the procession, and the collective feast, but also that like any other dramatic production, it is preceded by a time of preparation. These preparations are the invisible part of the spectacle, just as they are at the theater or the opera. In the village, only young men, in a space jealously guarded from all intruders, can watch the make-up and costuming of the actors. While it is possible to appreciate a performance without attending the rehearsal, it does not seem possible to arrive at an understanding of the functioning of a theatrical performance or ceremony without rigorously observing what takes place offstage. For in the case considered here, the sequence carried out behind the scenes is a festival within a festival, and some of the themes that emerge more or less consistently at this point will be developed later on in the public space or else abandoned for reasons that will require explanation.

For simple reasons of convenience, but also because it forms a separate time that is clearly demarcated by the actors' entrance "onstage," these preparations occupy a distinct place in my account, just like the other discrete stages of the festival process. I willingly concede that approaching the description in this way is already tantamount to interpretation. But this method has the advantage of breaking the action up into sequences whose limits are clearly indicated by the actors themselves. This question has to be addressed each time it becomes necessary to legitimize the analytical breakdown of the action and the interpretation based on it. For the moment, it is merely necessary to note that the divisions appearing in my presentation will be justified by the rhythm of the events themselves.

In addition, my predecessors were unable to see what took place inside the houses or to observe the dances that took place during the evening. Undoubtedly, one has to take into consideration the nature of fieldwork as it was carried out in the early part of the century, in a region that identified the ethnographer, always a Christian or culturally assimilated, with the colonial powers. But the facts suggest that the discipline could not shake off the prejudice of the time, which is readily apparent in the disparity that is presented between Muslim solemnity (the sacrifice) and pagan games (the masquerade). Nonetheless, such "oversights" are perplexing, even though they could be attributed, among other things (and with some likelihood), to the way in which local informants were interviewed—though it never occurred to this generation of ethnographers to discuss fieldwork conditions. The reader will find an example (chap. 4) of one informant's account of the festival, compared to the data provided by direct and systematic observation; this will offer a better understanding of the logic governing the "omissions" mentioned above.

Before going into more detail about the aims of this study, it is necessary to locate the actions and events I will be describing and interpreting. The Ait Mizane, who live less than a two-hour drive from the city of Marrakech, like Muslims the world over celebrate each year the feast of the sacrifice of the 10 dhu-Lhijja. In 1983, the year I observed these rituals for the last time, this date fell in the second half of the month of September.[4] Nothing out of the ordinary took place at this ceremony, except some local details that are given below, and the fact that a part of the prayers were said in Shilha Berber, which is the language of the Ait Mizane and all their neighbors to the north, extending to where the valleys open onto the Marrakech plain. In the morning the common prayer followed by individual sacrifices is carried out in an atmosphere of ritual purity, recollection, and gravity; in the afternoon and evening, the viscera of the sacrificed animals are eaten. The ensuing days are spent enjoying the victim's flesh, which is generally cooked in a stew. People keep late hours, contrary to their usual habit, and visits between families continue unabated. Everyone dons his holiday best, and children enjoy unlimited freedom.

The high spirits and good humor of those who are feasting and visiting offer a contrast to the atmosphere surrounding the sacrifice. But this is not the most noticeable difference. Still enjoying this atmosphere of abundance and relaxation, the young men (both newly married and single) devote themselves on the following day to their own festival, which in their eyes excludes both the older and younger generations; and they demand and obtain the participation of the girls and married women. A masquerade complete with theatrics, procession, and quest will occupy the village for three days. Theoretically, the "old folks" are excluded. The young take over, and they savor, along with the meat that is such a rarity at other times, what some of them here call the "time of freedom" *(lḥurriyet)*.

The description and interpretation of this whole, the sacrifice and the masquerade, comprise the central subject of this book, occupying parts 1 and 2 respectively. A systematic ethnography of the feast requires the presentation of earlier accounts (chap. 1). Although these efforts often went beyond simple narrative and included elaborate theorizing, today it will be agreed that the descriptions of my predecessors are of much more interest than their hypotheses, which are largely unfounded. These accounts familiarize us with ludic and ritual figures and form a rich tapestry that serves as a backdrop for the case presented here.

My description has been enriched to some extent by these earlier accounts and is better able to utilize what my predecessors were unable to bring to it. These deficiencies include their silence concerning the restrictions and the trump cards that give the participants choices for action. These variables, which shape the players' attitudes as well as their decisions, depend as much on their perceptions of their physical and social surroundings as on the cultural tools that organize it. Therefore, I have accorded the choices facing the actors the same importance as the feast itself (chaps. 2–7) and have described both at the same time; for the feast is only one kind of action among others. However, notions related to local theories about the material and invisible world are naturally included for clarification each time the exposition calls for them. Thus, instead of beginning with a simple cosmology and exegesis that, as will be seen, reduce the ritual to what can be contained within them, I hope to evoke a living context in which the action creates its meaning.

In fact, my approach takes these earlier descriptions of the sacrifice and masquerade to task, but not merely to call attention to their ideological and methodological omissions, errors, and biases. In addition, I intend to offer a systematic and in-depth description of a production by which this society says something about itself, just as it expresses and manifests itself through this process. These objectives include first of all the search for the relationship between this society and its drama, taken in their specificity and locality, as revealed in the observation of the festival in two village communities. Whatever their differences with respect to comparable festivals found elsewhere, it is the overall hypothesis of this book that the relationship expressed between these celebrations and the societies that enact them is of the same type that emerges from the description and analysis of the festivals of the Ait Mizane.

These societies share the aim of self-parody and utilize a script that can be compared despite differences in theme, identity of the characters and means used to represent them, and the rhythm and general economy of the scene. Underlying the action is clearly a matrix that, in the course of the "play," is capable of expanding, transforming, and heading off in every direction as it suits the actors' circumstances and personal resources. This flexibility gives it the means to attract all the talents of the group, as well as a surprising sensitivity to events. The account of the whole action as observed is immediately preceded by two individual narratives of the masquerade, provided by actors who happened to take part in it (chap. 4). The gap between these scenarios and what is actually performed in the drama makes it possible to see the extraordinary way in which the action develops from the basic matrix.

This sort of description is akin to and borrows from what Clifford Geertz defines as "thick description," from which it retains a taste for microscopic and detailed examination that constantly refers to the participants' actual doings and their cultural frames of reference.[5] However, I intend to furnish a clearer perception of the larger constraints that it indicates in the actors' system of reference. For example, the scarcity of food, the size of the group and its relation to resources, sexual segregation, and last, the relationships between men and women and among generations will all be discussed to account for the action described. Certainly, it will be admitted that most of the time such frameworks and constraints are unconscious. Yet they govern the shape of each act, even if they rarely appear to the actors as clearly formulated ideas. Nor does the observer directly perceive them as such. He is able to detect them because of his own referential system, by the analysis of the concrete but ephemeral actions of the human group.

At this point I would like to propose the term *reference* to denote the cultural frames of reference and what, for want of a better word, I have referred to broadly as "data" and "constraints." What human actions refer to will be conscious or unconscious, depending on the situation, and will pertain to what they have thought out and developed or simply to what is acted and undergone as a fact of structure.

The description of people and places found in the ethnography of the festival is an effort to provide the principal features of this structure. To accomplish this I stress not a theory of geographical conditions or social organization but instead focus on human actions in the real world, in part as they occur within and resist these geographic constraints, and in part as they occur as a result of and despite this social organization. At this stage— and throughout this book—the notion of structure guiding my argument refers to a combination of tensions and solutions—always provisional— between the elements of the material and mental context that the participants provide for themselves and within (and against) which they act in order to organize their existence.

When they reach the awareness of those who act upon them, these tensions and their solutions form the rules of the game; they also determine the game when the actors are unaware of them or lack any direct connection with them. This is to say, on the one hand, that here structure is inferred from concrete action and the institutions and organizations through which it is realized and, on the other, that it is in constant motion. The difficulty lies in grasping the dynamic pertaining to each that Georges Gurvitch used to call the different "stages" of social reality. Changes in technology— transportation, for example—have been extremely fast in the valley, since within fifty years people have abandoned (though not entirely, it must be said) animal or human modes of transport in favor of the automobile. Yet votive sacrifice or the concepts concerning the difference between the sexes seem immutable. The alterations affecting these are so slow that without modifying the scale of observation it is impossible to ascertain their movement. In this context, the invariable is simply that which changes very slowly.

People possess views and norms that explain and justify their external, everyday actions. Most often, of course, these are implicit. Whether implicit or explicit, however, they must be described with the same attention as the objects for which they furnish both a justification and a meaning in the eyes of the actors. At this stage, a simple preliminary presentation of a society in its surroundings, as well as later on, when the festival is described and interpreted, it becomes clear that among these rules are those which simultaneously govern ordinary actions, the acts presented in the drama, and the production itself. As is the case when dealing with facts about the environment and social organization, I seek to uncover intelligible groupings without first imposing any system on them. And I will not situate this analysis on the level of any fundamental structures of the human mind, either. For there too, if these exist, they must emerge out of the tensions and consistencies among these rules or groups of norms in use: in other words, as guides, frameworks, and constraints through which strategies for action either succeed or fail.[6]

Is there some relationship between ordinary strategies and those of the festival? Why do the second interrupt, disturb, or violate the first? And, finally, what is the meaning of the festival and the means it employs? These are the three principal questions that sum up and define the objectives pursued throughout this book.

By the end of my observations, I came to see these ceremonies essentially as a commentary, played out in either words or deed, that society makes about itself by means of the sacrifice and masquerade, two activities whose alliance, in the midst of the same ritual and dramatic grouping, only seems paradoxical. The rest of my analysis, indeed, reveals the profound connections between these two events, which in every way appear to be opposites. Beyond the differences between them, the two structures on which they are based echo one another, and behind the masquerade one finds clues leading to a system that develops a whole discourse on sacrifice. Finally, the sacrifice itself is endowed with some of the forces that the masks bring onstage.

The act that serves as the founding gesture of civilization, sacrifice, is brought into contemporary life; while the masquerade, under the pretext of destroying the existing order, in fact hearkens back to the original foundations. Each one lays out and coordinates not one but several discourses, some of which are always present in the minds of the actors while others seem to inhabit a latent space beyond their grasp. This is doubtless the case, for example, of the place of women in this scenario, in which everything transpires as if in response to a wish to transcend the structural contradiction between a patriarchal system and the physical reproduction of lineages. At the heart of this debate is no insoluble intellectual dilemma, but part of the stakes that can be revealed by analysis, which, if it is attentive to the concrete interplay of symbols on stage, keeps from reducing them to abstract terms.

This approach is far removed from the Frazerian legacy of evolutionary comparativism that the French North African school applied to the festival in the early years of this century, and from the eclectic functionalism with which Westermarck attempted to contest it. Since Westermarck allowed his analysis to encompass functionalist arguments, without first listening to what these writers said and attending to the means they used to say it, he paradoxically found himself assigning the same function both to the sacrifice and to the joyous theater that follows it: contact with the sacred, the expulsion of evil, the departure from the sacred, and so on. In short, his work displayed the very formalism of Hubert and Mauss, which it continues. For one could well ask, and with good reason, it seems, what such a "departure from the sacred" would mean for a society that instead seeks permanent contact with God—with the beneficent sacred that controls dangerous forces. Also, because of his eclecticism, Westermarck constantly allies this functionalism with the hypothesis that this festival represents the survival of an old paganism, resulting in the same hypothetical reconstructions of a primitive Berber religion to which a number of French scholars were so attached, particularly Edmond Doutté and Emile Laoust.

Indeed, following in Frazer's footsteps, Doutté and Laoust reduce the masquerade to fertility magic and the reproduction of natural cycles. This leads them to dissociate the sacrifice from the masquerade, on the one hand, and on the other, as we have seen, to seek their historical antecedents. In contrast, my approach abandons this arena. Not that it is necessary to deny the recurring themes linked to fertility, happiness, and the preservation of the group's good fortune; or that it is always impossible to trace the genealogy of customs. But in addition to the fact that in the case I observed I saw no one engage in sympathetic magic, it must be recognized that the "historical" stages according to which Doutté and Laoust claimed to reconstitute primitive religion are totally imaginary. Historical proof is sparse, and it is necessary to resort to heroic visions to invent the links between scattered facts, whose very rarity underscores our ignorance.

Of course it would be impossible for anyone observing the crazy behavior of Bilmawn and his odd pals in the village streets not to think of the Saturnalia and other ancient Mediterranean festivals. But even supposing that such an origin were one day to be established, first of all, it is unlikely that such a connection would contribute anything to our understanding of today's celebration. Second, today's celebration is related to the life that unfolds before our eyes in ways that should not be neglected in favor of vain and chancy reconstructions.

Despite all its failings, the mass of ethnographic data gathered by my predecessors deserves ample attention. It offers an opportunity to view the

phenomenon in its diverse manifestations, while behind and subtending
these differences the unique matrix I postulated earlier emerges all the more
clearly.

The Bilmawn depicted by the ethnologists in the first third of the twentieth century finds an echo in the Bilmawn that is narrated by two participants in the drama, which unfolds as a veritable script. Indeed, the scenes
reported early on by Mouliéras and others already suggest the presence of a
plot. Strangely, this is somewhat obscured in later accounts; however, these
reports are more often the result of direct, on-site observations. Undoubtedly, the nature of the portrait transmitted by earlier investigators is partly
the result of their reliance upon informants far from the scene and, in the
case of Mouliéras, of his own distance from the groups under study. But it
seems equally clear that the concepts and approaches that inform the works
of the time contributed to a separation of the components of a process that
my approach, on the contrary, seeks to grasp as a whole. The accounts of
the two participants are followed by a summary of the data that my collaborators and I observed, in which the entirety emerges as a theatrical performance having a script and action behind the scenes in addition to its own
staging. In this living totality, finally, one must not fail to note extraneous
details, the stakes that the game never totally eliminates from the scene.
This last characteristic of the festival distinguishes it from the theater and
its conventions and so conditions my reading of the whole.

Part 2 is devoted to interpreting the data, which in this instance are supported by comparisons with data from other areas. Not Morocco or even
North Africa but the world at large furnishes material to compare with our
own. The nature and dynamic of my search leads to the popular festivals
and carnivals of Europe, to rites of other societies that mark transitions, and
finally, to certain Greek rituals as they can be seen in the fine works of the
classical authors. Among all these examples, most interesting are those
which, despite many differences, seem to point to the same goal that animates the festival of the Ait Mizane. But simply comparing data is a dangerous approach, which has been condemned many times for reasons that do
not need repeating here. I seek instead to utilize the lessons offered by other
experiences to shed some light on my own observations. The differences
and likenesses that will not fail to appear will offer clues to what is specific
to this particular case. For my objective is first of all to understand what the
festival I am reconstructing is saying and what, in it and by it, the participants say to or about themselves. Once this is achieved, the next step is to

demonstrate the interaction of this festive ritual life with the society that produces it.

The course of my analysis traverses several major schools of thought. It remains attentive to the context and does not neglect any of the external markers that situate the discourse of the festival and the masquerade, particularly those which concern local societies (villages, valleys, linguistic groups) and relate by means of conflict or assimilation to global society and the habitual or scholarly systems of ideas by which this society organizes its action and its knowledge. Not that the internal structure of the festival will be ignored. But the festival is neither a bundle of logical propositions nor the resolution of the contradictions among these propositions. Both can be found there. Indeed there is no proof that these two elements form the basis of the narrative, even if it is true that they can provide the rules and the basic materials for it. Like most logical categories, they are empty rules that say nothing in and of themselves. Last, to speak of a project or an intention is to say that the festive action aims to realize an ideal, satirical, burlesque, or monstrous image of what it utilizes. Comparing these images with the images that govern ordinary life takes the relationship between festival and society further, by sidestepping the theory of reflection and its opposite, the theory of the festival's ontological status.

TOWARD A SYSTEMATIC ETHNOGRAPHY OF THE FESTIVAL

I

Colonial Anthropology on the Sacrifice and the Masquerade

In Search of a Lost Religion

1

The rituals, games, and masquerades that mark the annual cycle in the Maghreb, particularly in Morocco, began attracting the interest of outside observers in the late nineteenth century. Most of them were French, of course, because of that longstanding imperialist presence in the area; the notable exception is Edward Westermarck, who is discussed later in this chapter. As for Arab works of history, if I am not mistaken they breathe not a word of the festivals celebrated beyond the bounds of the official Muslim calendar. Are the traditional condemnations made by various Muslim literati on the subject of popular traditions, which were all classified under the general and commodious term "common customs," allusions to these celebrations? Their remarks never went beyond simple invective; too shocking or too familiar, these practices never moved North African intellectuals to take up their pens. In the early sixteenth century, Leo the African, alias al-Ḥasan ibn Muḥammad ibn al-Wazzan, makes note of the bonfires in Fez.[1] But at that point he was writing in Italian, as a convert to Christianity who had changed his name and begun a new life. In other words, he was writing as a Roman intellectual, brought up in the care of a papacy avid for information about Muslim societies.

Indeed, all revelations of the North African masquerades are the work of outsiders. The celebrations take place just about everywhere: in the Atlas Mountains, the plains of north Morocco, the Jbala, and the Rif. And they are not confined to rural areas, for observations are equally abundant concerning traditionally great urban centers such as Fez and Marrakech. In Algeria they occur in Ouargla, in the Aurès Mountains, and elsewhere. Laoust describes them in Tunisia, following the example of Monchicourt, who witnessed them in the Karouan region. Their trail leads into Lybia and beyond into Egypt.[2]

In Morocco most of these events take place between the great Feast of the Sacrifice and the feast of the Muslim New Year. In dialectal Arabic these two ceremonies are called 'id-Lekbir and 'Ashur, respectively; in Berber the second goes by the same name and the sacrifice is called *tfaska*. This is a particularly sacred time in the Muslim calendar. Since it is a lunar system, as mentioned earlier, this calendar has to be coordinated with the Julian calendar (or *filaḥi*), which in North Africa governs agricultural activities. These two months, known as dhu-Lḥijja and Muḥarram in the scholarly calendar, are marked by the pilgrimage to Mecca, the sacrifice, and the feast of the New Year.[3] All these rites occur during a forty-day period (between the first day of dhu-Lḥijja and the tenth of Muḥarram), highly charged with religious meaning, which culminates in the pilgrimage to the holy sites of Islam and the sacrifice and closes with the celebration of the New Year.

The processions and masquerades fall exactly between the sacrifice and the New Year's celebration, most often coinciding with the former in the country and more closely associated with the latter in town; like the sacrifice and New Year's festival, they signal a temporal transition. This is an observation that nearly all writers on the subject utilize as proof that these festivals are ancient pagan ceremonies for the renewal of nature which have come to be integrated into the Muslim calendar.

The nature of the symbols and other elements in these festivals certainly lends plausibility to the idea. This is not surprising; syncretisms propounding encounters between religious and cultural systems appear everywhere. However, the problem with the entire French North African school (who on the other hand are responsible for the finest descriptions of the masquerades) lies in their insistence of the notion of "survivals." Such an approach automatically dissociates pagan and Muslim festivals or, when it recognizes the links between them, denies the specificity of the latter to compare them to the meaning it claims to find in the former. This view obscures not only the significance of each festival but, perhaps even more seriously, conceals the meaning of their coexistence and dialectic within the same ritual process.

Beginning in the 1920s, this theoretical orientation, reinforced by the prejudices of the day, was contested by Edward Westermarck, who based his approach on the school of the *Année sociologique*. It is not necessary to summarize all these surveys here. Some of them are representative of the whole and make it possible to underscore the contributions and controversies and set them in their own context.

What Mouliéras calls the Djebalian carnival, a name that has been in use since the late nineteenth century, takes place after the sacrifice and lasts for three days.[4] The action can be described as two main activities: a round of questing that the author calls "a round of begging," and a series of scenes played in front of the houses by actors, all male Muslims disguised as several traditional characters. Both events are ongoing and form a single whole rather than two separate processes. The village population, which is also the audience, follows them both; sometimes they enter into the action, as when they pelt one or more of the characters with missiles.[5]

The masked figures take everything that is given them and play their scenes in front of each house:

The carnival takes place only once a year. It lasts for three days and coincides with the great Feast of Sacrifices. The first day, the masks spread out through the village, around noon, and they begin their round of begging, stopping in front of each lodging, incessantly replaying their filthy farces, after which they receive what people choose to give them: bread, meat, eggs, chickens, grain. Needless to say, the whole village is at their heels, surrounding them, admiring them, shouting with joy when they hear a joke more ribald than the rest.[6]

These "masks" represent ten characters: Ba-Shikh or Old Man Papa,[7] who for Mouliéras is equivalent to Carnival; his wife; the Ass; the Negress; the Jew and his wife the Jewess; the Qadi (Muslim judge); the Qa'id (governor); and the Guards. Ba-Shikh is a horny old man with a white beard, dressed in "sordid rags" wearing a "goatskin in the form of a hat" and counting a rosary of snailshells. His genitals are prominent: "A strip of woolly sheepskin and two eggplants between his legs serve as his reproductive organs." An "effeminate darling" in disguise plays his wife, with a hollow gourd for a female face and two others for breasts; last, a pot of tar "represents the perfumes of the Djebalian woman." The person playing the ass wears on his head a "veritable ass's skull, bleached and dried out and displaying formidable jaws and teeth." Two large stones sewn into two sacks and a club blackened with tar serve as his genitals.[8] The Jew is dressed in a filthy and disgusting burnoose; he wears the distinctive skullcap, and two cows' tails serve as the "temporal locks of the children of Israel." He must constantly dodge the blows sent his way, and he weeps and carries on. His wife protects him. She wears two gourds for breasts, and her body and face are painted with whitewash. The judge, on the contrary, is majestic with his enormous turban, which is maintained by a complex system of cords, and his rosary of snailshells. Under his arm a block of cork represents the holy Koran, which he uses to pronounce judgments that invariably contradict the most elemental common sense. The governor's face is bearded and "hideous." He wears a long red cap and keeps brandishing his saber ferociously. A complete set of pots and pans is at his feet. Finally, there are his guards: "sabers drawn, their faces menacing and full of hatred, disguised like their chief the qa'id, they wait for a word or a glance from their master to hurl themselves on their chosen victim." [9]

The negress and the thief are supernumeraries in the episodes performed by these characters. Here as well the scenes are of two main types: a satire on local mores, and scenes that turn the norms of ordinary life upside down. In the case Mouliéras describes, the reversal is primarily connected with religious life.

The governor sets his guards upon the victims he pressures. His favorite pastimes are prevarication and food. The old satyr Ba-Shikh is obsessed with his declining sexual prowess and is ready for action at a moment's notice. His wife drags him before the judge, who pronounces the divorce decree and, in same session, reads out the act of his own marriage to her! The husband then proposes a compromise: they will share her: "One heads, one tails." [10] The negress kneads mud to make bread and fixes couscous; as for the thief, he incessantly tries his tricks and, invariably caught and thrown into jail, he is at it again the moment he is released.

Like Ba-Shikh, the Jew is a repulsive old man, protected but also abused by his wife, who berates him for his impotence. They both speak Arabic with the accent and vocabulary of Moroccan Jews, pronouncing *s* as *sh*. The wife drags her spouse before the judge. Complaint: "His soul is dead" (he is impotent). The magistrate condemns the poor fellow "to mount her ten times a night" on pain of jail! Meanwhile, Ba-Shikh, still obsessed, mounts his wife. He is unsuccessful and begs her to guide him. She opens a sack into which he disappears; he comes out crying with fright, "That's not a vagina! It's a well, and I'm afraid of drowning and getting stuck in there!" [11]

These are the scenes that can be classed as satire. The use of inversion can be seen in the prayers, which are transformed from top to bottom. Everyone gathers to pray, except for the Jewish couple and the thief. Ba-Shikh makes his ablutions on his wife's face and the other faithful wash the ass's head. [12] They turn their backs to Mecca. The words of the judge who leads the prayer are gross and obscene instead of coming from the holy Book. Everything is done backward, and even people's hands, ordinarily joined for the invocations, are turned outward.

Mouliéras makes note of the fact that the activities thus described take place after the sacrifice. But he is vague concerning the origin of the skin that covers the head of the principal actor. Later the full importance of this detail will be seen. Indeed, he is silent about the man wearing the skins. Westermarck, visiting the same regions that Mouliéras describes on the basis of information gleaned from informants as far away as Oran, remarks that often a character disguised in the skins from the sacrifice appears next to Ba-Shikh.[13] This suggests a singular likeness to the ceremonies that I will describe in the Upper Atlas.

Above all, Mouliéras's description is limited to the scenes played in the streets, for which he proposes no interpretation. Some racist value judgments concerning the corruption of Moroccon society and power, which France must reform (the time of the conquest is drawing near), and a vague indication of origins serve as a frame of reference for his description. Thus he misses the poetic satire and carnivalesque grandeur of the spectacle, in which he sees "only a dissolute and abject game that was perhaps modeled on the ancient Saturnalia of the Roman people."[14]

Three key themes emerge here, then: the corruption of this society and the power that governs it; the coarseness and bawdiness indicative of a primitive or decadent state of morals; the memory of Roman customs. While the first themes will be more or less forgotten in later works, the notion of the survival of Roman and Christian customs, and especially that of an original Berber religion, will enjoy great popularity in the ethnographic literature of the first third of the twentieth century. This view has the advantage that it either avoids the issue of the relationship between these customs and Islam or that it emphasizes the tension between them. Westermarck among others will insist on what he calls the challenging of Muslim orthodoxy.[15] Edmond Doutté and later Emile Laoust set out on a quest for the primitive religion of the Berbers, believing they were able to reconstruct it from the "debris" that in their view can be detected in the annual festival cycle.

I will confine my discussion to these three writers. Not that they were the only ones to depict the masquerades. Others, such as Aubin and Diarnay, devote captivating pages to them as well—the former concerning a spectacle observed in Fez noted for its use of inversion and satire, and the latter about a tribe of the North where scenes comparable to those mentioned by Mouliéras take place.[16] However, the interpretations proposed by Doutté, Westermarck, and Laoust are the most coherent, and Laoust places Bilmawn in a ritual cycle that marks the various stages of the calendar.

In Marrakech, where Doutté made his observations, Bujlud appears in the streets the morning after the sacrifice, as is the case in Fez; but, just as in the capital of precolonial Morocco where Aubin saw it, the great entertainment (*fraja*) is given on the occasion of the 'Ashura, before the head of state or his governor. Doutté reports that in 1907 the same spectacle, which had been given at the sultan's court, was held at the court of the pretender Bu Hamara who, as is known, fought against the reigning dynasty and was trying to replace it in the name of protecting the country and the Muslim community from Christian domination.[17] Such a convergence between a legitimate but contested authority and a competing power reveals the institutionalization of the festival as a sign and prerogative of sovereignty. Perhaps this is why it has the character of a revue that lays out the whole of society before the prince's eyes; furthermore, a reading of Eugène Aubin's work suggests that this sovereign witnesses the portrait of a world whose boundaries coincide with those of the "fortunate Kingdom." [18] And according to Doutté, in this depiction satire, which spares not even the court, never loses its rights:

> In Marrakech, *Herema Bou Jloûd* is given at the *Aïd el-Kebir,* but it is at the *'Achoura* that the masquerades, and above all the little dramas, take place in the open air; this custom is highly developed, and some real comic gems are performed, particularly before the sultan. Indeed, the actors enter the court of the *mechouar,* and there satirical scenes, often full of wit, take place; like those performed everywhere else, they feature the qadi and the burlesque trial, but the greatest success is reserved for the European ambassador, with his mock interpreter and secretaries; and especially the ministers, who are directly portrayed and cleverly ridiculed; this satiric liberty is all the more remarkable in that it most often takes place before the very ministers it satirizes, and some of them are rather uncomfortable; but their colleagues and the sultan roar with laughter, and they have no choice but to put a good face on it.[19]

The spectacle recorded by Aubin and Doutté is a creation of the towns. Mouliéras depicts a rural event. In spite of everything, it is possible to note a distance between this "pioneer" of Moroccan colonization and his two heirs. The later works are characterized by a decrease in value judgments and a cooler sense of observation. Several scenes and characters appear in both areas: the qadi's comical, burlesque judgments, obscenities, and satires concerning the agents of the state. But the rural "theater" gives more place to sexual excess and the specter of impotence that age inflicts upon men.

Serving as a kind of complement to the description provided by Mouliéras, who concentrates on the north of the country, is the work of Doutté, who depicts the festival among the Rehamna, in the south and on the outskirts of Marrakech. There, too, in fact, the masquerade takes place not on the 'Ashura but on the Great Feast of the Sacrifice.

The scenes, which strongly recall those of the Jbala, revolve around the adventures of Herrma and Azzuna, his Jewish fiancée. The horny old goat vainly tries to "cover" her. But she is stubborn and insatiable. Hence the trial and judgment given by the qadi, who succumbs to the young woman's charms. At the end of the spectacle, the crowd leaps upon Bujlud, pretending to kill him. A procession and quest are other aspects of this version of the drama.[20]

Knowledge about the masquerades, which had already received rich contributions, comes into its heyday during the 1920s with the highly detailed and well presented surveys of Emile Laoust and Edward Westermarck. Laoust pursues his research along the lines of Doutté and, following in his master's footsteps, applies Frazerian hypotheses to the "Berber carnival." Westermarck is more concerned with concrete observation and contests the overall interpretations of his French colleagues.

Laoust's remarkable work on Berber linguistics and ethnography, in which he accords an important role to the festivals and games, is immediately followed by his other major survey, devoted to what an already well established tradition calls the "bonfire ceremonies."[21] Bilmawn holds an honored place in the second part of the study, while parts 1 and 3 are devoted to the account of rites in which a central character appears ('Ashur, Baynu, Tlghonja, Isli and Tilsit, Tislit unzar, etc.)[22] who is often feted only to be destroyed afterward. Bilmawn, celebrated everywhere at the Great Feast of the Sacrifice, takes his place in this venerable gallery, which indeed gathers together the ancient divinities of an original Berber pantheon.

A better sense of this pantheon can be obtained from a description in which Laoust seems to have reduced the festival to its essential characteristics, based on a number of cases directly or indirectly observed:

The word is Arabic and means "man dressed in skins." Its Berber equivalents: *bu-ilmaun, bilmaun, bub-tain, bu-isliyen* or *tagesduft* are, except for the last, formed on the basis of the same particle *bu* followed by a word meaning "skin." Bujlud indeed wears sheep or goatskins taken from victims that were sacrificed on the first day of the Aïd. These skins are placed on his naked body. The skin covering his arms is arranged so that the hooves dangle below his hands. His face, blackened with soot or powder, is hidden beneath an old goatskin container once used to churn butter which he wears as a mask. His head is adorned with the horns of a cow or with a sheep's head, the jaws of which are held open by a small stick to give him a most horrible grimace. An orange decorated with a bunch of feathers is often stuck into the end of each horn; sometimes his head or shoulders are covered with greenery, but this last accessory is only seen sporadically, in Tangiers, for example. Last, two or three necklaces, an enormous rosary made from snailshell beads, and powerful male attributes complete the outfit of the hideous character Bujlud.

As a general rule, one individual per *douar,* a village or part of a tribe, is disguised in this way. But in the towns, especially, one often sees three or four people putting on this disguise and playing the following role. Escorted by an orchestra of oboes and drums and a large train of children who hurl insults and stones at him. Bujlud makes his way in silence around the *douar* or the *ighrem*. He goes from one tent or house to another, sometimes stopping to execute a few dance steps and make a grotesque parody of Muslim prayers. He visits the important people in each locality: pasha, qa'id, *amghar,* or *ineflas* and even the marabout, the *moqqadem* of the *zawya,* who greet him with varying degrees of generosity but always with joy. He goes into the houses, chases the children, who flee in fright before his gaze, and always strikes anyone found within reach of his long sticks. For Bujlud always carries one or two long poles, which in some places reach a length of four or five meters. Hitting men and women and touching the *flij* of tents with his sticks even seems to be the most important part of his role.

When Bujlud is not armed with a stick, which is the exception, he uses his clogs or a stone attached to the skin covering his right hand. The fact that occasionally a sheep's or goat's hoof is firmly attached to the end of his sticks leads one to surmise that he prefers to strike with his feet. If people flee before him, it is only because they fear his blows; indeed it has been attested that the sick people he touches are healed and he keeps healthy people from falling ill.

Among the Aït Ndhir, Bujlud (called Bu-islikhen) goes inside the tents, where he has pulled up the stakes and overturned the pots and pans. He flings himself into the hearth *(almessi)* and raises a great cloud of dust by rolling in the ashes. He is greatly feared by the women, so they flee the moment they catch sight of him, but when he appears he acts in a manner with them that can be interpreted as a sexual rite. He shoves and manhandles them, striking them with the piece of skin hanging from his right arm; and they flee to dodge his blows. He strikes only women and children. It is likely that an identical character existed among the Aït Warain, who generally celebrate their Carnival on Aïd el-Kebir. Indeed, among the carnival types appears the so-called Bujlud's Fiancée, *Taslit u Bu-Jlud,* played by a man disguised as a woman dressed in a magnificent *handira*. This Taslit appears in the *douar* the moment the first sheep is slaughtered. Upon seeing her, men and women leave their tents and greet her with jeers and gibes whose meaning escapes them. The bride rushes at the spectators and brutally strikes whomever she can catch; she will not relinquish her prize until relatives intervene and tolbas come prostrate themselves before her, their hands tied behind their backs. At night this mock bride sneaks into the tents, where she betrays her presence by indicating to the husband that he must give her his place.

Bujlud's outings begin the very evening of the 'Ashura in the regions where the Carnival takes place on the occasion of this festival or, more commonly, on the second day of Aïd el-Kebir, the day called *ass n-buhsasen* or *nhar azellif.* They last for two or three days, sometimes even a week, and except on rare occasions take place during the day. Moreover, they are profitable. Players and musicians receive eggs, pieces of meat from the *tafaska,* and coins as they wander around. They share the money, eat the meat, or resell it if the search has been abundant and buy other food to serve in a feast. The Imjadh buy chickens and bring the feasts and meals to a close with an invocation of this sort:

> O God, give us ease!
> O God, grant us your pardon and
> bestow a good year upon us!

The Beni-Iznacen say in the same context:

> O God, give us rain!

The Carnival ends with a banquet and an invocation whose sacred character should not be doubted. It would be false, moreover, to consider only the ribald, burlesque side of Bujlud's procession. The Natives seem to attach a real importance to this practice, which cannot be justified solely by the attraction of the spectacle. The actors, chosen from people of humble status, shepherds, *khammas,* or thieves, or from the members of one family, do not always find it a pleasure to make this sort of public exhibition of themselves. Sometimes it is the *amghar* or the community that takes on the acquisition of the skins that Bujlud will wear. In addition to the proceeds of his search, he often receives payment. In the tribes of the Djebel, one or more individuals are hired for the seven days of the festival, they are dressed in the manner described above, and then they are walked through the *ddshar*. Bujlud's role is not of prime importance. He heals the sick and immunizes those he touches against danger. In other words, the ceremony in which he is the essential player seems to have as its object to attract blessings to the families and to shield them from misfortune and trouble throughout the coming year.[23]

Further on, writing of Bilmawn and outlining his notion of the death and resurrection of the god, Laoust insists on the relationship between sacrifice and masquerade; but we will see that it is at the cost of removing the Muslim character from the sacrifice. He notes the existence of the man garbed in skins among the Sektana, a tribe neighboring the Ait Mizane, and remarks that there one encounters the characters of the Jew, the blacksmith, as well as another one who operates the blacksmith's bellows. The presence of the Jews, he notes, is universal in the carnival processions of North Africa and is well suited to a festival where in fact, once the victim has been sacrificed, it would be fitting to see the sacrifice of the god representing the old year, laden with the evils that beset humankind. The Jewish characters and scapegoat themes would be naturally linked in the actors' minds.[24]

All the carnival ceremonies, whether they take place during the Feast of the Sacrifice or the 'Ashura, whether they mark a seasonal feast or a time in the solar calendar, are interpreted by Laoust according to the same hypothesis: the drama of the god's death and resurrection, which celebrates the year drawn to its close (worn out and dying) and the beginning of a new time. An old agrarian religion based on the renewal of nature adopting practices introduced by the new religions: Christianity and later, Islam. These views provide the target for Edward Westermarck's apparatus of empirical data and criticism, which is often penetrating and not without irony.

In 1926, after extensive visits to the region, Westermarck published his key work on Morocco.[25] His research focused on the north of the country, and the result was a clear and intelligent account, with many judicious observations. He employed a thematic logic that organizes observed and reported data by region.

This method gives his work the air of an immense file in which one seeks overarching interpretations in vain. However, Westermarck's views on the man in the goatskins are clear; he propounds them first of all in his *Ritual and Belief in Morocco* and returns to the subject in the lectures published in *Pagan Survivals in Mohammedan Civilisation.*

With many variations, this festival involves a central character clothed in the skins of sacrificial victims, his wife (who is Muslim), and a Jewess who replaces her when the Muslim wife is absent. Jewish characters and sometimes animals (lion, camel, mule, etc.) complete the picture. The women come up to Bujlud so that he will hit them; his blows make them fertile and bring them healthy children. Depending on the circumstances, either the goatskin-clad man or the Jews throw ashes on those who dare approach them. And the animals represented are most often pack animals. At times a decrepit and impotent old man who cannot satisfy his wife appears along with Bujlud and the Jews, and the presence of Christians has also been noted. In some instances, the bestiary includes pigs. Bujlud leads them all in a procession accompanied by a band of musicians. This is the band that goes from house to house or tent to tent to collect gifts and bless the women and children. Even though the skin-clad man chases evil away and is a bearer of *baraka,* he is endlessly teased, attacked, pushed, even beaten, and driven far away from men's habitations.[26]

Doutté and Laoust look toward the past. Not the Muslim past of the peoples whose customs they describe, but even further back, to Roman and Christian times, and earlier still, to an even more remote Berber past. Aubin and Biarnay left no interpretation of what they saw. Mouliéras, though, ranks the festival among the many signs he sees of decadence and evokes the Saturnalia—corruption, a paganism inherited from the Romans.

This quest for a past in which the Muslim history of North Africa becomes a simple, parenthetical episode will reach extreme proportions in the hands of Mouliéras's heirs. Among them, Doutté and Laoust lead the way and forge the doctrine. Then, too, English social anthropology takes little interest in North Africa; the Muslim Mediterranean is already divided between the colonial rivals, and the Maghreb has fallen to the French. However, Westermarck carries out extensive research in Morocco, taking an active interest in "pagan survivals," and from this standpoint, his approach hardly differs from the major "scientific interests" that inspire the other scholars. The study of Islam and its institutions falls in the field of Orientalism; the study of customs, mores, and popular conduct, especially Berber, falls to ethnology.

For Morocco in particular, after the exploratory phase, researchers engaged in the systematic study of "towns and tribes," then compiled archives, and, last, carried out inquiries that crossed over from ethnography to an attempt at some sort of theoretical interpretation.[27] This division of labor led Doutté to study all types of sacrifice, Muslim included, but to approach the subject not from the standpoint of Muslim theory but from the conclusions the author drew about sacrifices found in other traditions. Laoust follows suit and only mentions Muslim sacrifice when he believes he can demonstrate its compatibility with an original Berber religion. For both authors, sacrifice and masquerade are only the reproduction, half-disguised in Islamic colors, of the archaic, Mediterranean saga of the Berbers: the murder and resurrection of the god.

Should one add to this apportionment among the disciplines examining Islam under foreign domination the particular history of the ethnology of religion in the Maghreb? The story is still poorly known; one can only point out the marginal position of its practitioners with respect to the circles that gravitated around the *Année sociologique* during that time. North Africa and the Near East aroused little interest there, and for a long time ethnography and its interpretation remained the business of administrators, interpreters, and agents of the educational system. Their eclecticism, perhaps the result of distance, would explain their reliance on the works of both Frazer and Mauss.

This is far from saying that such a division of scientific labor is based on purely academic considerations. One can easily guess that it is linked to political interests and contingencies, to a politics of science that in this case is primarily concerned with finding a Berber religion enriched by Roman and Christian contributions which would bring this culture closer to Western values. Besides influencing ethnography, this attitude permeates the practice of history and leads to the theory of an evolution led astray by Islamicization and Arabicization. There is no need to dwell on a well-known fact that, all the same, colors the entire range of scientific discourse and goes well beyond the study of ritual practices and religious ideas, our sole areas of interest here.[28]

This search for specificity, motivated as it was by political considerations that set the boundaries for a scientific politics, accents certain areas of study. The great interpretative systems of the day naturally give rise to the concepts used to account for known facts or to steer the search for new data. Frazerian evolutionism and comparativism exercise a decisive influence on Doutté and Laoust. There again, the evolutionism they choose posits Christian sacrifice as the culmination of a trajectory that sets the standard for all other beliefs and practices. Were it not for the obstacles Islam placed in its path, the religion of the Berbers naturally could have evolved in the direction of this ultimate conception of sacrifice.

This point of view, parts of which are explicitly formulated by Doutté, can be devined in Laoust's work as well. Laoust returns to the themes of his predecessor, just as Westermarck is looking to the school of the *Année sociologique* for an approach that will enable him to challenge their findings. I will take a brief look at this controversy before offering an overall view that will serve to situate my research with respect to these earlier contributions.

Edmond Doutté is hardly unaware of the work of the Durkheim school. Quite the contrary, when he attempts to describe and interpret sacrifice in North Africa, he borrows the essentials of the project shaped by Hubert and Mauss.[29] But what interests him is less a theory of sacrifice, already outlined in their work, than finding the debris of ancient Berber religion in all types of sacrifice, including Muslim practices. Doutté calls the Muslim rite that precedes the masquerade "orthodox Muslim sacrifice" and compares, juxtaposes, and sometimes contrasts it to other sacrifices.[30] He pores over it to trace the "survivals" of an earlier magical period characterized by the effort to spiritualize fear and desire, which in his eyes are the two key mechanisms of original religious/magical behavior, in the Frazerian sense of the term. And so, despite the efforts of the doctors of law to replace primitive motives and sentiments with purification and nearness to God, he "discovers" in the Islamic sacrificial act the mark of primitive beliefs and practices.[31]

Even more, Doutté believes that Muslim sacrifice contains the three typical functions that Durkheimians find in all sacrifices: communion, purification, and expiation.[32] The last of these, through the theme of the scapegoat, then allows him to make a synthesis with the Frazerian credo and advance his own theory of North African sacrifice, which he describes in all the diversity of its actual expressions.[33] Naturally, there he finds the remains, which have been hidden, repressed, or absorbed by Islam, of a drama whose outcome he compares at the end with the course it took in Christianity. Indeed, for Doutté Christian sacrifice has evolved into its extreme, exemplary state because of its world-redemptive message. Islam has not come that far. Survivals of rites bear witness to the liveliness of its archaic forms of communication with the divine. Now at last a whole series of comparisons opens up in which various practices are likened despite the time and space separating them.

One might be surprised by the detour Doutté makes in devoting a chapter to sacrifice as a way to introduce his views concerning the man dressed in skins. However, this passage is necessary to understand the economy of his work and to contextualize his interpretation of the "Maghrebin carnival." Whether they are held during Muslim festivals or celebrations of transition in the solar or agrarian calendars, whether they present an old man being threatened and ridiculed, a fantastic creature clothed in skins, a bride of the fields and the wheat, or, finally, a character presented solely by calling his name, which is either chanted or lamented,[34] these masquerades and games cannot be understood without examining their link with the sacrifice. But it seems that Muslim sacrifice is not the issue here. On the contrary, the sacrifice must be stripped of any specific details so that it may be linked with what Islam is supposed to repress: an original pre-Islamic sacrifice. For this is the price to be paid so that the man wearing the skins, who is both venerated and abused, can find his kinship with the sacrificed kings and priests, with Carnival borne in joyous triumph and burned, and finally, with the bull of the Bouphonia, sacralized, killed, and revived in order to give the earth vigor and fertility.[35] Such, according to the author of *Magie et religion en Afrique du Nord*, would be the universal tradition that Islamicization had thwarted and suppressed!

Whether celebrated during the Muslim feast of the sacrifice or on other occasions, the Maghrebi carnival lends itself to comparison with European carnivals on the one hand, and with the murderous rites (accepted as factual) of the kings and priests of certain so-called primitive societies, on the other.[36] Now at last the Frazerian scheme is in operation, for we are in the presence of the ancient drama of the murder and resurrection of a vegetation spirit that would have progressively taken on a zoomorphic or anthropomorphic form. Doutté does not hesitate to conjecture that it may have originally been a human sacrifice tempered by later developments and notes that the ceremony utilizes "sympathetic magic" where, by the death and rebirth of a victim, men mime the annual death and renewal of the forces of nature.[37] Under these conditions, the Maghrebin masquerade would be composed of the debris of an immemorial rite in which the vegetation spirit is sacrificed. Notwithstanding the official, Muslim orthodox explanation of the sacrifices and New Year's celebrations, they are in fact ancient agrarian rites adopted by the Muslim calendar. And the sadness followed by the joys of the carnival characteristic of these festivals corresponds to the moments of the god's murder and resurrection.[38]

In such a system the functionalism of the Durkheim school is reinforced by Frazerian "geneticism," which moves to the foreground. Muslim sacrifice is interpreted by means of pagan "survivals" or pre-Islamic rites with which the new religion reached a compromise. In this process, the meanings the festival and masquerade might have for those who celebrate and organize them are forgotten. Since, as I have already said, Doutté's goal, and that of his successors such as Laoust, was to find a Berber religion with close ties to the ancient Mediterranean religions out of which Christian sacrifice arose, any historical or living Muslim significance, any function connected with present North African societies, was bound to be obscured.

The work of Edmond Doutté furnishes the program for Emile Laoust. His lengthy study of Berber ceremonies and bonfires is explicitly presented as an ethnography with two aims: to provide the empirical proof lacking in some of Doutté's arguments, and to amplify and defend the use his predecessor makes of Frazer's hypothesis, in opposition to Westermarck, who is challenging it at this time. The program is clearly restated in the body of the work, which attempts to show that the Berber carnival is a "more or less systematic" assemblage "of bits of ancient magico-religious ceremonies during which the Berbers celebrated the dramatic death of a pastoral or agrarian divinity, ceremonies that are juxtaposed and then blended with a number of sexual rites and practices aimed at the expulsion of evil, which is personified in diverse forms of human beings, animals, demons, or monsters."[39]

So begins an ethnographic investigation using linguistic evidence, as remarkable for its precision and attention to detail as for the fertile imagination it displays, which projects on the practices described rash images of a rare beauty. In fact, sympathetic mimesis, which in Doutté was restricted to the drama of death and resurrection, is enriched in Laoust by a collective sexual rite to favorize general fertility and the reproduction of nature. This is, moreover, a "hypothesis" that claims to illuminate all the reported data, including what Laoust had presented the year before in *Mots et choses berbères*. So that if one were to believe it, the two fundamental ritual acts of primitive Berber religion would be summed up in the slaying of a victim followed by an explosion of the vital forces manifested in sexuality: ritual murder and copulation.[40] The sum of these practices, which for Laoust constitute "the basis of Berber life," are intended to drive out evil and restore the fertility of the earth.

This is one of the fundamental postulates of evolutionist and psychological theories of primitive religion as elaborated at the end of the nineteenth and the beginning of the twentieth centuries. Religious man pursues the realization of a material goal. Attributing to the forces of nature a psychology in his own image, he attempts to influence them by means of rites, which (for Frazer, for example) are essentially a kind of mimesis, for at this stage of its development religion is merely sympathetic magic.

Laoust develops all these views with unprecedented fullness in "Noms et cérémonies des feux de joie." In the manner of his teacher and predecessor, Laoust brings out the full richness of the rituals of the yearly cycle: festivals and ceremonies of the Muslim New Year, sacrifices and masquerades, fires and ceremonies to mark the solstice, rites of the agricultural New Year, seasonal and other customs linked to drought and rain. Everywhere he finds a central personage whose function resembles that of Bilmawn.

Bilmawn is a scapegoat who resembles the Roman Lupercus in that he takes all evils upon himself and drives away evil spirits. Apropos, Laoust recalls the hypothesis that the sacred is transmitted by touch, which in the case of both Bilmawn and Lupercus means flagellation;[41] but he leans toward the notion of the scapegoat. Bilmawn, often called "the decrepit one" (Herrma), would have started out as the ram-god venerated by the Berbers in the days of their pastoral existence. An aging god, regularly sacrificed and revived in the form of a vigorous animal. It is of little consequence that the masquerade is now connected with the great Muslim feast of the sacrifice. The (lunar) calendar of the new religion simply appropriated it; the ancient Berber festival began with a sacrifice of the divine ram, and it is not at all surprising that the Islamic sacrifice came to replace it. The new festival is only a travesty of the old, which moreover would have been first disguised in Christianity's paschal lamb before it came to lurk under the cloak of Islam.[42]

He interprets all the rites he describes in the same way. The coupling of murder and resurrection captured by Islam would in fact be a spring rite accompanied by collective sexuality, the memory of which would be perpetuated in the group marriages celebrated by certain Berber communities at the great feast of the sacrifice. And if this feast is an ancient spring festival, these weddings must also quite logically take place during the same sea-son![43] Likewise the 'Ashura is marked by survivals of collective copulation or the cult of the phallus, notably during some ceremonies in the Anti-Atlas, where they would accompany the slaying of the *taslit*. Laoust, however, only reports one case of ritual copulation that he claims is real, which according to him was practiced at the mosque by two engaged couples during one night of ritual. And the intercourse was symbolic, since the girls' virginity apparently was respected.[44]

This reading, taken up by many others, particularly A. Bel,[45] provoked an energetic response from Edward Westermarck. Like his French colleagues, he examines the customs of the entire yearly cycle; and perhaps less preju-diced than they, he never hesitates to give credit to Islamic influence on ceremonies that seem the most foreign to it. I will limit the present discus-sion to his views on Bujlud, without going into details previously given in this chapter.

Westermarck does not attack the scapegoat function for which Bujlud and the Jews would seem well suited, and he does not deny that the rite could be a survival of practices antedating Islam. In this respect he agrees with Doutté and Laoust, and like them he firmly adheres to the theory of survivals. But that is where their agreement ends. For Westermarck, Laoust's hypotheses lack a historical basis. There is no proof, in fact, that a rite of the murder and resurrection of the god accompanied by collective sexuality existed among the ancient Berbers.[46] Furthermore, it is not neces-sary to look for the victim's ancestor (god), since his sacred character fits in with the Islamic credo; last, there is no evidence for the idea of the god's reincarnation in a vigorous body, while the notion of the resurrection of the sacrificed animal in paradise is clearly present in Muslim beliefs.[47]

Thus, Westermarck refutes the image of a primitive rite in which murder and copulation are combined, but he is also looking for historical anteced-ents, which he naturally finds in Roman Africa: the Saturnalia and later on, the Calends. These Berber–Roman celebrations could have been co-opted by the Muslim festivals.[48] Nonetheless, a full comparison with these prece-dents is impossible, since for Westermarck the Moroccan festival lacks what he considers the "key" to the Calends: the inversion of the master–slave relationship.[49]

Westermarck's historical alternative is not what interests me here. As a hypothesis it is only slightly more plausible than the original ritual as Laoust "restored" it. It is possible that the Romans influenced the Berbers, but I strongly doubt that concrete evidence of a historical route from the

Saturnalia and Calends to Bilmawn will ever be found. Moreover, while there are no masters to serve their slaves, inversion is not absent from the Moroccan festival; also, despite Westermarck's protestations, the term *tfaska* is specifically used, as Laoust notes, to refer to Muslim sacrifice in the Shilha areas. Last, one cannot deny, as Westermarck has done, the obvious link between the agricultural cycle and the masquerade, even if the latter has a connection with the Muslim lunar calendar. I will deal with each of these issues in my account of the festival.

Westermarck's arguments seem to be better founded when he avoids risky conjectures. It cannot be denied that the masquerade following the feast of the sacrifice, which is (in his own word) a "profanation," finds itself in an uneasy relationship with orthodox Islam (today we would say, the dominant idea of Islam). A profanation that is furthermore accompanied by a purification via a distancing from evil. Because of this argument, Westermarck partly avoids the ideology of a pre-Islamic, unchanging Berber substratum.[50] However critical one may be of his functionalism and his formalism inspired by Hubert and Mauss, his interpretation clearly links the specifically Muslim festival with the masquerade, thereby placing Bilmawn in a global social and ideological framework.[51]

Still, the theory of the substratum lingers on, and it surfaces in the only recent description of Bilmawn, from a valley neighboring that of the Ait Mizane. In a short study, Marie-Rose Rabaté revives the notion under the heading of a "common background." The cursorily described scenes involving the masked figures are set against this "common background" and cannot be understood without it.[52] Rabaté also bases her interpretation on a theory of origins, represented according to her by the masks, which incarnate the ancestors. The masquerade—in origin a mystery—enacts the universal fecundity of couples and nature.[53] It is impossible to find even the slightest foundation for these views in her ethnography, that of her predecessors, or even my own.

In addition to these pseudo-historical narratives linked to the largely ideological theory of a substratum, previous accounts display the vices of a comparativism in which details are isolated from a context that is often ignored in the descriptions. Neither the actors of the dramas nor the fundamental characteristics of the groups who play, organize, and attend the spectacle are noted. It is true, as Radcliffe-Brown will later maintain, that the function and general meaning of a practice can be discovered by comparing the different situations in which this practice appears. And one can maintain that, broadly speaking, this is what Doutté, Laoust, and Westermarck seek to do. Yet it is apparent that for the first two these comparisons are used to support not a function or a meaning, but a common origin; while for Westermarck, some elements are obscured by the initial interpretation. Such is the case, for example, of characters like the European ambassador, which he notes in his description of the masquerade but neglects in his overall analysis. Westermarck shares this attitude with his French colleagues, who wish at all costs to ignore the many aspects of "real" life reflected in the masquerades: ambassadors, interpreters, State agents, religious judges in action, steamships, and so forth. There again, the festival as I saw it, in the context of a village relatively isolated from urban life, reveals an amazing capacity to seize upon current events. This aspect is impossible to overlook and should be part of any interpretation.

Descriptions of the yearly festival cycle, which theoretically might shed light on the individual ceremonies, suffer from a lack of detail. Even more serious is the fact that none of these ceremonies has ever been depicted primarily as it is, a process with its own dynamic—a narrative that builds on itself and shapes its materials from everyday life. It will be readily admitted that a discipline that all too often relied on rough collections and classifications was not likely to manifest a feeling for living reality. My aim in the chapters that follow is to present the actors in their own surroundings and the festival as a narrative, in order to discover not only a structure and symbolic interplay but also, and above all, what the society has to say about itself.

Human Action in Its Environment
Concerning Some Structural Tensions

2

Here as elsewhere, festivals are only a passing occurrence. In the two villages where the sacrifice and masquerade were observed, as in the rest of the mountain region, they offer a break from ordinary life, which is marked by intense labor and a patient struggle for survival. In truth, since the festival occurs regularly, it is hard to avoid the impression that the Ait Mizane throw themselves into it with the same ardor with which they work the fields or climb the high mountains. In any event, these two activities, like many celebrations, are above all the affair of the young. But in both fields and festival there are a collaboration and exchange between sexes and among generations from which neither silent tension nor open conflict is absent. The young men are constantly engaged in backbreaking work; if they are to achieve recognition among their fellow men they must set aside some capital in order to marry, which is the first step in becoming a fully adult male. And if the women and unmarried girls performing their daily tasks outside the home dress and make themselves up as if they are going to a dance, this cannot disguise the harshness of the work that awaits them, both inside and outside the house.

It is about 20 kilometers and a gradient of 600 meters from Tamadout in the middle of the mountains, where the torrent[1] known as the Ait Mizane is joined on the right bank by the Imnan, up to Armd, the last village located at the foot of the high range known as Toubkal. The valley narrows as the altitude increases, taking the shape of a deep **V** that opens at the bottom into the Imlil basin. Of the two villages where the festival was observed, and which I will call Imi-n'Tassaft and Timezguida n'Oumalou, the first is located a short distance from the confluence of the Tamadout, in the middle altitudes of the mountains, the second one below Armd in the Imlil gap. From there a day's walk takes the traveler to the foot of Toubkal peak, at 4000 meters the highest point in the Atlas Mountains. The river locally called the Assif Ait Mizane has its source there, and in its northward descent, toward the Marrakech plain, it drains a vast area between Oukaime-dan to the east and the N'fis system to the west. After Tamadout, it crosses the Asni and Tahannaout basins before flowing into the plain where it is known as Oued Rheraya.

The two villages, despite differences discussed later on, are located in a zone influenced both by the Atlantic Ocean and the desert, where the altitude has a perceptible impact on the aridity. The winters are harsh. Snow is frequent, although it does not last long below 3000 meters. When the snow falls between November and April, it covers the ground for a few days, up to several weeks in the highest fields. As a general rule, although it quickly melts in the valley it remains for months, in rare cases for the entire year, on the highest summits of the Toubkal massif. Between October and April the high mountains (adrar) are inaccessible to men and animals because of frequent snowfall and the cold. However, in the summer the temperature can reach up to 30°C (which is rare), and sometimes the hot southerly and southeasterly winds (shergi) bring the temperature up to 40°C. In spite of everything these temperatures are low compared to the nearby plain, since the average annual minimum temperature in the Imlil basin ranges between 10°C and 12°C.[2]

The influence of the Atlantic and the altitude explain the relative humidity of this mountain area, where the average annual rainfall is from 600 to 800 millimeters, as opposed to 250 millimeters in the dry Marrakech plain. As a result the crests and slopes dominating the valley are covered with more or less dense forest. At mid altitudes, at Imi-n'Tassaft and somewhat higher, can be found green oak, red juniper, and prickly juniper. At higher levels the incense juniper dominates the forestlands (lghabt), with hardly any competitors; the tree line occurs at 2500 meters, above which the mountain is rocky, gray, and, on the high peaks, pink as the light of the setting sun reflects on it.

Only a slight distance separates Imi-n'Tassaft and Timezguida n'Oumalou. But the difference in altitude and the distribution of environments create important disparities in lifestyle. In the first village, the winters are less severe and the forest is almost always accessible for pasturage. In the second, between December and February people and animals must be confined to the inhabited area. This discrepancy is felt in all aspects of life. In midrange, around Imi-n'Tassaft, everything happens earlier: the return of the vegetation after the winter months, the harvests, the climb to higher pasturelands.

The systems of crop rotation used in the two villages clearly illustrate the differences between the two ecosystems. Throughout this land of terraced fields carved out of the mountainside, however, barley and corn hold first place. But the two crops, along with beans, are distributed according to the quality of the soil and the availability of water. In rich areas, where there is ample sun and water, barley planted in October is harvested in July, and the area is immediately replanted with a fast-growing corn *(amazuz)*, which is then harvested in September. Where the light is less favorable, and in poorer, colder fields, slightly more than half are planted with barley while the rest is left fallow *(issiki)* until March, when it is sown with a slow-growing corn *(amenzu)* harvested in July along with the barley. The first system generates two harvests annually; under the second, the farmer must be satisfied with three harvests every two years (figs. 1–2).

Both villages use both systems. But the first prevails in the richer ochre lands *(azugagh)* in Imi-n'Tassaft, while the second is more practical in the relatively poorer soils of Timezguida n'Oumalou and other villages of the high valley. The less intensive system is supplemented by the cultivation of beans, which are sown on some of the terraces that therefore lie fallow only in the month of December after this harvest. Of course, in practice things are more complicated: carrots, onions, tomatoes, and potatoes, grown on suitable terraces, contribute to daily sustenance and sometimes provide additional money for the household. And the annual crops coexist on narrow terraces with the walnut trees that shade the riverbanks, ravines, and irrigation ditches. For fifteen years or so cherry trees have been increasingly cultivated, especially in the middle altitudes, replacing barley and corn.

Still, only these two great annual crops, and the gathering of walnuts, punctuate the agricultural year; olive trees are on the wane in Imi-n'Tassaft, and cherry trees, which are being heavily planted, have not yet been integrated into the overall culture and are the business of well-off peasants. Barley and corn occupy the vast majority of fields, and the calendar of activities revolves around them. Barley *(tumzin)* is the indispensable grain for bread and couscous, a basic foodstuff. However, households able to provide enough of these for their own use are rare; and the majority must supplement their reserves at the markets on the plain[3] by using the surplus from the production of nuts and animals.

Bread, throughout the year, and couscous with beans, especially during the winter, make up the daily fare, where meat is rare. Meat is eaten once a week at most, on the day of the weekly market and then only in comfortable households. Others must be content with the butter and oil that dresses their bread and barley or corn porridge. This second grain is also the base

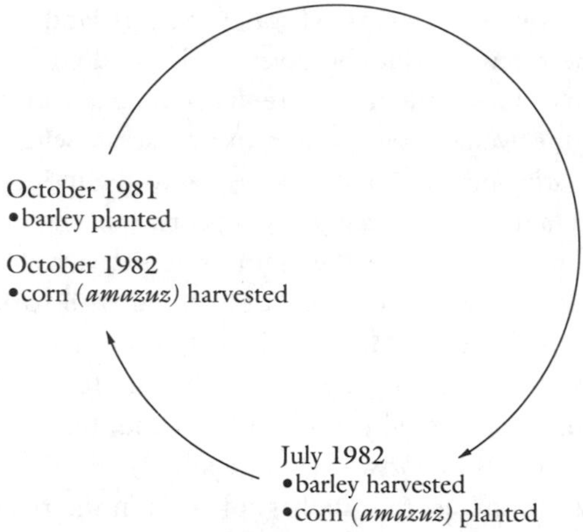

Figure 1. Crop rotation in the middle valley: two harvests annually (rich soil, enough moisture, and good sunlight).

amazuz: corn which grows in 3 months (short-cycle corn)
amenzu: corn which grows in 6 months (long-cycle corn)

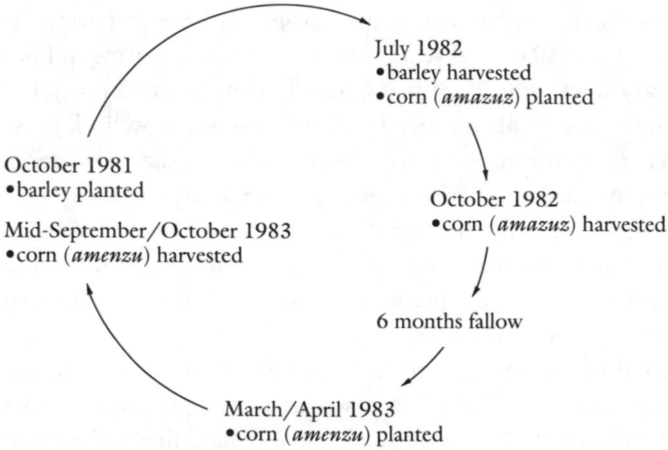

Figure 2. Crop rotation in the upper valley: three harvests in two years (colder climate, less fertile fields).

of the everyday breakfast soup *(askkif)*, which is drunk first before the coffee with milk. A type of porridge *('aṣida)* is the other basic food. It is prepared with whey, or with oil or butter. *Askkif* and *'aṣida* are the two distinctive elements of the mountain diet,[4] and during harvest time the first is served as the special dish.

This gives an idea of the importance of corn. Grown in spring and summer, its cultivation coincides with the beginning of the good weather that is also the time of intense physical work outside of the house, where the barley must be irrigated and the corn sown *(amenzu* in the spring and *amazuz* in the summer). While, except for weeding and some carrying, barley is the affair of men, corn involves closer cooperation between the sexes. Indeed the women thin the young corn plants and later remove the kernels from the cob after the ears have been dried on the terraces. Thus, unlike barley, which is threshed on a threshing floor *(anrar)* that is off limits to women, the grains of corn are separated by the women at home. In short, women play a key role in the harvest, while men carry out the lengthy and demanding tasks of plowing and sowing, as well as fertilizing and irrigation. While it requires a great deal of care, corn is a bountiful plant. It never fails; for each household produces a sufficient quantity, while shortages of barley are frequent. Ripe corn grows so tall that an animal or man can be easily hidden, which makes surveillance against thieves necessary[5] and leads to rumors of amorous adventures in the fields. Echoes of all this appear in the commentaries I have gathered about the masquerade, in which corn occupies a key place, as it does in the agricultural calendar.

All these crops are produced on an extremely small scale, for as in all the valleys of the Upper Atlas, the fields are tiny. According to a recent estimate around Targa n'Oumalou, there were 300 inhabitants per square kilometer of cultivated ground and an average of 2000 square meters per family.[6] A survey of the 44 households of Imi-n'Tassaft reveals that a majority (25) hold between 0 and 6000 square meters, and that among owners of more than 1 hectare of land (9), none hold more than 3. Even then in most of these cases it is a matter of brothers and sisters who often live separately but hold their property in common.[7] Of course it is necessary to make a distinction between property and cultivation, since the farmers can add to these holdings by means of various contractual agreements or renting. But the relationship between a high population and fields of dimensions that are modest at most restricts all the households to small areas. And not only here, for throughout the entire valley populous villages are established between scanty parcels of land that are irrigated, scrupulously maintained, and cultivated and the vast spaces devoted to animal pasture. According to the 1982 national census, Imi-n'Tassaft contained about 400 inhabitants and the average household included more than 6 people; Timezguida n'Oumalou housed more than 450 inhabitants, and the size of the domestic units was identical.[8] The two villages in fact are conglomerations of smaller units. For example, the second village produces two men dressed in skins (bilmawin),[9] because it is composed of two entities that simultaneously perceive themselves as unified and distinct and are physically separate.

What I call a household is in reality difficult to pin down. Locally the term that is ordinarily used is takat (pl. takatin) or, more rarely, the Arabic kanun. But this unit does not always coincide with the family, which frequently extends beyond it; nor does it refer in all cases to people who eat and live together, for married brothers having separate budgets and domiciles but maintaining the family property and farming together state they belong to the same takat. Then too, location and production can unite in the same takat couples who keep everything separate. In 1982 in Imi-n'Tassaft, out of 42 units answering to this name 20 of them shared property, jointly worked the land, and ate and lived together, as opposed to 15 in which individuals were united by land and production but separate in all the rest, and 7 in which the takat was based only on their dwelling and eating together.[10]

The units thus distinguished are grouped into more extensive and multifunctional groups. If we take into account the grouping (as is the case throughout the mountains) of all the takatin into a small number of lineages who people each village, the force of the bonds between them and the slight margin of autonomy left to each can be ascertained. Economic interdependence, blood ties, and the discipline imposed by a difficult environment reinforce the group's solidarity and cohesion. But on the other hand, hard times and daily contact exacerbate conflicts and lead to a responsible sociability. Religious norms, those of kinship and contiguity, and the sense of community moderate conflicts that often find a solution, or at least expression, in a ritualized framework.[11]

The village, formed of subunits that are spatially distinct or, on the contrary, gathered together in a compact entity, perceives itself as a great lineage that has integrated all kinds of immigrants who have come from elsewhere. Many indeed locate their origins in the Sous[12] or in another neighboring valley. Nonetheless, the image is that of a group having a common origin. They are part of a larger entity occupying a district which I, for want of a better word, will call a clan. Three groups of this level share the valley. At the highest elevations live the Ait Mizane, whose name also denotes the river up to the confluence at Tamadout; further down are the Ait Abdallah, whose territory begins at Taddart and ends a bit above Tiniitine; and below them are the Ait Ali, who occupy the last section of the valley. The village of Imi-n'Tassaft belongs to this last clan, while Timezguida n'Oumalou belongs to the Ait Mizane.

They are sometimes called *taqbilt*. An ambiguous expression, in some cases it designates the village and in others the federation of three clans to form a tribe taking the name Ait Mizane and coextensive to the whole valley; on rare occasions one hears *taqbilt* applied to the confederation that, before the days of the protectorate, the Mizane formed with their neighbors to the north and east to unite them with the valleys of Asni, Imnan, and Sidi Fares. At this level, it refers to an area of influence in which ties of solidarity were activated in conflicts and relationships between larger regional groups.

Under the French protectorate and up until Moroccan independence (1956), a single chief ruled this great gathering, aided in his task by a powerful Ait Mizane family and other neighboring chiefs and allies. His great house, situated on a mountain peak, had the aspect of a castle (*kasbah*) sealing the valley and dominating the land around Timezguida n'Oumalou; in Tamadout to the north, another chief's residence can still be seen a few kilometers away from Imi-n'Tassaft. The experience of this absolute potentate with his small court of notables and threatening black slaves who guarded the doors of his harem is a vivid local memory. He meted out his own form of justice, most often at the weekly market, and protected the Jewish communities of Tahannaout and Asni in exchange for sums levied on their incomes and businesses. But well before the twentieth century these groups had been familiar with the concept as well as the exercise of despotic power; furthermore, they were able to play a part in "great history," in the words of J. Berque, and frequently wavered between the chief's government and the local autonomy administered by the council of elders (*jma't*).[13] From this point of view, the characters of the masquerade (Bilmawn, slave, and Jews) are modeled on types found in the local reality.

Since independence, a family of notables connected by marriage to the former chiefs wields power in the valley. But they operate within the limits set by the central administration, whose control is reinforced by modern technology and its infrastructure. All these large entities, including the clan, are eroding. What remains is the village, a physical, moral, and historical community, the center for deciding and managing the resources of the land and communal territory. This development is identical to what has taken place throughout rural Morocco. The higher levels of organization—clan, tribe, confederation—traditionally played a political and military role that today is undertaken by the modern state. Vestiges of the old authority can still be seen in agreements concerning animals and pasturage, arrangements for the distribution of water, and the annual feasts *(mussem)* held around the great sanctuaries.[14]

Because of its ties with the land, however, the village retains a solid vitality. Perched on a promontory carved into the mountains by ravines that run into the main valley, it dominates its land. The site was originally chosen to combine the advantages of good light and easy defense, and also avoided using arable land. The human group made its own niche between the cultivated land and the pastures and forests.

Local knowledge and vocabulary make a clear distinction between three realms of human activity: *assif, lghabt,* and *adrar.* The first refers to the river, the valley, and by extension, whatever is inhabited and cultivated. The humanized and familiar world, one could say. The *lghabt,* or forest, is frequented by shepherds and their flocks when spring comes. In the winter, branches of oak and juniper are cut to feed the animals. Legal and illegal cuttings have decreased the wooded areas, and the areas surrounding the villages have been deforested. Charcoal makers carry out their craft here, often clandestinely. This is where artisans go in search of the materials for agricultural tools (plows and accessories), kitchen utensils, doors, windows, furniture, or even turbines for water mills. *Adrar* refers to the bare and imposing high mountains, where in May shepherds take their flocks; there they band into small groups and stay in crude shelters *(azib)* or gather in large numbers in pasturelands shared by several tribes and regulated by custom.

The *assif,* with its villages, is the human and controlled area. There the rhythms of varied activities engage the whole population. And since physical conditions are harsh, a collective discipline must be imposed by the council of elders, who exercise a flexible yet real vigilance. The system of terraces carved into the mountainside requires constant attention. Because of the rugged terrain, the network of irrigation ditches is extremely drawn out. Everyone must be able to water his fields, especially during the summer, when rain is scarce,[15] or when the water table is low and cisterns *(afra, tifruin)* must collect the water before it can be used. The three realms— village, forest, and high mountain—are differentiated by the style of activity that marks each one.

A cluster of notions justifies or simply describes the attitudes expected in each environment. In the center of Imi-n'Tassaft is the mosque, with its two rooms: the prayer room *(tamqsurt)* and the room where ablutions are performed *(takhurbisht)*. These will figure later on in the discussions of the sacrifice and the masquerade. The mosque occupies an elevated space, located on the edge of the central square *(asays)* where Bilmawn's drama takes place every year, and forms the terminus of the main street that runs uphill through the village. The slope is steep, and the houses, like the fields, are built on terraces. They are grouped into "aggregates" each belonging, at least nominally, to a patrilineage. Local symmetry calls for an even number of lineages, often four, as is the case here, to meet tax obligations to the group or the State. But if unexpected circumstances arise in which a man sees that it is in his interest to declare himself independent of his brothers, the lineages "disband" and suddenly proliferate!

Between the cultivated land and the edge of the forest is the cemetery, watched over by the patron saint of the village, and the adjoining area, called the mşalla, where the prayers and sermon precede the annual sacrifice. Everything there serves to define the village with its diffuse sacrality, the familiar places that it is unwise to leave and to which one must show one's devotion when one returns after repeated emigrations. It is the space belonging to the group, where strangers rarely venture, except the itinerant peddlers disliked by the men and who prefer to do business with the women. One proceeds with discretion, even politeness, in these one-on-one encounters that must nonetheless be shunned. Women and men avoid each other or, if they do meet, exchange terse greetings. Old men and those who are married and responsible for a household gather in one of the outbuildings of the mosque or, during the winter, on a sunny terrace or even in the warm room where ablutions are performed. In spring and summer the great amount of outdoor work, which is very intense, scatters the villagers throughout the fields, forest, and mountains. At that time the young men are all working or, when family resources are modest, out earning an income. During the day they must not be found in the village; and they keep their distance from the older men and the women. Daily life proceeds in an atmosphere in which young men and old avoid one another; and public encounters between the sexes are marked by distance.

Instructions come from the old men and one's elders. They are rarely discussed, and relations are of a formal nature, though neither stiff nor difficult; exchanges between old and young lack neither grace nor traces of humor. Do not imagine a Berber village in which people flee one another's contact, spy on each other from afar, hardly daring to look at one another, and where they confuse obedience with servility! No such village exists. On the contrary, daily interactions are marked by an undeniable serenity and remarkable ease. I want to stress that there is simply a sense of order and correctness that betrays profoundly internalized norms, which on ordinary occasions are rarely questioned.

Everyday life is bounded by a respect for rules that is, it must be emphasized, neither mechanical nor absolute. Tasks are clearly distributed by sex and age. The lot of women is no less onerous than that of the men, but it is probably more restrictive. While women do not perform heavy manual labor such as building and repairing irrigation ditches or digging and maintaining terraces, they are constantly occupied with household jobs and the many chores linked with cultivating crops and raising animals. The growing seasons of the agricultural calendar mean that the men's work is punctuated by slow periods of varying duration. Women's work, on the contrary, has an ongoing, unremitting quality. Women are responsible for domestic chores: cooking, housekeeping, childcare. They milk the cows, ewes, and goats, and make whey and butter. They weave the men's clothing and blankets, and they are responsible for the difficult and monotonous chore of grinding the grain.

But that is not the end of it. Women carry out other functions involved in production: they watch the cow, seek its daily fodder, weed the barley, and thin the corn. During the summer, women and girls help cut the hay grown on the man-made fields that border the streams. They regularly set off in groups on long hunts for firewood. They are not at all reclusive and must be extremely affluent before they are able to live the enclosed life associated with high social status.

In this division of labor, men rarely interfere in domestic chores. They take care of the flocks of goats and sheep kept in a shelter either attached to the house or located a short way from the village. Women feed the cow and lead it to the bull to impregnate it. Men are in charge of fattening the bull and are the only ones to take care of the mule. Women have little interest in this male mount and rarely use it; on the roads men and children can be seen riding while women trot along behind them.

Within the domestic group, both sexes share some aspects of production, most importantly, the cultivation of grain. The choice of grains and seed falls to the men. During the plowing, women help carry what is needed, and during the harvest they help bring in the crops; during all times of heavy labor, they prepare the meals and carry them to the workers, either to the roadside or the threshing ground. They dress their best for all these activities. Public appearances require it, and perhaps precautions for observing the ritual purity that is necessary when handling plants at the height of their growing period (weeding and thinning). In the spring the girls in particular spend the whole day in the fields. It seems that there, as at the dance *(ah-wash)* and ritual gatherings, they find a way to make themselves visible to the young men. "Contact" between members of the marriageable generation takes place at work and at the festivals. Songs and the obvious symbolism of flowers, such as the bouquets of *ghunbaz,* are the vectors of this dialogue. Both of these will be found in this overarching event that is Bilmawn's performance.

As already mentioned, men are responsible for the heavy labor without which the soil itself would disappear. Rain, snow, violent floods, and summer storms destroy the system of irrigation ditches and constantly threaten the fields. The bulkheads supporting the terraces must be rebuilt and the fields reworked each time they are washed away or strewn with debris brought down in the ravines. Plowing and harvesting require intense activity, for they must be undertaken during short periods, not only because of the rains and water, but also because local beliefs and knowledge divide the year into auspicious and inauspicious times. And after the first of October forces must be quickly mobilized to sow the barley, and in July, *amazuz* corn must be planted right after the barley is harvested. But once the grain is in, a short period of calm and relative abundance creates a time favorable for weddings and the large festival gatherings around important sanctuaries that influence the village and bring it into contact with larger groups of people. But in September the walnuts are ready for harvest. Then, from the ground or high in the trees, the men shake loose the nuts while the women stoop to gather them.

Whatever share men have in daily work, the differences between generations are clear and reflect the varying prestige and roles within the domestic group. The father, head of the household, supervises the group with the elders and rarely carries out the work himself. His place is on the council of elders *(jma't),* which administers the communal resources and village politics. It is the young men who toil. The other generations give orders and do not willingly work except during periods of intense labor. In general, as has already been noted, sons obey their fathers and young men their elders; but this does not always happen without discussion, which can deteriorate into conflicts that tear the *takatin* apart. For while local standards require one to show respect to one's elders, they also compel every male to "behave like a man." Thus work and farming offer young men a chance to develop their initiative by contesting the law of their fathers and the domination of their elders.

The price the younger men pay for their emerging autonomy is harsh conflict, especially since access to decision-making, inside the domestic group as well as the village council, does not automatically come with marriage. As already noted, this is but a first step. The birth of a male child is another. But for a man to have the full prerogatives of a head of a household, his own father must first die. This rule is sanctioned by Ait Mizane ritual, for after the sacrifice at Sidi Shamharush's *mussem*, when the sacred flesh is divided up, young married couples receive merely the leftovers. Indeed, they have the right only to a small portion. Even when the couple have their own separate house, the father claims the large share that falls to each household. To claim this portion, and the status it reflects, a man must wait for his father's death.

Once married, a man stays away from the young bachelors (*i'azriyan*, singular *a'azri*), but he is not yet a complete adult. He is a young man, or *afrukh*, in local terms, and is given only a "small share," so to speak. Like all the young men, he seeks to assert himself in the struggle with this stingy land and by standing up to his father.[16] Work and family ethics seem to be in total opposition, a situation that reveals one of the structural tensions that underlies the action of the masquerade.

The annual cycle of human activity slows in the winter, quickens in March and April, and further accelerates with the approach of summer. The slow period accompanies the cold weather when plants are dormant, while the heightened pace responds to the return of spring when vegetation is renewed. During the cold the flocks stay in the village, the barley is underground, and irrigation is impossible because of the cold and the risk of frost. People stay put. Humans and animals dip into their reserves, for nothing comes from the fields or from venturing afield. The animals grow thin, and when the snow covers the ground the trees must be trimmed to supplement their daily feed. People sell some of their goods, and it is not unusual for some of their animals to succumb to the rigors of winter and scarcity of resources. Humans are also affected by want, although starvation is rare. They have spent their cash on seed and to supplement their stores of barley.

The festival season comes to an end with the sacrifice that precedes planting (*tighersi n'l'ada*) and harvesting the walnut crop. Many chickens will be slaughtered in honor of the feast of the agrarian new year (*annayr*); but long months will pass before the celebration of the *ma'ruf*, in March–April, where several goats will be sacrificed.[17] In the spring, the livestock, which are now better fed, offer the households some relief, as it is now possible to sell a few head to replenish the dwindling stores of food. This is a vital matter now because the increased activity calls for renewed energy. In this context of scarcity, all sacrifices, Muslim and others, procure the meat that is so greatly desired. At the same time, the norm in this situation of want calls for discretion and a morality based on dignified sharing: thus ordinary behavior integrates, in this other tension, the ideal and the necessary.

For it must be remembered that this is a village, a humanized space where the values of the group protect it against all dangerous powers, be they human or natural, visible or invisible. This is not the case in the *adrar* or the *lghabt*. The latter is crisscrossed by uncontrollable forces, unlike the village where the community finds itself in regulated contact with its gods and demons. Not only is the forest traveled only by males; often they are alone and must spend only a short time there. Those who acquire a taste for prolonged visits are in danger of losing the habit of human commerce. Charcoal burners, woodsmen, and shepherds are marginal beings. The forest suits them, as it does wild animals. The *lghabt* and the *adrar* exercise their fascination on those who are unable to find a place in the human community. When, during the festival I describe, children are annoying, they are sent outside the village limits, and in the myth as is sometimes the case in the masquerade, Bilmawn is driven off into the forest.

The *lghabt* and *adrar* rarely contain any sanctuaries, with the exception of a few special sites: exceptionally large and rich communal springs or pastures. For example, there are *igudlan* (singular *agdal*), such as Oukaïmedan, where shepherds and flocks concentrate in the summer, after it has been opened according to the custom of the groups who use it. This type of site is protected by a great saint whose sanctuary is located in an inhabited valley, and custom is in the hands of his descendants and under the supervision of the local authorities.

Everything else is open pasture, under no one's control except at intertribal or intervillage limits. Shepherds tend to erect their shelters in groups of two or three but go alone during the day to keep their flocks separate. Like the peddler, the woodsman, and the charcoal burner, the shepherd is a solitary man. And unlike the rest of them, most often he is young and single.

Marriage introduces a youth to his new status as a man and is considered by all to be the first condition that he must meet to establish himself in the community. As a man's children arrive and he grows older, he gradually begins to take part in the council of elders. He sees his influence increase and, in his domestic life, strengthen next to that of the patriarch. The young married man will spend less and less time with those who have not yet wed, and if he does not, he is thought guilty of a propensity for "young men's things": alcohol, the quest for sexual pleasure, and other deviations that signal a "heedless life." Standards decree that instead he devote himself to the serious matters of the household and family. But there again, in addition to the opposition that is quick to appear between father and son in the fields, conflicts between brothers will occupy the married man who has become a full adult. And the friction is all the stronger when the brothers have different mothers.

It is not unusual for a man to have more than one wife. His first wife is sought as much as possible within the family and village. Here, as elsewhere in Morocco, the preferred choice is the daughter of the father's brother. She is the first wife (or *amenza*). This is the same term that refers to the first long-growing corn *(amenzu)*. But the harsh work in the field and the house, as well as frequent pregnancies, "tire out" the woman, to use a local expression. And if a man has the means, he does not hesitate to take a new, younger wife. She is the *tamazuzt,* the term that is used to refer to the short-growing summer corn *(amazuz)*. Then the *amenza* plays the role of the elder. She rules the house, goes about more freely, allocates domestic roles, and enjoys a certain degree of prestige if she has given several sons to the household. The *tamazuzt* must obey; but she is closer to the head of the house, and her children, younger than the others, usually enjoy favored treatment. The discord quickly engendered by this marital arrangement drives the first wife's sons to leave their father's house and go out on their own. But as a general rule the father keeps his lands together and farms them in common with his sons. And no matter what has been said of the patriarchal system of North Africa, maternal uncles help their nephews, while in theory the father depends on his own brothers. Thus women bring in an element that disrupts the solidarity and cohesion of the agnatic group. This is yet another tension coiled at the center of the physical reproduction of the guarantors of patriarchal rule and morality.

In a survey recently taken in Timezguida n'Oumalou on marriage and kinship,[18] young wives *(tamazuzt)* say they suffer from the impotence of husbands who are too old and who, in their words, "have no more milk." These husbands, on the contrary, see their younger wives as insatiable and obsessed with sex. The bitterness of the women is echoed by the criticisms that the young men aim at these old men, whom they describe as *herrma*. The term is widely used, especially in the plain of Marrakech, to refer to the equivalent of Bilmawn (called Bujlud). In the context of the Ait Mizane, it depicts decrepit old men incapable of moderating their desire who steal girls who ought to remain with their own generation.

This other structural tension is a source of conflict for young men, young women, old men and, of course, the first wives, who detest polygamy as much as the others. Young women may flee to a sanctuary or, in urban areas, depart in search of another husband: traditional solutions to the dilemmas caused by this situation. Couples commonly break up, and second marriages are not unusual, for a young man without any capital willingly marries a woman freed from a first union. In all cases, contact between the sexes remains difficult, and young men are haunted by the fear of a moment of weakness at that fateful meeting on their first wedding night. In their eyes all sorts of machinations may conspire to bring down the virility that is consubstantial with their maleness; the evil eye and another woman's revenge by sorcery are usually mentioned. The power of desire, the emotion of this long-awaited first contact, and the rarity of sexual relations outside marriage undoubtedly contribute to the drama of this highly ritualized encounter between man and woman.

If this description has led the reader to form an impression of immobility, now is the time to dispel it. For neither life in the valley, nor the festival that in so many ways takes its material from it, is immutable. Like everywhere else, demographic pressure has been felt. New crops are introduced and new fields created on the mountainside. Of course, access to the Ait Mizane country, especially in the winter, remains difficult. In the past, contact with the outside world was certainly limited by the rugged terrain, the state of the roads, and lack of safety. It was not until 1930 that a passable road for motor vehicles connected Asni to the route running from Marrakech to Agadir across the Tizi n'Test Pass. Before that only mule trails connected the region to the city of Marrakech in the north and to the country south of the Atlas. Consequently, a recent study, based on the reports of a few explorers, insists on the isolation of the Ait Mizane. But it must be emphasized that while even today they are far from the great modern highways, since their valley dead-ends at the foot of Toubkal, this does not mean that in the past they, like all the mountain people of this region, did not have ongoing ties with the town of Marrakech, several times the capital of the kingdom and the principal market of southern Morocco. The Ait Mizane valley is a tributary of the plain for its daily ration of food and due to mechanisms in the market that are dictated by insufficient harvests or speculative crops (barley and nuts, respectively). The city and the plains carry out an "unequal exchange" of grains, textiles, and manufactured goods for the valley's fruit, livestock, and some products of the traditional pharmacopoeia: the bark of the walnut root *(swak)* and iris bulbs.[19]

With the opening of the road, the valley of course has been infinitely more exposed to the outside world. The building of a modern school in the 1940s introduced the French language and contributed to the wider diffusion of Arabic. Former students occupy roles in teaching and civil service. And army recruiting during the last war and since independence has made a number of peasants aware of broader horizons. In 1942, in Imlil, the first commercial building opened; in it is what henceforth would be called *lgarage* (the garage). Regular transportation connects it to the main road. Today, fifty shops form a busy *swiqa* (permanent market). Some cafes, hotels, and a club for mountaineers attract many Moroccans and foreigners. Tourism,[20] excursions, and mountaineering, along with work in the mines, employ many young peasants who prefer these activities to the less lucrative work on the land. Over recent years vacation homes have been built, introducing a new style to the region.

This influx is countered by emigration to the great cities of Morocco or Europe. All these contacts, which strengthen integration with external networks, lead to the local changes mentioned above. These are the doings of young people who, on this point as well, find themselves in conflict with their elders. The planting of cherry trees is an instructive example. The colonial authorities unsuccessfully advised the peasants, skilled in passive resistance, to plant cherry trees; only in the 1970s did the trees begin to take over the fields. Young farmers succeed in overcoming the reluctance of the older ones, but growth is slow, for any modification affects the rotation of crops so tied to a collective management of irrigation waters. And there are the uncertainties of the market to be considered as well.

However widespread the innovation, local custom forcefully governs basic activities: eating, living, how to behave in the presence of a woman or other generations, getting married, or how to think about the physical environment, to cite only a few examples. The norms governing all these habits do not seem to be challenged by the modernism or theological radicalism of the new elites that have emerged since independence. Unlike any other ritual action, the feast and the masquerade the follows it deserve attention principally as a total event that raises all these issues at once in a visible fashion.

The Sacrifice

3

The inadequacies noted in the works discussed in chapter 1 are the consequence of a practice peculiar to ethnography and description in general, of the political ideas and contingencies of the day, and of the theoretical interests that inspired the interpretative systems that these investigators employed. The concept of survivals is a case in point, for it became an obsession, a painstaking enterprise transformed into a hermeneutics in which every detail becomes charged with revealing an ancient meaning and function; this renders the larger picture, as well as its contemporary function and significance, invisible. As a result, for these researchers each detail is literally a manifestation of an original system that is a product of their theoretical imagination.

In contrast, my approach is intended to depict the whole, which earlier readings have disjoined until it is unrecognizable. Thus I begin with a description of the Muslim sacrifice and follow it with the masquerade, since I view the two events as components of one and the same festival process.

Every year, like Muslims the world over, the Ait Mizane celebrate the feast of the sacrifice. It invariably falls on the tenth day of dhu-Lḥijja, the last month of the year. The old year has just ended and the new year arrives. Since the Muslims observe a lunar calendar, this feast has no particular seasonal associations; for during a complete cycle of lunar positions with respect to the sun, it takes place in every season. It goes by several names: the 'id-Umqqur, the 'id-Liekbir, or again, and this is the most frequent among the Ait Mizane, tfaska.[1] This last name refers only to the Muslim feast, and designates the ceremony, sacrifice, and victim all at once. All other ritual immolations—to the saints and the sanctuaries, to the victors of war, at the beginning of the seasons, and on the occasion of certain undertakings such as plowing, marriages, and so on—are designated by the same word, tighersi, which refers to both the victim and the act of sacrifice itself.

The tfaska that I witnessed took place in the year 1402 A.H., which fell on September 18, 1983. Special circumstances connected with the drought that beset the country for several years somewhat altered the "usual" format, as will be clear from the narrative below.

While under "normal" conditions the victim is often chosen several months ahead of time for fattening, this year nothing had been done because of the uncertainty about the feast itself. Since the beginning of the drought, the king regularly asked his subjects to refrain from sacrificing to avoid further diminishing the flocks, already severely affected by the scarcity of pasture and fodder. Even so, the sacrifice and pilgrimage to Mecca are a recurring topic of conversations for several weeks before they are supposed to occur. Livestock prices increase at the two weekly Saturday markets held in Asni and Tahannaout, meeting places for the villagers of the region. There they sell their products (animals, nuts, a few handicrafts) in order to obtain staples (sugar, flour, tea, coffee, matches) and textiles. Whether the sacrifice takes place or not, people stock up for the days of the festival, which generally see an increase in consumption. People repeat the names of those leaving for the holy sites of Islam, who will be given a joyful welcome when they come home several days after the tfaska. On the eve of the sacrifice there is a market especially for final purchases. Although held on the grounds of the weekly market, it is scheduled entirely according to the ceremonial calendar. In fact, it takes place on the day of 'arafat: the very day that believers who are making the pilgrimage carry out the halt during hajj (wuquf) before the mountain of 'Arafat, one of the canonical stages of the ritual of the pilgrimage to Mecca.

Since this year climatic conditions have been less severe, permission is granted to sacrifice. Families begin their preparations early. Men as well as women perform their ablutions. And everyone puts on new clothes. The men prefer to wear white to the mṣalla, a space in the towns and rural areas especially devoted to the prayer preceding the sacrifice. Here they make their ablutions with water. It must be recalled that this is not simply a matter of personal hygiene. The strict order in which the parts of the body are washed and the goal, which is purification (ṭahara), prove it.[2]

The prayer for the sacrifice takes place neither at the mosque nor at home but at the mṣalla. The area reserved for that purpose is sometimes surrounded by a low wall. Here only a pile of whitewashed stones marks the spot, which is next to the cemetery. Toward 9 A.M. the men, alone or in groups of two or three, ascend a sloping path that leads to this place. It takes nearly an hour for all of them to assemble. Then when the imam arrives, all the faithful chant praises to God. These words are repeated for about a quarter of an hour, after which the faithful position themselves to pray behind the imam, who in this case is the teacher at the Koranic school. They all are turned toward Mecca. The prayer comprises two prostrations identical to those of other Muslim prayers. After the ritual greeting ("Peace be upon you!") that ends the prayer, the imam rises to give the sermon *(lkhuṭba)*; he is followed in this by the faithful, who will then remain standing.

The sermon is composed of four parts. The first begins with the formula of praise to God and ends with a *takbir* that is repeated three times.[3] It deals with the beyond and describes with sinister and graphic images the fate of those who do not follow the way of Islam, who neglect their duties and commit sins. Their fate contrasts sharply with those who obey God's commandments and thus go to paradise, the resting place of the fortunate. Various *hadith* and quotations from the Koran evoke death, especially the first night in the grave, when the sinner is burned with a firebrand after being questioned by two angels named Munkir and Nakir. This brand, "applied to a mountain, would make it melt." Then the sinner is hung in the flames and set upon by "dragons and scorpions." The good Muslim is rewarded by God, who sends angels to keep him company in bliss until the day of resurrection. The whole section is a harangue in favor of strict observance of prayer, the other pillars of Islam, and obedience to the Koran and the Sunna.[4]

The second part takes up the idea of death. The theme is of a voyage for which one is wise to prepare. It repeats a divine admonition addressed to Adam, whom God has heaped with blessings but who has preferred to follow Satan. This is the explanation for his expulsion from the resting place of the fortunate and how he found himself tossed into "the house of misfortune" *(shaqa')* and expelled from the "house of eternity" to fall into "the house of annihilation" *(fana')*. This part ends with the formula, "God is the most great! God the great is truthful!" *(Ṣadaqa Allahu al-'Adim!)* Then the imam and the faithful sit down to rest for about three minutes.

The third part, the shortest of all, begins like the others with the *takbir* and insists on the holy, sacred character of this day and the feast: "Know that God holds you in his mercy!—that this day that is yours is a great day; God has honored it and has made of it a feast on heaven and earth, and feast between heaven and earth!" Then follow several discussions of the feast as a tradition inherited from the prophet Ibrahim (Abraham),[5] and then once again the *takbir*, the fourth and final one that introduces the last phase of the sermon.

Devoted to the actual sacrifice, this part describes the victim, its nature and characteristics, and the interdictions that limit and direct how it is selected. There is a preferred sacrifice and a whole series of criteria concerning the species, its age, and condition. The victim is a domestic animal, from the kind that may be eaten, and it must not suffer any infirmity. It goes without saying that it must be procured in a legal fashion. The time is also specified: the sacrifice must take place during a period of three days, including the day of the prayer, and no slaughter after sunset counts. The ritual killing must be preceded by the *basmala* and the *takbir,* two formulas that can be broadly translated as "In the name of Allah, Allah is the most great!" Last, the conclusion stipulates that no part of the victim may be subject to any transaction.

Another sermon, recorded at the village of Timezguida n'Oumalou, lays more stress on the account of the sacrifice of Ismail by his father, the prophet Ibrahim. As in the case of the text from the Imi-n'Tassaft already summarized, the preacher has inherited this homily from his teacher. Neither, then, is the work of the imam who gives it. The first was composed around 1930 by this imam's father; since his death, his son brings it out at each feast to read to the faithful. The second is more recent; it is a copy of a text written by the preacher's teacher only a few years ago. Its first part contains an admonition in general terms that gives way to a long passage devoted to the Abrahamic act as the exemplary sacrifice and ends with the traditional list of the victim's required characteristics and the enumeration of circumstances that must surround the sacrifice. Invocations to God for the benefit of all Muslims and on behalf of the king and his armies conclude the sermon.

The actual sermon now complete, the *du'a* or invocation on behalf of everyone is performed. The imam and his faithful address God for the pardon of sins. This pardon is extended to relatives, ancestors, and the entire Muslim community. It is a prayer that calls for a blessing on the prophet of Islam and all the messengers of God; last, God's blessing is asked for all the community enterprises.

Once the prayer is finished, at the end of the morning, the faithful greet one another with this formula, "God pardon us!" Afterward they all take the path to the mosque, singing, "Let the prayer and God's greeting fall on Lord Mohammed as well as on his people!" This procession toward the mosque is made in a certain order: the faithful walk in two groups with some distance between them. The first group sings the phrase and stops walking just before it reaches the last word. There it is joined by the second group, who takes up the phrase, and so forth.

Then a meeting is held in the room used for the Koranic school. There the register of accounts related to the *shard* is brought out;[6] it contains a record of what is owed each year to the imam for his services: teaching the children, leading prayers, and burials, to mention only the most important. Each one must pay his share, as the *shard* is divided among all the households of the village. Once the accounts are settled and the ledger is closed, the men split up into small groups to eat the *fdur* (breakfast). This is an ample meal especially prepared on this day, composed of a kind of crepe that is dipped either in oil, butter, or honey. Each household is generally supposed to offer the assembled men a plate of *fdur*.[7] The meal is accompanied by copious amounts of mint tea, which the men prepare on the spot. Afterward, the men stand up to auction off the harvest of walnuts, the proceeds of which will go the mosque for its upkeep, according to the classic Muslim system of the *habus*.[8] The men in attendance haggle over the merchandise, and the names of those making the best offers, who will receive what has been gathered, are recorded by the scribe in a small notebook. They will have to pay six months later, indeed all these accounts will be considered together at a gathering like the present one, which takes place at the feast that ends the month of fasting.[9]

The women are not present at any of these activities. They spend the morning cleaning house and making the *fdur*. Once in a while, there is a woman of special status with urgent business to put before the assembly who will come before the *mṣalla*. Generally it is an old woman without resources or a widow who comes to ask for help from the community or to make a complaint against someone who may have treated her unjustly. However, except for such cases, women go to neither the *mṣalla* nor the mosque. "There is nothing for them to do there, and," people add, "the sacrifice is none of their business."

Back home after this auction, the heads of the household themselves slaughter the victim or have it killed by someone more expert in this art. The animals's throat must be slit just above the uvula; otherwise the sacrifice is unacceptable and the consumption of the meat unlawful, like that of all animal flesh which has not been ritually slaughtered. The household where I observed the ritual is a comfortable one; the victim is a sheep. The two teenage boys, who attend the lycée in Marrakech, forbid their mother and the other women to apply "make-up" to the animal or to give it the traditional mouthful to swallow just before the fatal blow. The women have the custom of outlining the victim's eyes with a stick dabbed in kohl, as one would make up a person. This powdered antimony is the same substance women use to "blacken" their eyes during the festivals and on occasions where it is fitting to make oneself more attractive by using a cosmetic. In

Muslim tradition as reported here, it is an act of piety to darken one's eyes on Friday, following in that the prophet himself. The animal is offered the ritual mouthful in a big wooden spoon. Just before its throat is cut it is forced to swallow a mixture of henna (in the form of dried leaves), leavening, and barley, which then is found in its mouth or throat after its death.

The slaughter takes place in front of the door to the house, and the animal is laid on its side facing Mecca. A man steadies the animal to help the sacrificer, who exposes the animal's throat and, uttering the canonical formula ("In Allah's name! Allah is the most great!"), quickly slits it with a large knife *(tuzzalt* or *tajnwit)*—this is the knife for butchering large animals, not the small dagger *(lmus)* used for small animals such as fowl and which can be carried on one's person.

In spite of everything, the women rush over to collect the spurting blood in a wooden spoon. The animal struggles for a few moments. When the men drag it off to a corner to cut it up, the women come back and throw a few handfuls of salt onto the pool of blood, which is left to dry in the sun. Some of the collected blood will be sprinkled on the upper sill of the door to the house; the rest is dried and kept in the kitchen in a piece of cloth. It will be used for fumigations in cases of illness, debility, or accidents attributed to the work of spirits *(jnin).* It is often put in protective amulets that mothers like to acquire for their children.

The dead animal is dealt with exactly as if it were at the butcher's. First it is "inflated" by inserting a hole between the skin and the flesh below the knee of the hind leg, which makes skinning it easier. Then the skin is removed after the head is separated from the body. When it is opened to be cleaned, the gall bladder is carefully preserved. It will be hung on a wall to dry above the hearth. It is reputed to be highly efficacious in the treatment of all kinds of wounds, especially on the fingers and toes. At that time it is placed in hot water, and when it softens, it is only necessary to put the wounded digit into the water.

The skin is tossed up onto the roof, where it will dry. The viscera, especially the liver, lungs, and heart, are cut into small cubes and rolled in the fine part of the caul to be roasted on skewers over charcoal and eaten immediately (this is the traditional *bulfaf*). The head and feet are first cleaned by putting them into the fire and then are washed and cooked in the couscous that will be the evening meal. The fatty parts of the caul as well as the rest of the offal are minced, salted, and rolled into balls stuffed in little sacks made out of pieces of the stomach that are sewn up with the small intestine. These balls, known as *kurdass,* will be hung from a cord to dry. From time to time one or more of them will be removed to garnish a couscous. Formerly, part of the carcass was also cut into strips that were salted and dried in the sun. This is the custom of the *geddid* of the *tfaska,* which many people, including the family that had invited us on this feast day, have discarded.

I was unable to see for myself what became of the carcass. Indeed, consuming it takes several days. It is cut up as needed, and I could not—without offending custom—abuse the hospitality of the family whose life I shared on the day of the sacrifice. My hosts did provide some brief information concerning the fate of the carcasses. First the shoulders are eaten, then the legs. The principal dishes made with these meats are couscous and *tajine,* a stew made by simmering meat and vegetables together in the same sauce. In well-to-do families that kill several animals, sometimes a whole animal is roasted in the bread oven, or lacking that, in a specially constructed earthen oven (this is the well-known *meshwi*), and brochettes are carved out of the leg. In all cases it is necessary to avoid breaking any of the bones. Consequently, the butchering follows the animal's joints as much as possible, and carving at the table must be done carefully. The shoulder blade requires particular care. Fingers are used to remove the flesh, for one may not use one's teeth. Those who observe this rule may then, once the bone has been cleaned, use it for divinitory purposes. It is helpful in predicting the future, and some experts read in it events that may soon come to pass.[10]

The bones that are still intact, including those of the head and feet as well as the horns, are put in a basket that is hung from a beam in the ceiling of a closed room. They must be kept away from the dogs and cats. Later they will be taken far from the village and thrown into an isolated ravine. It is said that this is a way to ward off the accidents that cause fractures in domestic animals. After the carcass has been carved and prepared, the mistress of the house sweeps the victim's blood and excrement into a pile that she spreads on the floor of the stable.

Two events remain, which are associated with the sacrifice but already serve to link it with the masquerade that takes place the day after the feast. Sometimes the animal's skin is sold; goatskins are most often made into containers or churns, while sheepskins are thoroughly cleaned for use as prayer rugs. Since independence, giving the skin to the State is a gesture of solidarity with national or Arab causes.[11] The young men preparing for Bilmawn's masquerade make the rounds to collect gifts (*ziaras*) of money or in kind, and to obtain skins with which to clothe their character. When these skins must be given to the State, as was the case in 1983, arrangements are made to replace the fresh skins from the sacrifice given to the young men with old dried skins from the market or from animals killed at various times for meat. Last, another piece from the sacrificed animal apparently used to go to the Ait Bilmawn.[12] The large intestine is carefully washed and stuffed with eggs, butter, and flour. It is steamed in a couscous cooker. This kind of sausage is called Bilmawn's waterskin (*takashult n'bilmawn*). It also goes by the name of *sebt n'bilmawn* (Bilmawn's Sabbath), for it is given to his companions, who, as will be seen shortly, dress up as Jews and are referred to as such.

Narratives about Bilmawn

The Scenario

4

My predecessors' descriptions (chap. 1) present an incoherent game in which the general argument, preparation, and direction are impossible to discern. The two versions of the scenario given in this chapter betray the existence of a "text" that is created each year, as if by a director, by "Bilmawn's men." The relations between this scenario and the performance as it unfolds make it possible to track some of the improvisations as well as the logic presiding over the ad hoc development of this theater.

In April 1981, while working on agricultural techniques and tools, I met a young man of about thirty years of age. He was married and lived in the village of Imi-n'Tassaft, in the lower Ait Mizane, where I would later observe the sacrifice and masquerade. Over the evening meal we were speaking of local music and dance, which naturally led us to the matter of village celebrations. However, my companion did not mention the masquerade. When I asked him several questions on the subject, he hesitated and asked if we could save this discussion for another time. My interlocutor, whom I will call A., continued for several weeks to display a real reticence about discussing Bilmawn.

A. is currently the father of two children. He lives with his parents, who are still active, and his younger brother—also married—under the same roof. The family is of modest means; for many years the father worked in Marrakech in a small sawmill run by Europeans. But when the factory closed down several years ago, he was forced to return to the village, where he works several parcels of land he acquired recently and cares for his livestock with the help of his second son. A. looks for work whenever it is available, on construction sites in town and more recently in a mine that has just opened a half-day's walk from the village. When he cannot find work outside the village, A. helps his father and brother in the fields. The family claims the title of *sharif* (a descendant of the prophet), which it appears they were finally able to obtain after several requests to the guardians of the Sharifian genealogy.

A. took part in the masquerade, where he was given the role of the Jew. His younger brother, who has provided a second version of the masquerade, has never had a part, but like all the young men of the village he always enjoys following its progress. On June 16, 1981, approximately two months after A. gave his account, his brother gave his version. In both cases I began by asking these informants about Bilmawn, his identity, and the masquerade he leads. A. answered with the account given below and needed no further questions to prompt him. With his brother, more questions were necessary. His account, which is given after that of A., is less rich. However, it is worth noting because of the detail it contributes, especially concerning Bilmawn's character and costume. It also illustrates the differences that can be found in the degree of knowledge and mastery of the scenario.

In Berber he is called Bilmawn or Tamugayt. You take skins. Skins from the billygoat. First you spread them out. Then you arrange the head with the two horns. You cover his head [the person playing Bilmawn] with a piece of [burlap] sacking, which is sewn around him. His legs are covered up to the waist, each one with a skin, one on the right, one on the left. You cover his chest and back with two other skins. And his head with a goat's head from which the skull has been removed. You sew this last one at the neck to the two skins covering the chest and the back, so he has a complete goat's head, and a rope is tied around his waist. Before letting Tamugayt out, you put ashes on his shoulders, and he is supposed to go outside in a cloud of ashes. That is so that he will scare the kids. First another one who goes out; we call him Ismakh. I don't know what he's called in Arabic. . . . Ismakh is dressed in a black burnoose, that is, the *akhnif*.[1]

Ismakh has a stick in his hand, and his face is covered with soot. He wears whatever he wants on his feet. The others too, wear anything on their feet. Only their burnooses must not be black. They must be a little less so. Gray. There are four or five of them. They don't have any soot on their faces. They're called *udayan* (Jews). Yes, [to make] their faces, you take cardboard. Then you take egg yolk, which you mix with a little flour; [with that] you stick on hairs plucked from the goatskin [to make beards and moustaches]. Then you take a corncob (*aqurbash*) and sew it on the face to make the nose; that's the nose. You cut two slits [in the mask] for the eyes and a third one for the mouth. Then they go outside and start hitting people and throwing ashes at them. People yell at them, jeer, heckle, and laugh [at them].

It starts about nine in the morning. Ismakh comes out very fast. He has to be outside to scare the kids; especially to keep them from seeing who Bilmawn is [while he is getting ready]. He gets ready very fast. You bring the *ferrah;* you cover his face with soot, you give him his stick once he has his *akhnif* on and he goes out. To get [them all] ready, they are taken to the mosque and there everything takes place in the *akhurbish.*[2] First Ismakh is dressed, then the Jews, who all wear ropes around their waists, and then he is (Bilmawn). But when they go out, it's the Jews who go first. They are dressed and ready before him. But they must come outside and he must come out right after. They come out around two in the afternoon.

Right before going out you do *lfateh*[3] and say, "O God, pardon us . . . O God, pardon us for calling them Jews; for it's the festival; we're in the festival!" This prayer is said before going outside but also at the end [of the spectacle in the street]. [People also say] "O God, pardon us! O God, protect us!" They also say the *lfateh* once they are dressed. And then in the evening, after we have a good time, we go back to the same place and say another *lfateh.* Everything happens in the *akhurbish,* both putting on the costumes and the prayers. The young people of the *jma't*[4] are there. Not the older ones. They take care of business: They get out of the way; they stay away [from the spectacle] because they are ashamed. They have sons-in-law or in-laws [in the spectacle]. Some of them have sons there. They take off. First Ismakh comes out, followed by the Jews, followed by Bilmawn. Ismakh goes after the kids. He chases them and scares them. The kids must not know or guess who is [dressed as] Bilmawn. He doesn't [shouldn't] talk. The kids see him; he runs after them and they run away. Then he has to run all over, through all the streets. He doesn't chase the older people, just the kids. The Jews, when they go out, they have to shout and fill the air with noise. They say things that aren't nice. Not nice . . . [hesitation and laughter].

They go out like they are going to plow the fields. They turn (this way and that) and then go to a threshing ground (*anrar*). They work the threshing ground with a [real] plow to which they hitch Bilmawn-Tamugayt. Then they catch someone wearing white clothes [it doesn't matter who]. And then he is the *akhummas.*[5] The Jews cover him with ashes. With the ashes they are [also] planting. Then they make fun of him and jeer at him. They use sticks to lift up his clothes [to expose his nakedness]. All the people laugh at them [all]. Once the plowing is over, they get ready to harvest! Then they say to Tamugayt: "We've plowed and now we're going to harvest. . . . Go fix the meal for the workers! For we have just plowed and are going to harvest right away." They speak to Tamugayt the way they speak to a woman, for they make her into a woman. She finds a flat stone and piles dirt on it. She picks up little pebbles that she puts on the mound of dirt like they are meat and vegetables [this is couscous]. Sitting next to her hearth, she picks up another rock that she uses for a mirror. She looks at her face, puts some kohl on her eyes,[6] and makes herself look just like a woman getting ready to go out. She puts the kohl on her eyes with a little stick and arranges her hair. She makes everything the way it should be, puts the dish [of couscous] on her head, and walks toward the workers. Then the Jews shout to the crowd, "Line up to eat!" Tamugayt comes near; she walks a little farther, and all of a sudden trips on a rock, spills it all, and takes off. The Jews chase her. They catch her at the end of a street and bring her back to the workers who are waiting for their meal. These guys immediately start to hassle her by shouting, "Where is our meal, our lunch? Why did you spill it? Give us our lunch! Give us back our lunch!" The Jews turn to them yelling, "Here's your lunch!" and make obscene gestures at everybody. Then they go do something else.

Bilmawn lies on his back. One of the Jews gets on his chest, turning his back to him. He grabs Bilmawn's legs and lifts them up and moves them like the bellows at the forge.[7] Another [Jew] stands opposite with a stick and a bucket of water in his hands. He sprinkles Tamugayt [on his penis] and pretends to strike him as if he were an anvil.[8] Then he sprinkles water on him to harden (isqih) him. While striking, he shouts, "May you grow, may you prosper, may you get longer!" (Ka-ttgui ma-ttirgui!)" Then he opens his fly and urinates on Tamugayt as well as on the Jew who is working him like a bellows. The action is at its height. The women on the rooftops go crazy with laughter, as well as the men, and the children laugh. During this time the Jews shout and move about [around Tamugayt]. For all this they choose a threshing ground in the middle of the village so that everybody can watch.

Then Tamugayt leaves and everybody follows her. She stops in front of the doors and sometimes takes the passageways going into the houses. She leads the dance, for they dance every time they stop, and they yell, "Do the dance (Amlu urssa)!" The women give [the group] many things: sugar, bread, meat, rabbits, chickens, eggs. They give them everything [that they want]. They offer them things to eat and drink everywhere they go. Even

Tamugayt eats; for there is an opening [in his mask] that allows him to eat. The Jews run up and down the streets. Each one carries a sack (*asgers*) filled with ashes that they throw on the people they meet and those who dare come near them. The ashes are taken from the *akhurbish* or elsewhere. As they please.

Here, the guy playing Bilmawn has ringworm; Ismakh is played by a big fellow nicknamed Ḥarrgat. The two are single. Both of them are bachelors. Up to now they haven't gotten married. They are poor. Those who do one or the other thing (Ismakh, Bilmawn, Herrma, and the Jews) do it because the young people (*drari*) keep on asking them. . . . You can't say no.

When Tamugayt runs through the streets, she yowls like a dog, and if she meets someone, she hits him hard with her hooves. She runs like this until about eight at night, then it's dancing all the way back [with the whole entourage], Tamugayt followed by the Jews, and then Ismakh and the whole crowd of young folks, to the *takhurbisht*. They go back after the *lfateh* to pick up some money. In the *takhurbisht* they wash. The drums (*bendir*) are left outside. They aren't brought back to the mosque. Everybody goes to eat and relax somewhere, at a house. And when it's late at night, they meet again on the *assays* for the *ahwash*.[9]

The dance lasts two days. The women come out at night, and people dance until two or three in the morning. What has been collected every morning and cooked is eaten [by the young men]. People eat and dance in the evening, and in the afternoon they play. They begin the morning after the Feast [of the Sacrifice] of the *'id*. Not the same day as the feast, it's the day after and the day afterward that they play. The fourth day of the festival it's all over. The skins are donated by the people of the village; these are the skins from the sacrifice.

In Azzaden, they play [Bilmawn] for a week. Until the skins rot on the players. At Timezguida n'Oumalou, it's for three days, and for us two days. We always start with plowing the threshing floor (*anrar*). People pretend they don't like it [Bilmawn]. But that's just talk, for they love Tamugayt. The Jews shout, "O Baba! O Baba!" When someone meets one of them, he asks him, "O, Jew, how is the year going? How does the harvest look?" "It will be a good year," the Jew answers, and he changes the subject to shout at his questioner, "It looks like you have fleas," and at the same time covers him with ash [to kill the fleas]. That's called the *kafur*. As for Ismakh, he doesn't talk.[10]

They choose someone else and dress him in rags. He covers his head with a hat (*ṭarbush*) and carries a basket with several things inside: small

stones, pieces of plastic, bones, goat hairs, corncobs, and rags. He carries
an old shoulder bag in which he puts his notebook. He looks for the
women and offers them his wares: "Look, madame! Here is *ikhan n'tfullust, ibjir n'ugru, izuran n'umdlu, idarn n'tfullust.*" The woman who has
been addressed in this manner laughs and answers *"Wakha ya 'at-
tarnnu."*[11] Then the peddler gives her some of the hairs and tells her, "Go
burn all this under you! But be careful! Lift your pants up high!" No matter how old the woman is, he says it. Nobody can take offense. During
these two days, it's total freedom. You can say anything.

In other valleys, it's even worse. They do anything. They even go as far as
to take a woman away from her husband. A man desires another man's
wife? He waits until that day to dress as Bilmawn, for he can go into anybody's house. And on that day nobody but the women are in the houses.
We haven't played Bilmawn for two years here. We avoided it because [this
game] provokes hatred and troubles. There are people who use this means
to take advantage of the women. If you see a woman in this situation, you
cannot stand it. Here in our village, our relatives had given up Bilmawn for
a long time because our ancestors were burned on this occasion. They were
heating their drums *(bendir)* over big fires that they would jump over [as
custom demanded]. Two of them ran into each other above the fire. They
fell in and were burned. The tragedy took place when my father was still a
child.

In Msouft and Aguir, the play lasts for two days; in Timezguida
n'Oumalou, three; in Tamit, two; but in Imnan it lasts seven days, and in
the Nfis,[12] eight. Until the skins rot. During this time, the women don't go
anywhere. They go onto the terraces and rooftops and keep track of Bilmawn in this way. They don't do anything for these two days. It's a rest.
They have to stay in the house. The men [the mature and married ones]
leave the village; they look after the animals and go out after water and
wood. They are ashamed. They cannot stay in the village. They cannot listen to the [obscene] things said in the presence of their children, in-laws,
and relatives. For those two days, it's democracy!

The face [that is, the mask] of the Jews is made of cardboard. Before we
had cardboard, we used sieve skin.[13] This skin has many little holes in it.
The beard and moustache are put on with egg. The mask isn't covered with
soot. Only Herrma has his face and his feet covered with soot. The Jews
don't have any soot on them anywhere. There are slits cut [in the masks]
for eyes.

They do another piece: the workers. They must line up, and each one has a name that the boss must put on a list before they go to the plowing and harvesting. The boss shouts the question and the worker the answer:

Boss: What's your name?

Worker: Snake's Ass!

B: What's your name?

W: Rooster Ass!

B: What's your name?

W: Hedgehog Head!

B: What's your name?

W: Cow's Ass!

B: What's your name?

W: Monkey's Ass!

B: What's your name?

W: Hedgehog Prick!

B: What's your name?

W: Bull Prick!

B: What's your name?

W: Goudman's Ass's Face![14]

B: What's your name?

W: Cock-Sucker!

B: What's your name?

W: Prick Head!

B: What's your name?

W: Match Head!

Everybody has names like ass-something, prick-something, or something-fucker. Every time you get to a person who has ringworm, they're called Prick Head. Match Head is a name given to bald guys, especially.

The workers pass before the rabbi-boss in this way. One of the Jews is the rabbi, and is called *Iḥazzan Ikhan addikun.* For the moment, he is the boss. The workers work for him. When the game is over, the *ḥakham* must pay and clothe his workers. Then he sits down comfortably and with dignity on his seat, which is nothing but his stick. So everyone can watch with undisguised glee while the stick goes into the boss's asshole.[15] He holds a piece of paper that he uses to cut out [on the spot] his workers' clothes. Amid gales of laughter he slowly tears the sheet, accompanying this act with a noisy fart that he sounds with his mouth. Then, to finish up, he bargains with the workers.

Ḥakham: How much do you want for the harvest?

Workers (together): Three, plus *ṭuz* and the buttermilk!
(*tlata uṭṭuz ulban*)!

Three, that's the prick and the two testicles; *tuz*,[16] that's the fart that can
be made by penetration. The buttermilk is sperm. This game is the tough-
est of all.

This is the end of A.'s narrative. As already mentioned, about two months
later, on June 16, 1981, I obtained a second account of Bilmawn's doings
from A.'s youngest brother. Here is what he has to say about the masquerade:

The second day of the 'id-Lekbir, Tamugayt is led by his friends into the
akhurbish at the mosque. Not the prayer room but the place where the
water is heated for ablutions. There they take two skins. One is a goatskin
and the other a sheepskin. With the skin used to cover the back, head, and
face, they keep the neck open as well as the part that covers the skull, with
the horns, eye slits, nostrils, and mouth. To make the muzzle work, you
take a little stick that has a fork at one end. It's no more than a few centimeters long. The fork is placed on the player's lower lip. So Bilmawn can
work it with his jaws and open and shut the muzzle while he makes noise.
It works just like the jaws of an animal. Tamugayt pulls the goatskin on
over his feet; he uses the sheepskin for his head, face, and chest.
    All morning long, Tamugayt's friends get him ready. The Jews and
Herrma[17] get ready at the same time. Herrma wears a black burnoose; his
face and hands are covered with soot. The Jews wear the *akhnif* and masks
on their faces. These masks used to be made of bark. Now they are made of
pieces of cardboard. Moustaches are glued on with flour mixed with egg
yolk. Slits are cut for the eyes and mouth. Egg yolk is mixed with flour into
a kind of glue to hold the goat hairs on the masks. The Jews' hands as well
as their feet are covered with soot.[18] Before going outside, they attach
sheep's feet to Tamugayt's hands [The skins cover his arms and hands.]
    Late in the morning, Herrma is the first to go out. He runs all around,
yells, chases people and kids away, and hits everyone he meets. Tamugayt
follows him, shouting. He scares people. Women and children. He runs
everywhere, yelling, goes into houses, jumps from one terrace to another
and from one roof to the next, and hits everyone he meets with his sheep's
feet. He doesn't hit the women as hard. The men get some pretty hard
blows.
    Then people try to get him away from the village. The Jews follow him.

They carry sacks full of ashes and throw ashes on the people they meet. Before Tamugayt goes out, they put ashes all over him, and in the beginning they run after him sprinkling him with ash. He leaves [he is supposed to go out] in a cloud of ash.

At nightfall, they all go wash and stir up the *aḥwash*. While they are running about, people give them sugar, tea, meat, and all kinds of presents. In our village, this goes on for three days. But in Azzaden, it lasts seven or eight days, until the skins start to smell. They throw a big party with what the group collects and people danse the *aḥwash*.

Question: Who plays Tamugayt?

Answer: Anybody [the narrator's words are confirmed by his mother, who has just come into the room where we are talking].

Question: Married or single?

Answer: Anybody! Married or single. . . . It's not important [this is again confirmed by his mother].

In the old days, the masks were made of skin or something else. . . . Now, since people go to France, they bring back plastic masks, real ones. . . . And people wear them. Also in the old days, the Jews wore the old *akhnif*. Now they don't.

I asked many people about the Feast of the Sacrifice and the masquerade. Rightly so, my questions about the sacrifice were greeted with astonishment. Wasn't I a Muslim like they? Everybody knows about the sacrifice, and there is no need anywhere in the entire country to discuss it. They also responded that if I wished I could come observe it there. The topic of the masquerade provokes laughter and very often discomfort. Or again a few laconic sentences when I insist. Si Brahim, a friend of many years who is very pious but also fond of dances and hikes in the high mountains, retorts, "This isn't the time to talk about it. Bilmawn and the *aḥwash* have their time. It's not good to talk about them when it's not that time. And then, before, it was done everywhere in the valley. Now it's not done because of the authorities. Now everything is being lost. The people in Ardem (a village in the upper valley an hour's walk from his house) have the best *aḥwash* and the best Bilmawn."

Later I asked his son, who is married and lives with him. He maintains that people don't like to speak about those days during everyday life, "for that is when people do and say obscene things. And also, we haven't sacrificed for *tfaska* for several years because of the drought. In the village of Aguer, they haven't done it for several years. They are all *ṭolba*. They know

the Koran; almost all the men of the *jma't* know the Koran. They have decided not to play Bilmawn any more."

I was aware of the decision made by this village before this conversation
took place; and, having met one of the men from Aguer, I asked him about
it. This is his answer: "We follow the king's advice. We didn't sacrifice this
year [1981]. We didn't want to disobey the king, who is God's lieutenant on
earth. Therefore we didn't play Bujlud that year. It belongs to the *jahiliya*.
Now you're not supposed to do it. It was from before; these are customs
from before. Bujlud, these are the *jahiliya*. In Azzaden, it lasts eight days,
until the skins rot on the people who wear them. In Taourirt n'Oumalou it
lasts for three days. But it's not good. How come? The people are Muslim,
and all of a sudden they call themselves Jews and rabbis! It's not possible.
And then, someone who imitates a people afterward belongs to that
people!" [19]

However, this imitation is undertaken with great enthusiasm by all the
young men of the villages where I was able to watch Bilmawn. Lengthy preparations behind the scenes enable them to shift to the side of "this other"
people who take over the village, to the great dismay of the literati with their
rigid moralism.

Bilmawn Observed

His Preparation and Accession

5

In this chapter and the two that follow, I present two systematic accounts of the masquerades, which I observed in September of 1982 and 1983 respectively, and which brought the research I began in 1981 to an end. During my final visit to the site, I had the opportunity to profit from the collaboration of a scholar native to the region,[1] who willingly agreed to observe Bilmawn's feast in Timezguida n'Oumalou while I observed the same event in Imi-n'Tassaft. The valuable information he obtained in the first village will be given at the end of my presentation to complete and enrich the account of what I saw in Imi-n'Tassaft.

This narrative does not present the events in the order in which I originally observed them. While I first saw the scenes played in the streets and square of the village, I was immediately convinced that serious preparations had preceded the masquerade. Yet early on it was impossible to see what went on behind the scenes, for the young men—who are specialists in the matter—were hardly eager to divulge this information. Consequently I had no opportunity to watch the entire process until September 1983, when the young men accepted my presence "backstage." Here is how the scenario given in the preceding chapter is actually performed.

At approximately 10:30 A.M., young men, most of them unmarried, arrive at the soot-darkened room where water is heated for ritual ablutions. This is the *takhurbisht,* which they take over for the duration of the ceremonies. This long room, oriented toward the west, opens onto a terrace overlooking a ravine running along the south side of the village. It contains a fireplace, over which hangs a metal basin for heating water. It is fitted with latrines and a small cubicle that serves as a steambath. In one corner is the stretcher used to carry the dead to the cemetery after their ritual cleansing, which takes place in this room. Matting covers the ground near the fireplace, and a stone bench occupies the side opposite the hearth. The walls are covered with soot, and daylight penetrates only through the door, the sole opening to the outside. The *takhurbisht* adjoins the prayer room *(talmaqsurt),* with its whitewashed walls and neat and tidy mats. In the winter, once the members of the great *jma'a* have gone home after the last prayer, the young people congregate, sometimes until far into the night, in the *takhurbisht.*

On the terrace, a young man removes the animal's skull from the skin, carefully saving the horns. Two others cut masks out of cardboard for the Jews and make openings for the eyes and mouth. They attach a beard and moustache to each "face" with a glue made of flour mixed with egg. Surrounded by laughter, they attach a corncob to one of the masks to serve as a nose: it is the rabbi's face. Children hover around outside and try to enter the dark, warm room to see the preparations. The young men repeatedly chase them away and tolerate them only for a moment when they tire of the fight, and then they shoo them away once more. Occasionally a child will pick up a mask to try it on. The young men snatch it away and send the child packing without further ado.

By noon it is already crowded in the *takhurbisht,* where most of the young men have assembled. Not everyone takes an active part in dressing the actors or choosing the costumes and roles. Many, like myself, simply sit on the stone benches and watch the operations. The room is abustle with people constantly moving to and fro, and the air rings with discussions and disputes. Many ideas founder the moment they are mentioned because of misunderstandings. Children are constantly peeking, trying to invade the room, while the young men keep them out. Running in all directions, they seem mainly to be trying to keep up with all that is happening. Collecting the skins takes a long time. Some of the young men are asked for them. But no one complies, and those who have made the request burst out in reproaches and imprecations against the unwilling. "This lack of generosity! . . . It's proof that we can't do anything here [collectively]. . . . No one gets along any more!" Nevertheless, the skins pile up on the terrace, where for several hours a small group has been playing the drums. The drumming is not always well coordinated, but the sound carries.

Three men who are older than the rest—two are married and have children—set about preparing the skins. One of them is mature and poor in appearance. He is a charcoal maker who spends most of his time in the forest burning wood—often secretly—to make his merchandise.[2] Throughout the morning, the group has attempted to persuade a young man, who has obstinately refused, to wear the skins. By all appearances, he is between twenty-five and thirty years old. According to my neighbors, he is married and has children. His wife lives in the village with his parents while he looks for work wherever he can find it. This year he has returned from Casablanca for the Feast of the Sacrifice. Confronted with such obstinacy, his companions have threatened—according to what I am told—to make the sacrifice on the threshold of his house.[3] But he has apparently accepted his role in order to avoid these extreme measures.

The man strips to his underpants. He is supposed to wear the skins, which have been neither washed nor cleaned, against his own skin. First he is sewn into the skins that are supposed to form his "pants." The pouches for the sacrificed animal's testicles and phallus are positioned in back, hanging over his buttocks. Someone explains to me that this is "because everything on him is topsy turvy" (*ka igalbu lih kullshi*). Then he is dressed on top with two other skins that cover his chest and are joined to the pants at the waist. His arms and hands are also covered. His right arm is hung with two goat's feet on a stout string. In the middle of Bilmawn's chest protrudes a single enormous breast. The skin covers the man's chest, and care has been taken to sew the "head" of the skin to the pants and to attach the feet to the feet of the skin on the man's back over his shoulders, like suspenders. In this way the testicular pouches can be filled with corncobs and this breast can be made. Laughing, the "designer" of this costume points to the breast with the simple commentary, "The breast! The breast! . . ."

The character's head is covered with pieces of crumpled burlap, especially where the two horns will protrude. A forked twig is placed in his mouth. To be precise, the fork is placed on his lower teeth, while the other end pushes against the animal's upper lip. When he opens his mouth, the actor closes Bilmawn's muzzle; when he closes his mouth, he raises its upper lip. As a result he has to clench his teeth when he cries out, so that the sound emerges from his nose and throat. The specialist takes some time to adjust this outfit and arrange the eyeholes. At last he ties a belt around Bilmawn's waist, the way women wear it, while another one (*ḥmala*) encircles his chest under his armpits, the two ends tied in back. As the preparations come to an end, the good mood in the *takhurbisht* increases, and as they try on their masks the Jews multiply the jokes on the assistants.

The "faces" of the four Jews—which is what the four masks are called—have been drying all morning, set in the sun against the wall of the *takhurbisht*. While I saw no one competing to wear the skins, the roles of the Jews raised serious discussions and even violent exchanges. Several councils were held to decide who would play the rabbi. A neighbor explains to me that "to play the rabbi, you have to know . . . to know how to make people laugh." They entreat one of the young men to wear the costume. He refuses, then accepts. But a few minutes later he casts off his rags on the pretext of fatigue and refuses to go along with the game. For a short while the role is the subject of acrimonious dispute. The moment one of the candidates overcomes the rest by putting on the mask, his older brother enters the room. Everyone turns to him to make him take the role. He makes little show of resistance, but the younger brother, furious, refuses to remove the disguise. After labored bargaining, in which the rule is stressed that precedence is given to one's elder brother, the younger brother acquiesces, throws the costume on the ground, and goes into the steam room. He puts on his clothes and heads into a corner to sulk about the preparations until Bilmawn goes outside. His companions find his attitude "somewhat extreme, for his brother is more competent than he is." Meanwhile another young man is asked to accept the role of the slave.

One of the Jews puts on a mauve women's tunic, over which he carelessly drapes a torn and dirty grey vest. On his head, over the mask hiding his face, he wears a green bonnet. Torn pants full of holes complete the costume, and over his shoulder goes a plastic bag blackened with filth. This bag, like those carried by the others, will be filled with ashes just before the actors go outside. The second Jew wears a long, ragged, gray cape; a burlap bag hanging from his neck reaches down to his buttocks. He sports a yellow bonnet on his head. His yellow pants, made from shiny oilcloth, are too big for him and drag on the ground; he looks like he is walking in a bag. The two others bundle up in long capes, wrap rags around their necks, and hang their bags over their shoulders. Of course all of them wear masks, which are attached by a string tied around their skulls. The rabbi's corncob nose sets him apart from the other Jews. They give the general impression of repulsive bundles of filthy rags, which move like extremely agile puppets. The slave wears a black cape and covers his head with a hood tied around his neck with a rope. His pants are torn and dirty and are held up by a belt from which hangs a piece of red plastic hose that flaps over his fly like a penis. His face, of which only his eyes, nose, and mouth can be seen (the rest is covered by the hood) is completely blackened with several layers of soot. He wears, like girls do, a small corsage of marigolds. His hands and feet are painted exactly like those of the four Jews. All of them, including Bilmawn, wear black rubber boots.

When the preparations are over, the Jews begin their games and jokes even before they leave the *takhurbisht*. One of them rolls in the fireplace, raising a cloud of dust and ashes. Then, getting up, he throws himself on some young men whom he caresses and pretends to undress. The victims struggle, pummel him with a few blows, and leave the room. He goes after some others with an incessant laugh and cries of "Over there, you son of a whore! Ah, these thighs! . . . Such lovely flesh! . . ." This sort of scene will be repeated several times.

Then all the Jews fill their sacks with ash and grab their long sticks. The slave does the same. Bilmawn then lies down in the fireplace, on his left side, facing the wall. Two men squat next to him and without speaking a word, apply ashes all over his body. "He is supposed to go outside in a cloud of ash," they explain, "it makes people laugh." By the time he gets up, the disturbance in the *takhurbisht* is at its height. The Jews are running everywhere; shouts come from the crowd that earlier had been busy with the preparations or, like myself, had been watching the proceedings seated or standing in the overpopulated and overheated space. It is September, and the weather is fairly hot. Outside, other young men play their drums even more loudly, and the children have gathered in droves, insolent and fearful. The Jews await their victims on the terrace. The noise subsides a bit when the rabbi stretches out his joined hands, followed by one and all, in a short prayer:

> God, forgive us! We are only playing . . .
> If we dress as Jews, it is only for play! . . .
> May the year be good and auspicious!

Once this invocation is complete, the slave literally bursts out of the room. The children flee like a swarm of sparrows. Bilmawn runs out after him, followed by the four Jews. It is a crazy race that carries the whole company along. Laughter and jeers explode everywhere. The children shout out, "O the Jews! O Tamugayt!" The slave goes after them and then back to Bilmawn. The Jews chase the young men, dealing sharp blows to all they meet or to those who make a show of resistance. They shower their heads, even their eyes, with ashes and in return receive copious blows from switches of green wood. They join forces with the slave to protect Bilmawn, for he is sometimes hit and repeatedly pulled over and harassed. The children keep entering the fray and flee before the slave who pursues them until they reach the ravine bordering the village. Over and over he chases the children away, and once they have gone past the ravine the slave lets them be, so they return to the company.

This business leads everyone to the first house to be visited, which is located in the upper part of the village at the limit of the developed and inhabited space. First the slave enters, through a wide-open door. He inspects the house as he races through, jostles the women, takes the stairs up to the principal terrace. There he tips over the water jars as well as every pot or pan that he finds. Then he goes onto the roof and stomps about in a comical dance that shakes the whole house. He comes back down and goes outside to post himself, brandishing his stick, in front of the door and bars all from entering. Only Bilmawn, with the four Jews still in tow, may come inside. In theory such visits, which will continue until every house has welcomed the company, are made exclusively to the women, for the men must absent themselves from the village during these days of games and "freedom," the rule being that if one of them is "caught," the Jews will mock him in public and divulge real or invented secrets—particularly those of a sexual nature—to all: women, children, and the young men who relish the scene.[4] The visit is short. The rabbi addresses the women, especially the mistress of the house. He pretends to ask her about her husband's health; then he demands presents. Bilmawn jokingly goes after the women, as if to touch them. They back away and hide, but if the pursuit lets up they immediately reappear. The company are given eggs and flour. One of the men in the family, who is there, removes part of the shoulder from the animal sacrificed the night before and offers it to the group. Custom dictates that the first house visited give this present.[5] Then the rabbi, surrounded by the three Jews, recites a parody of the prayers and invocations said on behalf of the family: "God, master of the worlds, be praised! The ravine has collapsed and has fallen into the Wad Issil!"[6]

Again out of doors, the band picks up speed. The rabbi chases the children, then turns to the young men, whom he hits with cries of "Sons of whores, what are you doing here, start chanting and do the *ahwash!*" Insults and blows rain down. Children take off, crying, "O Jews! O the Jews! O Tamugayt!" Again the rabbi attacks the young men, who respond by pounding him vigorously. One of them picks up an old skin rotting in the sun and hits the judge on the head with it. This stinking weapon is fought over, grabbed, and used by many in turn until it completely falls apart.

The brawl rages on; the rabbi, aided by the other Jews, succeeds in gathering some young people around the drummers, who have just started playing. Now the *ahwash* begins, and it will follow Bilmawn and his group everywhere they go. Once the young people are together, they stand in a semicircle around the drummers. In theory, when the dance begins, no one can remain outside the circle. Unmarried girls are supposed to join in. The Jews encourage them, urgently pushing them to take part. Do they dare put up any resistance to the wild chorus? They are immediately discovered, whether hiding in their houses or gathered on the terraces, and shoved into the circle. However, for a long time the girls manage to escape and refuse to join the game. People drift away, and the visits to the houses continue. The girls follow; the Jews succeed in blending into the scenery and let them wander even farther. And then, coming upon the girls from behind like a band of demons, they push and hit them, pull them and hurl them until they stand opposite the young men. One of the girls receives a blow that sends her flying several meters onto a rocky platform. She picks herself up only to be set upon by one of the masked men and shoved into the lines of dancers. Some of the girls are crying. Then they relent, and the *aḥwash* begins. However, the continued singing in the sunlight, with only brief stops for rest, tires the girls out, and soon they are dripping with sweat. Some of them seek the shade, only to be brought back to their task. Swearing, they draw back, displaying their ill humor. No matter, the dance continues. After a time they all get into the spirit, adjust to the rhythms, and relax, while the joyous, powerful music everywhere accompanies Bilmawn on his noisy round of visits.

Women, girls, young men, and children are decked out in new clothes for the feast of the sacrifice. The women and girls are well dressed; some wear corsages of freshly picked marigolds,[7] Bilmawn also wears one, and so does the slave. After the visits, Bilmawn regularly stations himself among the girls to enliven the dance. His gestures are not those of a man but recall those of a woman, except for the contortions that shake his genitals which, as was mentioned earlier, hang over his buttocks. Meanwhile the slave is inspecting the next house that the company will overwhelm. The Jews harangue the dancers with shouts of, "Dance, sons of whores! Dance, or I'll bugger you!" and take after all those who stop or give signs of leaving the parade. In this brouhaha the slave comes out of the house, which he has turned topsy turvy, and as usual stands at the entrance to keep anyone but Bilmawn and the Jews from entering. I saw him at work in a house belonging to a friend in the village. First he pursues the women, who flee to the terrace, where he goes up to join them. There he comes close to them, touching them on the shoulders and chest with his hooves and making a few gallant gestures. The women then play a game of approach-avoidance. For a few minutes everyone enjoys this vacillation, then a pot of basil attracts notice. Bilmawn picks a few sprigs, which he offers to a young woman. She backs off, but nevertheless is careful to receive the gift. The man wearing the skins executes a few dance steps and goes after the others, whom he lightly strikes with his hooves.

Meanwhile, after eating and drinking what they were served, the Jews seek the mistress of the house demanding their presents. This time they want more than the traditional gift of eggs and flour. The rabbi cries that he wants a chicken (*"tafullust,* o Madame, *tafullust! . . ."*). The woman turns a deaf ear. But the Jews go after the fowl. The rabbi keeps on repeating his request, each time with more vehemence; the woman gives in. The chicken is then handed to one of the young men, who serves as porter and carries a large basket that is already half filled with an array of products: for in addition to the flour and eggs, people also give tea, coffee, sugar. The Jews filch whatever they can get their hands on with impunity.

In the course of a visit that I was personally unable to observe, the Jews exit a house after grabbing a rabbit, despite the bad temper of their hostesses.[8] The oldest woman, the mother of the head of the household, who normally is in charge of the others and administers the provisions, presents a terrified child to Bilmawn. Then, following the rabbi's orders, the *aḥwash* becomes more lively. The child struggles and drowns out the music with his yells. Bilmawn touches him several times with his hooves, and the parade moves on to another house. Here are some of the words addressed to the women inside the house:[9]

> Show yourself, daughter of a whore,
> Do you want to be fucked?
> This one has no shame [spoken to the woman
>   who collaborated with me and who wears glasses]
> She wears glasses.
> Do you want me to start with you?
> What beauty do you bring to us [to her husband
>   and myself]?
> Allah give you aid deep in your house [addressed to
>   the husband—an allusion to the sexual act]!

Then the rabbi turns to the mistress of the house:

> In the name of the clement and merciful God!
> The *sha'ba* is thrown into the *sha'ba*
> And was carried off by the Wad Issil.
> Si Abdelkebir is in your hands, lift it up for him,
> By God, o madame, two eggs and not three!
> The Jew is lying on top of you,
> They all have nailed it into you.
> He has returned and gone into the back of your house,
> This year, you are desirable.
> O madame, tonight undo the belt of your pants

So that I'll give it all to you!
O Madame Khadduj, who do you want to fuck?
God made Sidi Ali consent [to give you to us]
Sidi Mohammed wants a new wallet [a new vagina].[10]
Put it there with your own hands,
Quick, serve the Jew,
If not, he'll spend the night on top of you!
O madame, your merchandise [that consists]
Of gold goes well!
Do you hear what we need? The ass!
O madame, let God give Si Ahmad [the husband]
A prick twenty centimeters long,
Then you'll feel it and see!
Here's [the recipe] for the fumigation;
A little *fasukh,* a little benjamin, a little coriander;
You mix that all with Bilmawn's wool.[11]
Do you understand? You take off your pants. You need it

Soon the procession reaches the central square of the village, next to the mosque. About a third of the houses have been visited; the dance and the music stop. The Jews take the drums and stand with Bilmawn and the slave in the middle of the square. Young men and women stand around the scene. The married women watch the events from where they stand on the terraces overlooking the square. Now begins what is called the play *(alla'b).*[12]

Bilmawn Observed

Street Theater

6

In the center of the main square, the rabbi stands to address the crowd in these terms: "O assembly! How should one properly begin? With the wedding or the plowing?" And without waiting for an answer, the slave goes off in search of a plow. He is gone for a good while, during which the Jews trade blows, insults, and jokes with the young men. Children throw stones at them. The Jews pursue them, and those who come near receive a shower of ash on their heads and faces. At last the slave arrives, carrying the implement on his shoulder. He puts it on the ground, and the participants immediately proceed to the annual repair of the plowshare, which normally proceeds the plowing. The air is filled with shouts: "Sharpen the plowshare! It has to have a good edge! It's got to dig! It has to have a good edge."

The blacksmiths go to work. Bilmawn lies down, belly up; the rabbi sits on his chest, with his back to his face. He grabs his legs, which he raises and works as if they were the handles of a bellows.[1] People ask him to make the wind to fan the fire, saying, "Fart, daughter of a whore!" Then one of the Jews notes that perhaps the pipe is blocked; he tickles Tamugayt's anus with his stick. The scene is repeated several times, to the crowd's great mirth. When the plowshare seems to be red hot, it is taken from the fire to be struck and sharpened. One of the Jews takes it and, making as if to put it on Tamugayt's phallus (which serves as an anvil), orders his companion to "strike the iron." The latter strikes several blows, crying, "May you grow and prosper!" His companion, as if to encourage him, answers, "Hit him on the head! The whole head will be for Tamugayt!" Once the plowshare is sharpened, it has to be doused with water to cool it. The Jews then open their flies, brandish their penises, and urinate (for real, this time) all over Bilmawn as well as the blacksmith. The uproar is at a peak; laughter and jibes fly back and forth. Shouts and noise emerge from the terraces, where the women miss nothing of the spectacle.

Now it is time to begin the plowing. Tamugayt is harnessed to the plow.

For the moment she is the cow that pulls the plow, and for the moment the rabbi has become the landowner. "Bring the *khammas*. Where is the *khammas (awid akhummas!)?*" The slave takes by surprise a young man in the crowd who vainly struggles to escape before finally giving into the game. He takes the handle of the plow and the labor begins. The *khammas* is called all sorts of names: "Wet ass! Donkey dick! Do you want some milk, whore's son?" Tamugayt pulls, hesitates, and falls down. She is brought to her feet, insulted, and ordered to pull. The Jews poke their sticks into her backside and act as if they are striking her. Meanwhile, one of them flings ash in the air. Then the *khammas,* taking advantage of the momentary distraction, disappears. Another one is selected. This one makes as if to continue the work; then suddenly he pivots the plow around on its base; as the beam skims over the ground it mows everyone down: Jews, owner, slave, and Bilmawn. The scene makes a hit and is repeated until the actors are worn out.

As it should be, the plowing is immediately followed by the harvest! Tamugayt then becomes the rabbi-owner's wife. She fixes couscous for the fieldhands working under the watchful eye of the owner, who stands next to the field. A few handfuls of dirt serve as semolina, and stones are the vegetables and meat. The dish cooks on the makeshift hearth while the woman is preoccupied with her appearance. She makes up her eyes, face, and mouth with special care and from time to time arranges her dress. Taking advantage of her husband the owner's absence, the slave turns her on her back and frenetically copulates with her. Then the first Jew arrives, beats him and throws him on the ground to take his place; he is treated the same way by the second Jew, who is quick to undergo the same fate. These brawls and couplings continue in the general tumult until the master's voice is heard. Then the assailants disappear, and the woman places the food in a dish that she puts on her head to take to the workmen. On the way she trips over a stone, falls, and spills all the food on the ground. She flees, and the workers go after her, crying, "Give us our food! Where's our food! You've lost the food, whore!" As soon as they catch her, she gets away.

Then the rabbi-boss must pay his workers. Custom also requires that he give them clothing. At that time, to make himself comfortable he sits on his stick, which causes him to give off a sonorous fart. The workers are called one by one. All answer to absurd and obscene names. The boss rips a piece of paper to make the workers' costumes. A long (simulated) posterior noise accompanies each tear. At last he speaks to them to negotiate their pay: "How much do you ask?" And without waiting for a reply, he makes an obscene gesture while saying, "Here, take it! Take all three of them and multiply it by two"—a sentence understood by all to mean a multiplication of the penis by two testicles. The children repeat the words, along with the gesture, until they have had enough, all of it spiced with insults addressed to the rabbi and all his companions, who quickly regroup into the procession to continue visiting the houses.

All at once the game gets carried away. The Jews head off at a frenetic pace and soon vanish into a house where Bilmawn is chasing the women, and the slave, as the rule has it, is posted in front of the door. They tear around, leaping from terrace to terrace and jumping from roof to roof, much to the annoyance of the master of the house, who is not far away. Their actions are highly visible, since these roofs, which are in the center of the village and below the level of most of the houses, offer an admirable view, easily seen from all around. After this comic race, the four Jews, headed by the rabbi, line up and, brandishing their sticks like penises, pretend to make love to each other, amid laughter, shouts, and hoots. They trade roles with an intense pleasure betrayed by repeated orgasmic cries, clickings of the tongue, and urgent encouragements to push "still deeper."

Then the Jews order the young men and women to make another dancing circle; they overcome all resistance with their sticks. It is already five o'clock in the afternoon, and they still need to visit several groups of houses, one of which is separated from the main village by a deep gorge. The music accompanies the procession, which makes many stops because the participants are growing tired. At the end of the day, the rules are less severely enforced, and many accompany the festival as spectators, since the Jews and the slave are now powerless to force them to take part in the game and the *aḥwash*. Still there are a few young men who "squeal" for the rabbi. They whisper in his ear the names of those who are not taking part and show him their hiding places. The Jews surprise them and violently drag them back to the procession, not without giving them a good licking and covering them with ashes. But the Jews are also regularly attacked, though never by a group. An individual suddenly falls upon them, giving them a few sharp kicks. They respond with their sticks and call the slave to the rescue. These attacks and counterattacks will go on until the end of Bilmawn's rounds, at about nine or ten o'clock in the evening.

Custom requires that after a short period of rest they all come together again to celebrate; the common meal is prepared from the goods collected during the day's rounds. Then, once the meal is over, everyone meets for a dance in the central square. Yet in fact, because of the general weariness, on some nights neither the group meal nor the *aḥwash* take place. Only once, on the last day of the festival, was there a common meal, which was very festive, held in one of the village houses; after which everyone, including married men and women, went to the central square for the dance. It is to be recalled that during the day the village is off limits to married men. They return to the village at night after carrying out some of the jobs (gathering wood and grass, overseeing the cows, etc.) normally reserved for women. At this time Bilmawn is in charge of the festivities; his skins, which are decomposing due to the combined effects of heat and sweat, give off an unbearable stench. Every night he is the director of operations. He moves around the circle of dancers, chasing away any nuisances, sometimes replacing worn out drummers or dancers, and leading the entire group. Sometimes an auction is held after Bilmawn's last day. Part of the goods that have been gathered are sold. The rest is kept for a banquet (*tinubga*) that brings all the young people together in a sometimes ribald atmosphere of excess. The money that has been acquired is partly spent to hold this last feast; the rest of it is shared among the players.

The rule dictating that all mature and married men leave the village has not been strictly respected. Likewise, it should not be thought that the spectacle and village tour follow a set schedule. Indeed, like any sort of activity the pageant is marked by peaks followed by moments of relaxation in which the music stops, and the actors seem to be searching for the next move. Similarly, while laughter and gaiety predominate, they often make way for nervousness, a lack of cooperation, and sometimes out and out fighting.

A rather nasty dispute arises as the procession heads toward a hamlet that, although considered part of the main village, in fact forms an offshoot recently established at some distance away. To get there, the procession first takes the trail down to the river, which they briefly follow before climbing a narrow overhang to reach the houses hanging over a cliff. The jokes are in fine form, and the Jews and young men constantly trade blows. One of the followers, who has come from a neighboring village to take part in the procession, receives a number of sharp blows. He rebels and pulls back. An ill-tempered fellow, he takes a second licking. He responds violently, only to be seriously manhandled by the Jews, who quickly enter the fray. The playfulness becomes a veritable brawl, and soon the usual insults rain down. Almost everyone is against the intruder, who furthermore has dared to refuse to play by the rules. He is the son of a notable who since independence has often performed the duties of *moqaddem*.[2] The drummers attempt to calm everyone down, for two camps have already formed, as a few people who are connected by marriage or kinship to the recalcitrant party have gone over to his side. The traditional arguments are invoked, concerning the festival and the celebrations that no one is supposed to disturb. An appeal is made to the feeling of brotherhood, to the rules and obligations of neighborliness. Nothing works. The Jews, without removing their masks, have the strongest words for the troublemakers: "If you don't accept [our rules], get the hell out! Besides, this isn't your village here!" Repeated several times, the threats and curses become so heated that for a moment all seems nearly lost. A few people, beside themselves, take up the cry, "If they don't accept, they shouldn't be here!" Then one of the drummers visibly looses his composure and sets out after the young man. A third individual manages to separate them and drag the outsider away from the procession, in the direction of his own village. The group continues on its way, but everyone talks only of the incident. Bilmawn has stayed out of the trouble. Since he is forbidden to speak, he hasn't said a word to anyone.

However, during the masquerade, speech is like everything else. The rules can be broken to some degree without invalidating the masquerade and the ritual. For example, while walking up to this hamlet along a very steep path littered with sharp rocks, I find myself in the dark with Bilmawn (night had already fallen), away from the others. He bends down to adjust his torn shoes and complains of his fate: "I can't take it anymore," he tells me. "If my friends didn't insist on it, I'd never do this. The skins smell awful. And do I ever sweat in them . . . it's hell!" He lifts his skin to show me his leg dripping with nauseating sweat. In the meantime, we are joined by a man of the village who works in a big hotel in Casablanca and who comes home regularly for the festivals. He advises Tamugayt next time to wear underclothes to avoid direct contact with the skins!

The men from the village who live elsewhere and return only for vacation and the festivals become veritable censors of the masquerade. Students, civil servants, emigré workers in Europe, or employees in the large Moroccan cities, they dress either in European style or in the manner of the traditional middle class of the old imperial cities. The emigré workers are particularly fond of the second style of dress. While the students and civil servants are content to watch the events without taking part, using the rationalization that this is part of their "heritage," they nonetheless agree with the emigrés (who are active participants) in wishing "to avoid certain things that don't do [us] any honor." In any event it is the emigrés who have kept the marriage scene from being played and who have tried to shorten the others, especially the exchanges of obscenities. My presence, especially the second time with a photographer, seemed particularly to embarrass them. While those who have participated in the masquerade many times consented to our presence, the emigrés made us promise several times not to make our findings available to television.

The constraints I noticed in Imi-n'Tassaft did not seem to operate in other villages, or at least not with the same rigor. In Timezguida n'Oumalou the young people delight in playing all the scenes they like. However, I will not furnish a complete description of the festival in this village but will simply offer a summary of the variants between the masquerade enacted there and the one I observed in Imi-n'Tassaft.

In Timezguida n'Oumalou two men wear skins. While the group thinks of itself as a single entity, and its members insist on their solidarity, in practice it is physically divided in two. Two groups of buildings separated by a river, each one housing several lineages, form what the villagers themselves think of as a single village. The masquerade is celebrated jointly, but the people insist on the presence of two Bilmawin. This unity and bipolarity is observed on other levels as well. Furthermore, while in Imi-n'Tassaft Bilmawn had no contact with other villages, this is not the case in Timezguida n'Oumalou, where the Bilmawin serve as intermediaries between the inhabitants of their own village and their neighbors and rivals in the village of Agadir. Each of the two groups tries to outpace the other and by trickery succeed in being the first to send Bilmawn to a place that marks the boundary between the two units. The one who succeeds in overtaking the other leaves him *ballush*. The term is difficult to define and covers a range of meanings having to do with sickness, bad luck, and all sorts of difficulties— rather like the idea of being jinxed.

Our interlocutors were unable to provide names for the scenes we observed. To simplify matters, from this point on I will borrow Hesiod's title and refer to them as "works and days." Indeed they may be seen as a powerful evocation of the myth immortalized by Hesiod and for that reason merit the familiar title the Greek gave to his work. In addition, sometimes a series of scenes is played that is given the name of *tiguryu*. Generally placed at the end of the "works and days," they resemble a kind of revue devoted to anecdotes or events that have taken place in the village during the preceding year. The *tiguryu* was not played in Imi-n'Tassaft; likewise, the "works and days" of this village left out the marriage, even though it was announced at the beginning of the performance. Preparations in Timezguida n'Oumalou are as serious as in Imi-n'Tassaft. There as well, one or two "directors" can be found. But in Timezguida there is a veritable team, led by an older man, who coordinates the ensemble and conducts a kind of rehearsal before the actors go outside. It seems that not all the scenes from the traditional repertoire are enacted each year. This year the walnut harvest is omitted. However, the scenes are supposed to occur in an unvarying order: plowing, impregnating the cow, harvesting, flailing and threshing the grain, gathering nuts, and the wedding. In addition to the scenes observed at Imi-n'Tassaft the *tiguryu* played at Timezguida n'Oumalou were the marriage and impregnating the cow.

As already mentioned, the impregnation of the cow takes place immediately after the plowing. Someone holds the cow while another one shouts: "Let the women come to hold the cow! Bring on the bull!"

Bilmawn bellows. Suddenly a young man cuts through the crowd and stands next to the cow. He acts as if he is pushing the bull away, shouting, "I beg you, let me go first!" The crowd answers with a barrage of obscene gestures and yells of, "Here's one of them, here's two. Here's three, here's four!" after which he is violently shoved aside. Then the whole company throngs around the bull, feeling and palpating his genitals and crying out: "Blessed be God! Blessed be God! He's got big ones. Feel him! Let's measure him! . . . Let's weigh them! . . . Be careful holding them so he doesn't hurt the cow! . . . That's it!"

Then they sing:

> God help [him]
> He doesn't go out or in
> He's stuck in the entrance.

The bull mounts the cow in the general enthusiasm amid shouts of encouragement. Then, at the moment the bull penetrates the cow, the Jews recite a well-known Koranic verse:

> In the Name of God, the Merciful, the Compassionate
>
> Praise belongs to God, the Lord of all Being,
> the All-merciful, the All-compassionate,
>   the Master of the Day of Doom.
>
> Thee only we serve; to Thee alone we pray for succour.
>   Guide us in the straight path,
> the path of those whom Thou has blessed,
> not of those against whom Thou art wrathful,
>   nor of those who are astray.[3]

All the scenes invariably end in a fiasco, and in the disorder everyone improvises feats, stage business, and dialogues of his own choosing. Of course the action must be repeated to repair the failure that inevitably recurs! So the scenes are played until all have had enough. In the melée everyone tries to make off with the girl who at the end of the cycle will be asked for in marriage. Every time, she allows herself to be overcome in public; and invariably her father beats her to death. Furthermore, each occasion that takes the men away from the village brings business to the peddler, who comes to offer the women his wares and, when the opportunity arises, seduce them. The most sought-after merchandise is the mixture of ingredients burned as an inhalant that is described in the Imi-n'Tassaft cycle.

Two men are disguised as women to play the marriage scene; one is young, the other old. It is the mother and daughter, going about their daily tasks inside the house. Someone knocks, and the young man introduces himself. He holds his stick erect like a penis. The daughter stands next to her mother, who opens the discussions.

Mother: Who is there?
First Suitor: It's me, Ḥwizzine, Lalla A'isha! I want to get married . . . (he approaches the girl). I want her.[4]

He walks around the girl, penis erect, and starts braying again and again, in imitation of a donkey in rut.

Mother (feeling the penis): It's quite enough . . . Yes, quite enough! Blessed be God! Blessed be God! Bring it here! Let's measure and weigh it!
Jews: It is big! He's got a real big one! . . .

Then they sing the verses that will be regularly repeated until the scene is over:

God! Help him!
He doesn't go out or in
He's stuck in the entrance.

Someone else knocks at the door.

Mother: Who is it!
Second Suitor: My name is Uncover [it] so I drip . . .
Mother: What do you want?
First Suitor: He wants 'Atiqa.[5]

The second suitor looks dumbfounded.

Mother: Welcome! You're number one hundred! Don't you speak Berber? You don't know it? Here, take this!

She makes an obscene gesture.

Second Suitor: Stick it up your ass! I don't know Arabic. But I'll stick it here.

He comes up to the mother who, instead of defending herself, takes on an alluring air.

Mother: Welcome!

The whole company sings:

God! Help him!
He doesn't go out or in
He's stuck in the entrance.

Meanwhile, some one else has arrived:

Mother: Who's knocking [on my door]?
Third Suitor: It's me . . . Hairy Ali! O Lalla Aïsha Qandisha,[6] I seek your daughter in marriage. Is somebody else here?
Mother: No, no! Only ten and you the eleventh. Where's Omar? Bring Omar, too!

Someone knocks at the door:

Mother: Who is it?
Answer: Pot-bellied Ali!

Everyone who wants the daughter introduces himself in the same way. So there are two Long-Fingernailed Alis and some others. This time the choice turns out to be difficult. Unable to overcome their impatience, all the suitors try to take Khnata[7] immediately; her mother makes a feeble attempt to defend her. But what actually saves the mother and daughter are the brawls among the suitors; for the mother herself arouses visible desire, and she would certainly succumb if not for her wish to come to an immediate decision over who should carry off her daughter. Then she states that nothing can be done until she consults her husband, Pot-Bellied Ali. So they go off to see him at once.

The husband doesn't know what to do with all the suitors pressing him to offer Khnata. At last the mother gets him to make up his mind—after giving the young men a thorough looking over. They line up and hold their stick-penises erect. The mother goes down the line, looks, takes her time measuring, and feels them, all the while commenting: "No, it's not enough! Next! Now . . . that one, if it could just be a little longer . . . ," and so on. While this is going on, the candidates give her a serious once-over and urge her to try them; each continues to wage a veritable war, in an attempt to carry the daughter away. Khnata, who is quite docile, willingly lets herself be carried off. Because it is so difficult to choose, the suitors decide to cast lots. But once the happy winner is named, the family must contend with the others' ire, as they energetically reclaim the presents they brought as suitors.

The family does a fairly good job of extricating itself from the situation, and the marriage is celebrated. But the young men continue to take advantage of the slightest moment of parental inattention to whisk the daughter far from any onlookers. Still, the ceremony continues, and all sing the traditional couplet:

Grind, o mill
Peace and *rihane* on [to] the bride![8]

The singing accompanies the sacrifice of a cow *(tamugayt)*. This is one of the Bilmawin, who becomes a cow for the occasion. The mother invites all the men of the village. She wishes to renew her ties, as is required, with the *jma't*. She prefers to speak to those who have been her lovers. Then it is time for preparing the bride, especially the combing ceremony *(asraf)*, which always takes place under a white canopy. It begins with:

In the name of God we comb the bride's hair
We begin in the name of God.

The girl who has been readied in this way must be carried to her future husband. Some young men approach, but instead of picking her up as custom requires, they chant the following couplet as an aside:

I ask you, which of you can pick the bride
Up to toss her?

Two bearers balance her on a pole they support on their shoulders and rush to toss her, after which everyone dances and sings these words:

God help [him]
He doesn't go out or in
He's stuck in the entrance!

"May the year be a good one" *(Assuggas bi khayr!)* is the typical expression with which these actors, like those in Imi-n'Tassaft, bring to a close the dances, the visits to the houses, and the events I have just described. These end with the marriage, to be followed by the activities collectively referred to as *tiguryu,* a term that conveys the idea of "what's left."

The scenes of the *tiguryu* are announced beforehand, and care is taken to specify the name of the family or persons involved, as well as the circumstances of their lives that are to be enacted. Each performance ends with *"Afallas Ihlef rabbi!"* [9]

One of the village notables appears on center stage. Everyone recognizes him. He has a hotel that caters to tourists and is a pious man, respected by all. But here he is rushing forward to open the doors of a bus for a throng of European women, who get out. He starts speaking French, which unleashes a torrent of laughter. He serves the guests something to eat, and when a dance begins, he grabs them and begins to dance with them!

An old man is riding peacefully on his donkey in the sun. The animal abruptly stops halfway up an incline. The man urges it on; the donkey raises its head to heaven and refuses to budge, despite its master's orders. The master addresses the animal like a friend; the animal doesn't move; he begs it again and then, beside himself, starts to beat it. The donkey lies down and throws the rider on the ground; he curses and gets up to hit it some more. Worn out, he sits on the prone animal and laments his fate, which has burdened him with such an obstinate and skeletal mount. Finally, a man with several marriageable daughters appears. A quarrel breaks out among brothers who all desire an immediate union. The old man tries for a long while to reason with them. Nothing works, and he is reduced to having them draw straws.

To complete this description, it is necessary to add several details that I did not observe in the "works and days" at Imi-n'Tassaft but were seen in Timezguida n'Oumalou.

The peddler (a familiar figure in both villages) takes advantage of the absence of the head of the household, off preparing the fields, to make advances to his daughter. With her make-up on, she has already stirred the desire of the crowd of young men (actors and spectators) who touch her, shower obscenities upon her, and so forth. The peddler's flirtation is, however, brutally interrupted by the "dog" that hurls itself, barking with rage, on the unfortunate seducer, biting him all over and beating him black and blue.

In these regions, plowing is done in accordance with the widespread custom of mutual assistance. But the workers have trouble with the draft animals (the Bilmawin), who pull backward. The men scold them, but the animals respond by lashing out with well-aimed blows. Their duty done, the men are invited to the boss's house for a common meal. They make a mess of things and throw away the food that is offered them.

I cannot repeat too often that sometimes the linearity of this account is deceptive. First, as I have emphasized, our observations did not begin at the beginning, that is, first with the sacrifice, then the preparations associated with Bilmawn, and finally the events linked to his visits and tours of the villages. On the contrary, the events in the streets gave rise to the hypothesis of a preparation time and action "offstage." Above all, in reality the scenes are sketched out, begun over and over again, aborted, then replayed in an atmosphere of freedom and relative disorder that reveals an underlying suppleness. The only constants are the general scenario, which dictates the order as well as the themes of the first series of scenes. Those grouped under the name of *tiguryu* occur in no particular order and require additional improvisation. Likewise, the names can change: thus the daughter answers to the name of Ti'azza (in the past a name often given Jewish women); the old man, Ashibane (old man). In the play he is called either this name or Pot-Bellied Ali; the daughter can go by Khnata and even 'Atiqa, names associated with urban Arab contexts that would bring ridicule on a Berber girl. Last, there are the playlets, such as the kidnapping of the girl, which are frequently repeated, without any connection to the main action, as well as characters who perform some task without attracting any attention. Such is the case of the "Negress" *(tawaya)* who goes here and there, busying herself at milking a cow or making bread, and who finds herself the butt of tricks played on her by other actors who themselves play no specific part. Thus, the account just presented must be taken for what it is: a framework imposed on the action for purposes of clarity.

Local Exegesis

7

During as well as after the festival I asked the actors, as well as some of the older people, who as I have seen are excluded from the masquerade, for their commentaries. My questions elicited only vague answers. In Timez-guida, people often made the kind of evasive answer one often hears about other practices: "It's an ancestral tradition; a custom (*'ada*) that we follow. Our parents did it too. It's the young people's business. A chance to have fun." Less often the answer was that it was "a habit inherited from the Jews." My informants also tell of confrontations between the Koranic schoolmasters and Bilmawn's supporters. For example, in an important village in the upper valley the schoolmaster attempts to forbid this custom, saying that it is a pagan relic. The men of the assembly refuse to follow him. The dispute becomes rather heated, since it appears that the schoolmaster threatened to quit serving the mosque and the village. He is an educated man of about sixty, who learned the Koran in the village and then studied for a time at the traditional Islamic University of Ben Youssef in Marrakech. There he devoted himself to the study of grammar, Koranic exegesis, and Islamic law.[1] Therefore, people consult him on issues generally considered beyond the competence of the other local schoolmasters, whose knowledge most often is confined to memorizing the Koran. His opinions are highly valued, and a rift with him would have been felt by all to be a loss and a stigma for the village. Nevertheless, the villagers make it understood "that it is better for him to take care of the mosque, which should be his only concern, and let the youths have their fun." It is difficult to foresee the long-term results of such a dispute, which has been momentarily resolved in this fashion. During an interview with him in his village mosque, he made the following comments:

It's a practice of corrupt people (*fasiqin*). They take advantage of this occasion to settle their scores. Someone who has an old score to settle with someone else uses this situation to beat him up. And there is more to it than that, I swear before God; here like everywhere else, the masquerade is the opportunity to make a contact with a woman one has desired for a long time.

I'm going to tell you a true story; we are in a mosque, and God will be severe with me if I make anything up. A man, who is still alive (I won't give you his name; he lives in a neighboring village) came to confide in me one day. He desired a woman, and he had tried every possible means of seducing her. The woman was married and didn't want to lose her honor. The woman—it must be said—truly defended herself. She had resisted all the ploys that Satan (Iblis) had inspired in her seducer. At the end of his rope, the man took advantage of the Bilmawn festival and made arrangements to wear the skins. . . . When he went into the woman's house, it was stronger than she, she succumbed. You realize what an obscenity this is. Where is the husband, you ask? But because [it is during] Bilmawn, he has to leave the house; the men give their houses over to the Bilmawin! In this case, all that was needed was a little arrangement with the group accompanying him for Bilmawn to take advantage of his time alone with his beloved. The woman had defended herself well, however, but the scum has sullied her dignity. This woman is now beneath the ground (dead), and I cannot make up stories about her. The man is still alive; he regretted his actions after I gave him a long [moral] lecture. Every time we meet, he lowers he eyes.

In this village *(dwar)* I've often shown them the right path; I tell them over and over again that they are falling into error. My words fall on deaf ears. Bilmawn encourages debauchery—that is the [disastrous] result of this conduct.

During the *tiguryu* a man shouts about his daughter's sluttish conduct in the forest. It's shameful, I told him, to speak that way about your daughter in public. . . .

Another educated villager offers a brief "history" of Bilmawn and insists on refuting current opinions about him:

Bilmawn was a practice of the *majus* who lived in these mountains before the arrival of Islam. As you know, these mountains did not yet know the religion of our Lord Mohammed, . . . and the populace lived in *jahiliya*.[2] Bilmawn, that is *jahiliya*. Our parents did the same; but they didn't know any better. It makes no sense that in our day people continue to disguise themselves, to make themselves ugly and run around the countryside hitting one another. They answer yes to whoever calls them a "Jew." As youngsters they saw their parents wear the Jews' skullcap and they want to do the same. That's what the infidels used to do at the time of our Lord Ibrahim; they answered that their parents did the same thing. Suppose that one of the guys disguised in this way drops dead; then he would come back under the *sunna* of the Jews. These people have no sense. You shouldn't believe them when they sometimes say that they have seen Bilmawn here or there. It's not true; it's inconceivable. They're thieves who start rumors. The people who believe them stay home, leaving their fields to them. And then, it's unthinkable that skins would stick to guys who have broken the *ḥorm* of a *zawya*.[3] For since the birth of our Lord Mohammed, metamorphosis has been suppressed [by God].

A third educated man, describing Bilmawn as Satan's work, stresses the relationship that he sees between the "monster" and the mosque:

Bilmawn is a mountain wind: *adu d'Udrar* (it's a wind, as they say). It's necessary to ask the people who celebrate it after the 'id-Lekbir sacrifice. These *dwar* hurry to dress one of themselves up as Bilmawn and run to neighboring villages to throw *ballush* on them. They also say that the annual celebration of Bilmawn prevents all sorts of sicknesses (*tamogt*). Iblis, God curse him, does not fail to get involved in such affairs. Think for example that Bilmawn puts on his costume in the mosque! It's Iblis who has dictated this choice. "Listen!" he suggested to the group, "the mosque doesn't belong to anyone, it belongs to the *jma't,* and nobody can chase you away." Then it happens that Bilmawn scares the little boys most of all. They see him come out of the mosque in the morning and see him going back inside at night. They say to themselves: "So the monster lives in the mosque." The children, having come to that conclusion, don't want to come to the mosque any more to learn the Koran, and in this way Iblis turns the little ones away from Islam.

Throughout the valley Koranic specialists and the guardians of Islamic norms rise up against practices that they judge non-Islamic. The campaign is aimed particularly at festivals devoted to saints and seasonal sacrifices or the countless regional sanctuaries. "Ordinary" people, as we have already seen, are content with shorter explanations: for example, this shepherd, whose opinion can be compared with those preceding it:

Bilmawn is an amusement (*l'mudhika*). After the sacrifice, some people wear skins, as you saw the other day; the ones who want to; nobody has to. I don't know anything about how it got started; I've never heard anything about it.

Many people say that they detest Bilmawn but do nothing to suppress him. In Imi-n'Tassaft, while the scene of feigned homosexuality is going on under his own roof, the owner (a man over sixty) hides not far away. He gazes fixedly at "these young devils," and his fulminations against them never cease. When asked why he didn't keep them out of the house, he answers, "Who can do such a thing?" In response to my amazement, he points to some ruins on a nearby hill: "The people of that house forbade Bilmawn from entering. Everything went sour for them, and their family has disappeared from the area. He has to go into every house. Haven't you seen that the people he's forgotten come to ask him to visit their houses?"

Informants have sometimes offered details (during conversations in which *jnun* and other invisible beings are brought up) or told a myth concerning Bilmawn's exact nature and the origin of the drama played out every year in the village square; above all, they do not hesitate to enlarge upon the appearance of these beings, which take on human characteristics of a special kind. Very often they are black women (*tissamkht*) nursing their babies. The bilmawin are genies (*jnun*) like the others. Their existence must be believed like that of all beings who inhabit the darkness. "Once," a man says, "a Bilmawn was moved by hunger to enter a house. It was night, and the master of the house was getting ready to eat some corn porridge. He offered the visitor half his porridge, which the visitor ate right away, and then he asked his host for the rest. The man got sick after Bilmawn left. I tell you that you must believe these things. When my grandfather was alive, people often saw Bilmawn. Nowadays, I don't think he can survive. My grandfather died a long time ago." Then, someone explains: "They are two poor fellows who have gone into a *zawya* where the women live under the *hjab*.[4] The saints got angry and cursed them, so that the skins (which they had worn to disguise themselves) would cling to their bodies for all eternity. Which is what happened. Since that time the bilmawin have wandered in wild places and appear here and there." This conversation ends with a summary of the myth of Bilmawn, two versions of which will be given here: I recorded the first in the village of Imi-n'Tassaft, and the second was gathered by my collaborator Mohamed Mahdi in Timezguida n'Oumalou.

In the Isuktane[5] country, two men who were passing by a sanctuary saw women entering the sacred precincts. It is said that they were women of high morals, veiled and of Sharifian descent; but as to this last detail, God only knows. They followed the women into the sanctuary and spied on them there. God changed them into bilmawin, and since that time they were forced to live in the forest. They approach the village only at night to ask for food. It is said that every year, when the grain is ripe, Bilmawn appears in the fields.

The informant who gave this account says that he has never seen this in person. But he states that others have met Bilmawn a number of times by accident. He walks on all fours like a billygoat, and when you get near him he disappears into the corn.

A man from the village of Timezguida offers another version of the story, in which narrative and commentary are blended:

It is said that in far-off times we of Ait Ouaouzguit used to celebrate Bilmawn. Two men were disguised (as usual) with skins the way we do it. They made the mistake of entering a *zawya* in which women (of holy lineage) were cloistered. This sacrilege brought a curse upon the sinners. Since that time the skins stuck to their bodies. They couldn't remove them and were compelled to live far from humans. They are called *bilmawin n'Sus* or *bilmawin n'Imezgur*. They are called *bilmawin n'Imezgur* because they make their appearance in the corn season. During this time, rumors circulate about their appearance in the cornfields and encounters with them.

Early in this century, E. Doutté collected another version, close to the preceding one, in the valley of the Nfis, bordering that of the Ait Mizane on the west. His informant, a great regional chief who for a time played a role on the level of Franco–Moroccan relations, says he met Bilmawn in the fields. The account as he gave it contains two variants with respect to the version from Imi-n'Tassaft: the injured parties are male children, and Bilmawn appears at night to ask for food. He says to the woman who receives him: "I cannot come during the day because I frighten the children, so I come at night."[6]

Last, should the appealing observations written by a French-speaking Moroccan writer of Berber origin be seen as local commentary? This is how Mohammed Khair-Eddine views the masquerade, particularly the character of the "clown":

> This faun in rut was the living symbol of vulgarity and insolence. Crudely he laid bare everything the hypocrites camouflaged under the frippery of dubious morals. His miming electrified the crowd. The general hilarity broke through the heavy bonds of morality. It was a kind of public psychotherapy, the honeyed remains of the priapic festivities of Hellenic Antiquity. As a way of showing the extreme importance of these nights, people everywhere prepared dry wooden branches, which they set afire beneath the shimmering heavens. These gigantic blazes were fed constantly. Over centuries and millennia, transcending racial beliefs and the tumult of history, men were repeating the acts of their common ancestors, worshipers of vital energy. They were communicating in secret with the elementary cosmic principle, as if some essential atom in them reflected the critical moment of the primordial big bang, when the universe was created out of the explosion of incalculably dense matter into an immeasurable conflagration.[7]

Some young Ait Mizane (who have remained peasants on their land or who have gone away to school to the large lycées in Marrakech) are surprised at such a commentary. For them, Bilmawn is above all a celebration and an amusement, as well as a chance to say anything they want—but not to challenge or question ordinary habits or behaviors. Those who have had some education and found an enviable job in town shun the proceedings. But this is more because norms of modesty and respect are being infringed; above all they behave in this way "because it is an impious innovation" (bid'a). Khair-Eddine's vision of a masquerade that radically challenges everything is shared by no one. As for the theories of catharsis and the renewed contact with a primordial energy, no one here can even understand them. Of course people say that "laughter is good" and that it "eases the heart." And the young men must have their days of freedom (lhurriyet). Beyond these few statements, no one hazards (and with good reason!) the kind of metapsychological theory popular in France, particularly since the work of Roger Caillois, ideas that a certain type of psychoanalysis, paired with renewed interest in popular culture and its virtues, have helped to spread. Local commentary, when it exists, is in fact interested in origins, as is that of Khair-Eddine. But, unlike Khair-Eddine, the people I talked with in the village have little use for explanations or functions. I will return to this point when I advance a global interpretation of the sacrifice and masquerade. But first, a look at the identity of the actors engaged in these scenes will provide a better fix on the theater that they bring to life.

Who are they? And is it possible to establish their profile? It is not enough to say that Bilmawn belongs to young single or recently married men. In Imi-n'Tassaft as in Timezguida, while the majority of the troupe is composed of young bachelors, it must immediately be added that the role of Bilmawn is taken by young married men who are sometimes fathers. Furthermore, the other roles are never given to either children or adolescents, but to youths ready for marriage, who are perfectly described by the term *i'azriyan* that is used to refer to them. It happens that young bachelors try to don the skins, but others stop them. Offstage in Timezguida, a discussion begins among a few married men who are busy, as we have seen, readying the skins and the masks. Can the skins be given to the *i'azriyan?* The answer is no, for you never can tell what they will do: "They are capable of defecating in the skins!"

In Imi-n'Tassaft, almost everyone who has a role comes from lineages that are reputed to be old—a source of prestige—but that have slipped somewhat on the social scale because of the upward mobility of others after the changes occurring since colonization and independence (emigration to the cities and Europe, education, etc.). For several years Bilmawn has been played by members of an old but déclassé family. It belongs to the group that here is called *assuqi* and elsewhere *aqabli* or *hartani*. They are found just about everywhere throughout the Atlas and the southern oases; they are dark-skinned and either work the land or engage in labor involving water (e.g., well men or canal specialists). They exercise certain trades, some of which, like smithing, are feared and disdained. Traditionally they lived under the social and political domination of the Berber- or Arabic-speaking whites. The young man from this group is married and has children of his own. However, since his people are of modest condition, he has spent the past several years as a laborer in Casablanca. Some lineages, on the other hand, "never wear the skins." In Imi-n'Tassaft, five groups can be counted, of which four never take the role of the slave. Yet all accept the Jews' masks. Finally, the *issuqiyan* lineages play all roles. The reasons that some groups are banned from wearing the skins are somewhat mysterious. Among the excluded lineages are three that are powerful and "rich" (one of which has recently achieved high social standing). Another lineage seems to have given

up the role after a change in status that came about when some members
furnished proof of their Sharifian origin. They explain that their ancestors
"gave up the skins" after an accident (chap. 4). This information suggests
that the roles of Bilmawn and slave are associated with the marginality that
results from downward mobility caused by recent arrivals in the village
(a dialectic of old/new lineages) or the marginality that is linked to status
(issuqiyan). This last observation is largely confirmed by the trades practiced by the players.

In the village we counted eight persons who have worn the skins, two of
whom are now "too old" and no longer play a part. The two "former Bilmawin" are a charcoal maker and a woodseller. Of the six others, two work in
a neighboring mine; the other four are a mason, a seasonal worker, a woodseller, and finally, a jack of all trades. The latter is, among other things, a
sorcerer specializing in amulets, a traveling peddler who sells cheap goods
and wood. All are poor or very poor; they possess no land and survive on an
irregular income supplemented by the few resources offered by modest
flocks of goats.

It is harder to account for those who take on the other parts—slave, Jew,
and woman, when the latter is part of the masquerade. The roles of the Jews
seem less connected with the social and economic hierarchy than Bilmawn's
part. In the masquerade played in Imi-n'Tassaft in 1983 two of the four
masked figures belong to farming families of some means, while the third is
from a line of poor people and the fourth lives off a small livestock business.
Only one of the four is married. Finally, the slave belongs to the issuqiyan
group and usually works as a mason.

Overall, the data gathered in Timezguida overlap and confirm the observations made in Imi-n'Tassaft. With a nuance, however. It seems that marginality with respect to sources of influence and prestige in the village is the
decisive characteristic of those who direct Bilmawn's drama. On the one
hand, prestige and influence arise from social status; on the other, from
ownership of lands and animals, business, positions with civil institutions,
and Koranic or secular knowledge—that has already been or is being acquired (in traditional or modern schools). Of eighteen "stage entrances"—
including characters played once by a single actor, the same character
played several times by several actors or, which is more common, the same
actor appearing in different roles—not one of them is played by an individual of the local community who enjoys even one of the abovementioned
sources of prestige and influence. Among the players are six day laborers,
five shepherds, three muleteer-guides who make their living guiding tour-

ists and mountaineers, three masons, and a worker in town. Even when they come from families that are said to be well off, as is the case for five of them, they have found work as shepherds, masons, or laborers because their parents consider them to be less capable or even slightly backward. By age they are mostly under twenty-five (10 out of 18), and a very few of them are over thirty (3 out of 18). Finally, half the actors are married. With one exception the single men are bachelors because they lack the money to marry. Either they have not managed to set aside a small amount "to make a claim to marry" or they are still working to accumulate it. Bachelors take most of the parts in all roles except Bilmawn (3 out of 5 roles for the Jews, 6 out of 9 for the others, while Bilmawn is played by a bachelor only 1 time out of 4). However, of the total number of roles, the number of bachelors, surprisingly, is equal to that of the married men (9 vs. 9). Last of all, the four Bilmawin (the same two people played the role for two days) are played by members from two old families, one of which has seen its circumstances deteriorate for many years and is presently trying to improve matters by enlistment in the military, while the other is comfortable but from an *assuqi* lineage that in the past specialized in smithing.

Undoubtedly, more could be discovered concerning the actors' identities. For example, almost nothing is known to me about their individual biographies. Nevertheless, the data gathered here help situate categories and groups with respect to the masquerade and both enrich and clarify earlier comments. But this is not the only value of these social profiles, which anthropologists, unlike historians, all too often neglect. When it comes to interpreting the masquerade, they make it possible to better focus on the words and function of ritual by offering a closer look at those who perform it onstage.

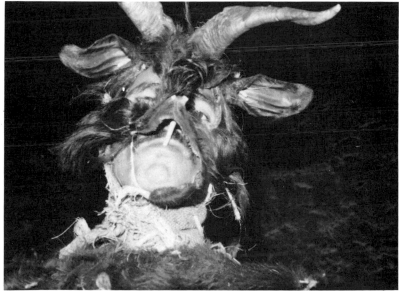

1

2

1. Bilmawn. Note the white stick that is used to open and shut the character's muzzle. Photo courtesy Ali Fdal.

2. In the village streets. The youngsters follow, but at a safe distance. Photo courtesy Ali Fdal.

3

4

5

3. Ait Mizane village. Houses made of
earth, which blend into the landscape.
Open terraces are characteristic of the
western part of the Upper Atlas. Photo
courtesy Marfin.

4. Ait Mizane terraced agriculture.
Photo courtesy Marfin.

5. Ait Mizane landscape. In September
the summer (short-growing) corn is
ripe. Bilmawn appears in the cornfields. Photo courtesy Ali Fdal.

6

7

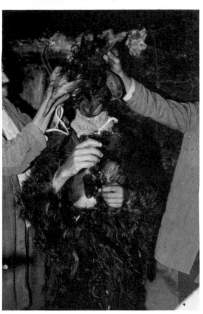

6. Billygoat sacrificed for the great Muslim Feast of the Sacrifice (*tfaska* or *'id-Lekbir*). Photo courtesy Marfin.

7. Dressing the actors backstage (*takhurbisht*): Bilmawn. Photo courtesy Ali Fdal.

8. Dressing and making up the actors: the slave, his face covered with soot. Photo courtesy Ali Fdal.

9. Making the masks out of doors. Photo courtesy Ali Fdal.

10. Making the rounds of the village streets and houses. Photo courtesy Ali Fdal.

11. In the courtyard of a house. As part of the game, the women have vanished into the rooms. The Jews hurl insults and demand gifts. Photo courtesy Ali Fdal.

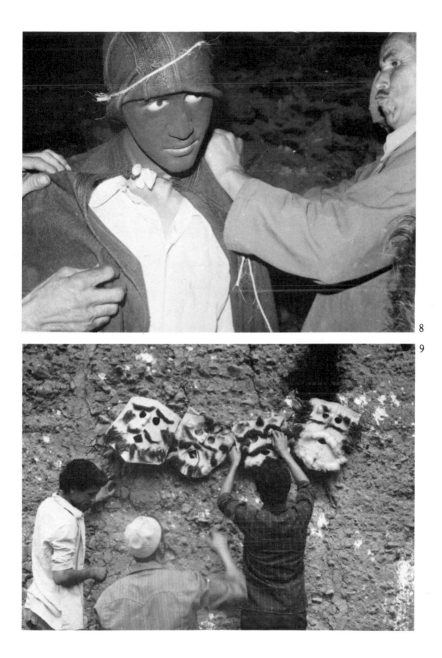

10

11

12

13

14

15

◄ 12. Bilmawn on the terrace. Photo
courtesy Ali Fdal.

◄ 13. The procession dancing in front of
the door of the house they are visiting.
Photo courtesy Ali Fdal.

14. "Works and Days." Bilmawn as the
blacksmith's bellows. Photo courtesy
Ali Fdal.

15. Procession in one of the village
streets. Photo courtesy Ali Fdal.

THE SACRIFICE AND THE
MASQUERADE INTERPRETED

II

Theoretical Approaches

8

Is there a way to interpret this festival without being arbitrary and at the same time accounting for all the data? Obviously, we are confronted with a cultural manifestation that marks the passage of time. The old Muslim year—a lunar year, let it be recalled—ends, and the new one begins. This passage is celebrated by the pilgrimage to Mecca and the sacrifice.[1] The Ait Mizane, like Muslims the world over, practice both of these. Seen in this context, the festival is not connected with an agricultural cycle, which clearly weakens the Frazerian interpretations discussed and criticized in chapter 1.

This is not to say that the festival is detached from all agricultural concerns. On the contrary, invocations are made to God to ask that the coming year be good and bountiful; and plowing and harvesting figure among the key dramatic scenes featuring Bilmawn. Finally, it is possible to speculate that the masquerade could have been taken over by the Muslim festival and calendar as the result of little-known historical vicissitudes; and there are good reasons for supposing that this is the case, in light of the analysis made in the following pages. On the other hand, the murder and resurrection of a vegetation god—the central thesis of the colonial ethnologists who followed in Frazer's footsteps—have no factual basis in the festival process I have described.

Without a doubt this is a rite in which the ritual stages noted by Arnold Van Gennep are easily discerned. Separation, marginality, and aggregation, which create the characteristic rhythm of any rite of passage, are found in both the sacrifice and the masquerade. In the context of the sacrifice these stages are the prayer and preparation of the victim, the immolation, and the feast; in the masquerade they take the form of young people acting apart from the larger group, along with games and rites expressing marginality, the final meal, and the return to community. And the totality is marked by the same three parts: the prayer and preparation of the victim; the immolation; feasting and play are phases of a process that resists division into two separate festivals.

But if this outline accurately conveys a rhythm, it offers little information about the identities of the actors and characters appearing onstage and even less about the meanings expressed in their words and deeds. As utilized by the functionalists, the "theory" of the rite of passage leads to the socio-psychological function of the ritual as catharsis.

Thus Gluckman classifies all ceremonies in which ordinary rules are violated as "rites of rebellion," whose function, by expressing conflict within an institutionalized framework, would be to let off steam and thereby consolidate the established order. Such would be the case in certain African rituals, whether annual or initiatory, in which sex roles are reversed and women take on male prerogatives and burst out with obscenities.[2] And the same would be true of a royal rite of old Swaziland, where during an annual ceremony the king seems first transfigured and endowed with superhuman qualities, then suddenly is the butt of his people's invective, and at last, at another stage, is the object of their love songs.[3]

To interpret the first example, Gluckman notes that it would be necessary to begin with the ambivalence men feel toward women, who are the source of reproduction and conflict. Ordinarily dominated, once a year and on special occasions women are authorized, even encouraged, to break the rules. The ritual reinforces social cohesion by inverting the rules and bringing underlying conflicts to light. Men and women, following established customs, would be submitting to a rite from which the community hopes to benefit in the form of anticipated prosperity and harmony.

Likewise, the royal ceremony described above would consolidate political cohesion. If the king authorizes and encourages behaviors that invert the usual rules, it is because on the one hand, the rite is indispensable to the kingdom's well-being, and on the other, the rebellion it fosters occurs in the midst of an institution (royalty) that no one would ever dream of challenging: it is a catharsis whose social settings require study. Settings that Gluckman here consolidates into two contradictory societal demands: to obey in a hierarchical environment in which questioning is difficult, and to question within a system in which rebellion—but not revolution—is conceivable.

In the case of the Ait Mizane, the notion of catharsis is tempting, for the masquerade appears to completely overturn the sacrifice. Especially since this capacity to live simultaneously in antagonism and harmony, to which Gluckman attributes the persistence of social and political organizations, seems to emerge full blown: on the first day in the victim's immolation according a rule accepted by all; and on the days that follow in the license and violation of the behaviors based on that rule.

Even better, the rite of passage found in this festival is played out on two levels: domestic and political. The sacrifice simultaneously involves both the household and the community, and the masquerade engages a generation that, acting in its very marginality and liminality, takes over the household and the community, thus upending the hierarchy and the proprieties. The catharsis operates on two levels, then, to purge conflicts about authority: between young and old within the community, and between father and son within the domestic group. Therefore, in this view, one function is fulfilled by a single process based on two sorts of rites: those which involve only individuals or a certain class of individuals, and those which indicate the passage of time by mobilizing an entire political community.

Nevertheless, it is not at all clear against whom or what Bilmawn's gang is rebelling. For if indeed the generation of the heads of household is excluded from the proceedings, they freely give their consent and leave the freedom to the young who, moreover, rarely attack them, unless it is to portray their elders' weakness concerning the female sex. Women, however, are regular targets. And they are in total complicity with the masqueraders. They welcome them into their homes, feed them, go along with their advances, give them presents, and accept on behalf of the household the benediction of the monster and his impure fellows. Consequently, could it be that everyone—young and old, women and men—violates his or her own organization and rebels against it?

Indeed, a series of inversions is evident, but they cannot be attributed either to the general principle of harmonious living and underlying conflict or to a catharsis resulting in the purgation of tension. First of all, why would such a purgation happen so infrequently? It would be necessary to either coordinate it with ongoing mechanisms for resolving tension or admit that it is impossible to understand the mysterious efficacy of a technique applied once a year or on rare occasions. And if one wished at all costs to find in social settings the tensions it would relieve, one would have to find their traces in everyday culture. Now, nothing of the sort can be found in the description of the rites that Gluckman uses to support his arguments. Inversion appears in the ceremony, but there is nothing in his account to make the connection between the celebration and the abstract social setting presented to explain it. Gluckman deals with ritual much in the manner of a hurried psychoanalyst who forgets Freud's lesson and relates the action of the dream to a theory of the dreamer's life without taking the dreamer's own associations into account.

Roger Caillois, who has widely popularized this "theory" of catharsis, encounters the came problem. His approach is very seductive as a reflection on Ait Mizane ritual, for it provides an instant key to understanding it. Just as in Caillois's view of the festival, the Ait Mizane sacrifice and masquerade go back deep into the mythical time of the ancestors and the origins. The acts of Abraham and the metamorphoses of Bilmawn took place in those heroic times. Similarly, just as Caillois would have it, their reappearance signals the work of the "rite of transgression" that unleashes excess and immoderation; then the prohibitions that define the "rite of respect" are swept away, up to the all-powerful rule governing the relationship between sexes.[4]

As in Caillois's model, throughout the year the society has abided by this separative, restrictive rule; this is the very separation that serves to keep the two spheres of sacred and profane apart, and that maintains authority, once they are separated, over the group and sacralizes it.[5] The mosque, the house, women, and last, the assembly of elders function according to this norm of separation.

This would lead one to think that in our villages as elsewhere, the annual return of the founding ancestors of civilization unleashes the breaking of all rules and establishes the primordial chaos, a fountain of youth in which the group bathes. Sacrifice and masquerade would appear here too as domesticated witnesses of a primitive festival that would nevertheless purge an everlasting human instinct of excess.[6]

However, it is unclear which instinct would be satisfied by our festival. And if the time imposed by this festival is indeed mythical time, it will be noted that its characters are far from being indisputable representations of the ancestors. The Jews wear beards. Is this a sign of venerable age? It is also an ethnic trait. They lean on sticks when they walk. Is this a sign of disability? Perhaps—but the ritual action highlights sexual attributes and weapons in the same way. The excess introduced by this ceremony is, in the long run, completely relative; a radical violation of the norm would have been, for example, to join young and old together in the festive frenzy and to conjoin what ordinary life keeps apart. This is not at all the case, and my analysis reveals instead that the festival operates according to the same categories and classifications that govern everyday relationships within the group, particularly the relations between the sexes, the generations, and those indicating degrees of authority. In their efforts to reduce the festival to a catharsis, Gluckman and Caillois miss seeing the process as a production of meaning by ritual acts and thoughts.

This search for latent functions has rightly brought about a reaction in the name of analyzing human action based on what the actors themselves think and say. I will refer to this position, forcefully developed by Evans-Pritchard, in my interpretation of Muslim sacrifice. More recently, Victor Turner has enriched the study of rites of passage with an abundant ethnography and has insisted on the importance, central in his eyes, of local exegesis in the development of any interpretation. Curiously enough, he nevertheless ends up with the hypothesis of reflexivity among the actors provoked by the monstruous nature of the liminal characters and their extraordinary actions; this undoubtedly owes less to their exegesis than to an utterly personal "discovery" of being in ritual.[7]

However interesting such a hypothesis may be, in addition to its unprovability it presents another difficulty, for despite Turner's own insistence on the "positional meaning" of the components of the rite, it focuses the analysis on the central characters and certain internal qualities of the ritual components. Finally, the concern that Evans-Pritchard, Turner, and those who follow them display for interpreting every ritual in its own context is too often reduced to providing a picture of the actors' cosmological and theological ideas, which is taken as the only context. Thus the possible relations between ritual and social organization are overlooked. Such is the case, for example, in T. O. Beidelman's interpretation of the royal rite of ancient Swaziland (called "Ncwala"), in which the entire emphasis is placed on mediation with the supernatural, discounting the relationships stressed by Hilda Kuper between the rite and social hierarchy and the latent dualisms (the king's strength and weakness) on which the ceremony rests.[8]

In the case we are considering, the local exegesis—i.e., what the actors think they are doing and the meaning that their own acts have for them—is rather sober, since it often amounts to a denunciation. However, etiological myths are available. Analyzing them sheds light on the ritual action. Not that I am postulating that myth is a justification and explanation of the rite. On the contrary, I will first examine each one separately and only then compare the series of statements at work in each one. At that point certain relationships between them will emerge, relationships that, all things being equal, bear a resemblance to the connections between conversations before bedtime and the language of dreams. The second transfigures the first without changing all of the details, and utilizes contrast and opposition to evoke the same or similar references.

But first of all it is necessary to establish this series of statements. I have adopted in this matter the method tested by Claude Lévi-Strauss.[9] First the rites and myths will be systematically analyzed as units of action; in order to minimize the inherent arbitrariness of the process, actual pauses in the action will serve to demarcate each discrete entity. A second time through, these entities will be rearranged according to affinities in their meaning. However, in both the definition of the pauses and the attempt to find kindred meanings, the context, local and global, ideal and social—in short the culture of the people under consideration—plays a decisive role. No universal function of the human spirit underlies this analysis, which is guided first and foremost by whatever this particular culture combines or sunders in its own way.

"Context" in this sense does not merely mean the addition of a sociological code, when such a thing exists, to the interpretation of the message of the rite or myth that is hidden and revealed in various codes. On the contrary it reflects an attempt, on the one hand, to discern in the ritual, religious, and mythological codes the echo of the debates stirring the group and, on the other, to record what this group says about itself and its relationship with anything that is not part of it: global society, religious community, or the visible and invisible powers it attempts to approach or avoid. J.-P. Vernant and Marcel Detienne, who carried out their admirable analyses of Greek sacrifice along these lines, discover in the rite a classificatory and separative function that first distinguishes men from gods and then men from men in the midst of a city in which sacrificial, culinary, and alimentary codes reveal relationships and tensions.[10]

However, it must be remarked that in classical studies the ritual context is obscure, for the obvious reason that the only available data are fragments reported by ancient authors. The ethnography arrives second-hand and in bits and pieces, so to speak. And while the works that contribute to the interpretation may resonate with echoes of religious and social debates, nonetheless overall they belong to a literate and literary culture. Here, on the contrary, it is in everyday thought, loosely structured and barely distinguished from everyday activities, that the cultural context is sought. And in this arena the debate about consciousness versus the unconscious is of little importance. For this problem, which seems to matter only to anthropologists, is not raised in the habitual (nonscholarly) use of concepts and the actions that cannot be completely disjoined from it.

Describing the total spectacle that is the Balinese cockfight, Clifford Geertz notes that it is at once a game about social structure (rank and prestige), a game played in the same way that every other activity is carried out and which thus reveals the ways of being Balinese, and last and most important, a self-portrait that the group provides for itself. When, in a socially charged fight, the portrait is successfully realized, it is clearly and forcefully imposed by the bloody drama that, through these animals set against one another, actually pits man against man in mortal combat. It is a kind of language the society speaks to itself about itself by means of concrete and highly visible objects.[11] The sacrifice and the masquerade easily lend themselves to this kind of analysis. But it will be noted that their "language" appears in a more or less clear and organized form and that for this reason it is impossible to demand that everything the two rituals communicate be perfectly transparent to the minds of actors and spectators. Some acts of this play resort to deliberate and corrosive satire; others make reference to the structural dynamic of the group just as I have defined it, although it is not possible to ascertain whether this is premeditated. For this reason, actions in the second category will be constantly examined in their extreme proximity to the structural tensions that can be inferred from the actual performance. Finally, the units that will be isolated may be viewed as discrete entities if one considers the fact that the process under analysis has a direction and certain "bunches" of actions can be separated from the economy of the whole by a period of calm that clearly indicates a pause.

Perhaps rearranging these units in the tables below will pose more problems than dividing them up according to the divisions I have already indicated. I have attempted to place them along the vertical axis of the tables (tables 9–12) according to a common denominator. And this is where the pertinence of the cultural context appears, of the dilemmas of real action, and of responses that are reflected in or brought forth by the tradition found therein. For, it must be repeated, it is this context which permits us to find what have been called kindred meanings. The whole ritual process, including etiological myths, will be divided into units of action set along a horizontal axis, and they will simultaneously be reorganized along a vertical axis according to the affinities of their meanings. The structure that emerges will be less universal than that of the structuralists. Instead, it is intended to reveal the highly specific structural tensions of a single society. And it will have the advantage that it lends itself to comparisons based not on the work of the mind but on that of societies, which reveals their images of themselves.

In addition, I do not have any preconceived notions about where these dilemmas function, or their formulation or solution, whether symbolic or real. Do they appear on the level of thought, cognition, emotion, or practice? It is impossible here to make any sure claims about their location.

In any event, examination reveals that the basis of ritual as posited by Lévi-Strauss, the reconciliation of faithfulness to oneself with the passage of time—synchrony with diachrony—is inadequate to account for our festival. For if, in the sacrifice, commemoration claims to transcend history and locate in the present an ideal community that was founded in the past by an ancestor close to God, this commemoration nonetheless betrays tensions among ritual roles that hearken back to the relationships among the positions and prerogatives of daily life. And if the masquerade is intended to plunge us back into a past where a sacrilege was committed that today has been expiated in some way by the play, nevertheless it also offers the enactment of everyday life, with all its real and threatening ambiguities.

The masquerade creates and brings into the light of day beings marked by essential mutations who spy on the identity of individuals, even that of the group itself, which in other respects is subjected to the upheavals and evaluations of world society. Perhaps this is the source of the unusual emotional power of this whole dramatic evocation.

Especially since such a dramatization, in a poetic movement that rebels against every social sense of moderation, brings us face to face with some of the logical contradictions found within some of the classifications that regulate ordinary behavior. In so doing, society says something about itself. But it must be immediately noted that society does not present itself as a speaker exchanging words or ideas with someone else or as an actor giving a monologue about himself. For the very element that defines a conversational posture is missing from the relationship between the drama and its audience. No clear boundary is there to make it possible to decide whether this or that scenic "formulation" is undecipherable and consequently incapable of generating a response.

All regard for an exchange of clear statements is alien to this ritual and its drama; perhaps this is characteristic of all types of theater and would lead to the creation of forms shaped by tradition and constantly recreated and modified by the actors and circumstances. Hence the emergence of what will be called the "dramatic operators," which tell us that what the festival has to say cannot be directly communicated. Needed are a backdrop and a convention that resemble sleep and dreams in the sense that they unleash an activity that is unthinkable and inaccessible during the waking state. This will be a way of working with the drama that is analogous to what Freud has called "dream-work." [12] As in the case of dreams, the real is never entirely banished, and thus one accounts for the fact that the inversion of the described ritual is incomplete. It is partial; what counts is not the ritual itself but the mixture of the ordinary and its negation, the departure from the serious and the burlesque escapades so typical of Bilmawn, and the intermingling, revealed by analysis, of the sacrifice and the masquerade.

Prayer and the Preparation of the Victim
Ideal Community and the Division and Hierarchy of Ritual Roles

9

The activities connected with the sacrifice are divided into three principal phases: the collective prayer in the open air in a place especially set aside for that purpose; the men's assembly, in an outbuilding of the mosque, and their communal breakfast *(lafdur)*; and, the slaughter of the victim, as well as other actions constituting the sacrifice in the strict sense of the term and the distribution of the flesh. Each of these stages includes a series of units that are distinguished according to the criteria that have been set forth, summarized in table 1.

At the end of the sermon, the men disperse. But before that, custom decrees that they greet one another in a special way by clasping each other by the hand and wishing one another God's forgiveness. For this reason, the prayer is the consecration of an expiatory victim. But what sin, what disobedience, are they attempting to "wash away," to use their term? Of course, each one desires to receive divine mercy. But it is difficult not to see this as a collective redemption. The offerings and sacrifices that compensate for individual faults exist and are clearly distinct from this sacrifice, falling in the month of dhu-Lḥijja and so tied in other ways to the pilgrimage.

The prayer that consecrates the victim brings the sacrifiers together, since this is a rite that—locally—is undertaken neither by women nor by young unmarried men.* Muslim law does not decree it;[1] one cannot stress this point too much—local practice imposes its own norms. Thus we are in the presence of sacrifiers who have collectively returned to God by means of a prayer in the open air. One might as well say that the consecration and

---

*According to the distinction made by Henri Hubert and Marcel Mauss in *Essai sur la nature et fonction du sacrifice* (1899), the sacrifier *(sacrifiant)* offers the sacrifice but may employ a ritual specialist, the sacrificer *(sacrificateur)*, to carry out the sacrifice for him.—Trans.

Table 1. Steps and Units of Action of the Sacrifice

Units of Action[a] (3 Steps)	1	2	3	4	5
1. M	Gathering at the mṣalla	Prayer	Sermon	Return to the village	
F	Cleaning house and preparing breakfast (lafdur)	Same	Same	Same	
2. M	Meeting and accounts at the mosque	Communal breakfast (lafdur)	Dispersal		
F	Sending food to the men	Preparing the ingredients and utensils	Waiting and preparation of the victim: kohl		
	Waiting	Waiting			
3. M	Preparation of the victim: short invocation	Immolation	Dismembering and emptying the carcass	Roasting liver and heart: bulfaf prepared and eaten	Eating the head, feet, stomach, and other offal
F	Preparation of the victim: water, salt, henna	Collection of the blood, salt thrown into the spilled blood	Preparation of the brazier and charcoal	Eating the roasted viscera (bulfaf), except the spleen, large intestine	Cooking the same offal in a couscous stew
					Eating it

[a]M = male, F = female

sanctification of the victim are valid for the group itself as it is represented there, and as projected outside of their dwellings. This last aspect of the prayer is similar on the one hand to the ordinary prayer for the dead, and on the other to the prayer preceding a martyr's burial. In the case under consideration here, the chosen space is adjacent to the cemetery. Hence a clear association: in the sacrifice, it is a soul freed by the murderous act of slaughter that is going to rejoin other souls in their places of eternal rest.

Unlike the Friday prayers, the festival prayer (*salat al'Id*) comes before the sermon. The sermon I observed is given in two parts, separated by a moment of rest when everyone sits down, for the faithful remain standing around the imam as he instructs them. Standing in a circle, they listen to a homily that focuses on two questions: the justification of the sacrifice, and the requisite qualities of the victim. This concludes with admonitions to follow the straight and narrow path, accompanied by terrifying images of the fate awaiting unrepentant rebels and sinners. Later on I will analyze the justification of the sacrifice, which is given as a commemoration of Abraham's primordial act as he offers his son to God in this bloody rite. For the moment, let us consider the criteria that must govern the selection of the animal to be slaughtered.

Sheep are the preferred victims, and rams are more highly prized than lambs or ewes. Then come the billygoat and the nanny goat, followed by the bull, the ox, and the cow. Lastly, male or female camels may also be sacrificed. Four domestic species, then, in which the male always occupies the first place.[2] Finally, the sermon stresses the need for the victim to be perfect and whole. It must not suffer from any wounds or infirmities.[3]

Essentially, the sermon given in Imi-n'Tassaft takes up the story of Abraham's sacrifice as it is found in the Koran and the vulgates.[4] The same is true of several homiletic texts coming from the western Upper Atlas that I had the opportunity to examine. All the prescriptions given are respected in practice, as well as the order of preference concerning the victim, except when material conditions, such as in Imi-n'Tassaft, dictate a nearly exclusive slaughter of goats. Indeed, sheep are rare in these rugged mountain areas with their harsh climate, and they are raised primarily for their wool and for trade with the markets on the plains. In any event, goat meat appears on the ordinary menu with almost no competition. Very often people will choose a castrated goat, despite the canonical preference for perfect victims, and in large families a female is acceptable for want of other choices.

The relationship between the victim and sacrifier can already be discerned in this scale: a whole male, uncastrated if possible. Within each species the female is at the bottom of the scale. Locally, people are aware of the preference for rams and understand why: wasn't it the animal that God himself substituted for Ismail, who was about to be slain?[5] In Imi-n'Tassaft as in neighboring villages, people choose a male goat. In the scale of local values it replaces the ram, which as we have noted, is a rarity. Sometimes it is a castrated animal. Although it does not contradict the religious prescription, such a choice is, however, less recommended than others. Here once again, in addition to the relative availability of the species, family size and the need to provide it with animal raw materials, in an environment where these are rare, enter into play. The feast provides the opportunity to eat one's fill and often the chance to set food aside for future times. According to local criteria, the castrated goat is the animal of choice to sell or sacrifice on other occasions, and it is often the victim slaughtered to seal and ratify a marriage.

The prayer and the sermon form the climax of a series of rites leading to the immolation. Full ablutions[6] that are made upon awakening and other observances of the previous night form the passage into the ceremonies: people abstain from sexual relations, avoid cutting or plucking their beards and hair or biting their nails. The night, or at least part of it, must be devoted to prayer, for it is particularly holy.[7]

The complete ablutions—which are identical to those performed after every seminal emission—both conclude and announce a radical purification, which is achieved when one cuts one's hair, shaves, and cleans and files one's nails either before or after barbering. Each of these biological growths is cut off, or ended, with the intention of bringing about a meeting with God. If, as universal tradition and local thought would have it, these are impurities of which one must be rid, then it is all the more easy to understand that the *ḥajj,* as a "washing of sins" and a commemoration and expiation, is accomplished by the faithful who are burdened with these signs of impurity, and thus with sin. The prayer of the sacrifice purifies after it causes one to renounce all these forbidden parts of the body. What is not one's own is given up so that one may stand forth, purified, with what one has. The sacrifice will be the other ransom; closer to the soul, and thus more radical, if one considers it to be a gift of life itself. In this way the rites preceding the prayer and the commemoration of the murderous act reported by the holy text are connected. The first are reflected in the bodily evidence signaling biological growth and its rejection, the second announces the birth of the son and the necessary separation from him. In both cases, the process takes place away from human habitation. For the most popular version of the Abrahamic myth states that the sacrifice of the son must occur far from the paternal home, in a space devoid of humanity, and the *'id* prayer takes place outside the village, in the *mṣalla* located beyond the village precincts.

Also in both cases, those at the center of the drama must carry out practices to beautify them. Indeed they must fit an ideal of perfection. Ablutions, costumes, attention to the body, and purification embellish the sacrifier. This same requirement is imposed on the victim. The parallel is so strong that often the victim is made up and adorned with products such as henna

Table 2. Signs of Privation and Signs of Compromise

Acts of the sacrifier	Privation and sacrifice	Renunciation of the world	Compromise with the world
Sexual abstinence	+	+	−
Abstinence pertaining to bodily "growth"	+	−	+

(ḥanna: Lawsonia inermis), ordinarily associated with perfumes, ritual scarring, and the preparation of the bride and groom. I will return to this point. A summary of the first series of relationships appears in table 2.

Abstinence is a clear sign of a rupture with the pleasures of this world. In the devotion of the learned, just as in ordinary and popular thought, it is a synonym for asceticism, purification, and a return to God in a movement of repentance. It can be described as the mastery of the fundamental pollution that overshadows all men. From this standpoint, it is also a sacrifice, in the ordinary meaning of depriving oneself of something. It is a gift to God and is accompanied by a certain number of other privations: not cutting or plucking one's hair, not chewing one's nails, even. But sexual abstinence is listed among these privations only to be set apart from them all as a sign: for if it is a standard of purity, all these bodily growths, all this biological increase that one is compelled to undergo, can only turn out to be filth and impurity. Hair and nails are signs of impurity, although of a weaker sort compared to the emission of sperm. Even in cases of sexual abstinence, they are evidence of an unavoidable state of sin that is practically consubstantial with life itself. Hence their role in mourning practices. It is not enough for the sacrifier to renounce the world; he must also show by some sign his irremediable compromise with it.

So, when the most holy of days arrives, the sacrifier is in that ambiguous state which he will ask prayer and sacrifice to remove. All at once, it is no surprise that everything is reversed. All signs of pollution are literally shaved and washed away, by ablutions identical on the one hand to those required after sexual relations and on the other, to those needed after death to prepare the corpse for burial.[8] It is a consecration to God that resembles a total surrender, something akin to death. Prayer, which is carried out beyond the community walls, is a sign of this total break with the world that is also a departure from it. The gathering of the sacrifiers at the mṣalla is the spectacular culmination of this rupture sought by the now-ideal community. In the villages as in the towns, the entire *'umma* surrenders to its creator.[9] This is without a doubt one of the high moments of the festival.

Evidence of this are the legalistic sermon that follows and the return to the village where, once again, it is necessary to settle a few practical details before everyone goes home to immolate the victim. But it is a group that is transformed and renewed that eats the first meal of the new life foretold by the year that is about to begin. This *fdur*,[10] which is eaten together after a morning of fasting and prayer, is the true communion of a group that expresses its renewed fraternity by eating together. Indeed, everyone has experienced a quasi-rebirth whose symbolism is traced by the wanderings before and after the prayers. The men go to the *mṣalla* one by one, each taking the path of his choice. They return to the village in a group, all by the same route, which means a change of itinerary.[11] A review of the transformations affecting the sacrifier and sanctioned by the law of the group makes it possible to readily discern the passage from a state of ambiguity and penitence to a state of absolute purity that abolishes the distance between man and God—a true resurrection into a sanctified world. It will be noted that this is no sacralization—which moreover is impossible—that denies the life of the body and earthly needs, but a sanctification of this world whose ambiguous nature no one claims to hide. At most the believer is re-armed to confront it (cf. table 3).

Let us turn to the sacrifice and the victim to follow the transformations

Table 3. Transformations of the Sacrifier

State of ambiguity; Privation and signs of sin	Renunciation of the world	Compromise with the world	Total break from the world	Return with a new personality
Sexual abstinence	Sexual abstinence		Ablutions	Return to the village following a new path, common to all
			Walk to the *mṣalla* and prayer	
			Cleaning, shaving . . .	
			Common prayer	
Abstinence concerning bodily "growths" (not cutting hair, etc.)		Abstinences concerning the body (not cutting hair, etc.)		

the animal undergoes. Set apart from the flock or purchased weeks or even months beforehand, the sacrificial animal has shared the life of the household. The woman watches over it with special care; it is treated with respect, generally the way in which one would treat a human being. Its bed is clean, it does not leave the house, and it is fed barley and bran. It has no further contact with its flock or with nature. Thus it is not only a domestic animal in the sense that it belongs to a species that has been domesticated; it has been taken away from the animal realm to be brought closer to the life of humans.

The evening before the day of the immolation, the wives and daughters of the sacrifiers put henna on their hands and feet. In the family where I observed the rite, the male children's hands were also stained. Some of this henna is put on the animal's forehead, and the next morning a mark remains of the same red that colors the women's hands. This marking nearly completes the series of small acts of identification that for some time have been part of taking care of the victim, which end with the application of kohl to the animal's eyelids and the gift of barley, salt, and henna that the creature must swallow at the very moment that its throat is slit. In the case I observed, it is true, the sons of the house, educated at the modern school, forbade their mother to "make up" the animal's eyes. But throughout the mountains the two practices are widespread. Here is a description recorded by a writer early in this century:

The women . . . take trays made from dwarf palm fronds; they pour a little barley onto them, into which they add a few leaves of henna, walnut bark (*swak*), and powder taken from the flask of *kohel*. Seizing the sheep of the Aid, the men open its mouth and pour the henna and barley into it. Immediately afterward they add some water and hold the animal's muzzle shut with their left hand. Then the women, holding the flask of *kohel* in their right hand, offer it to the men, who grasp the brush and dip it into the flask of *kohel* to apply it to the sheep's right eye.[12]

Except for the *swak,* today the victim still swallows the ingredients noted by the writer, and is "prettied up" under the same conditions. Whatever the men's role in these operations may be, it is clear that they are masters only of the rituals of prayer and immolation, while the final touches are the province of the women.

Let us pause for a moment to examine this exchange between woman and victim. Publicly, and if one may say it, politically, the sacrifier is a man, the master of a household. In the house, to which he rightly returns after the public ritual, his wife in her way takes charge of the victim. She shares with it her henna,[13] a purifying and prophylactic substance—in local exegesis, it is a paradisaical substance. Its virtues and its perfume doubtless attest to this origin.[14] And this combination of traits makes it an indispensable element in all celebrations, including certain rites of passage that use it intensively: circumcision and marriage, for example. In the marriage celebration, henna literally readies the bride and groom for one another as well as for the radical change in their status. In addition, the fact that many circumcisions and all marriages are sealed by the immolation of a victim completes the image of a system in which spilled blood and henna are constantly associated.

A minor ingredient compared to henna, kohl is the other finishing touch that the woman shares with the victim. The pairing of the two makes the victim into a marginal creature, to use Van Gennep's term, comparable to all of those put into this position by the rite of passage. Here again, circumcision, marriage, and death naturally come to mind.

Thus it is as if the men, by their ablutions and bodily preparations, put themselves in the same marginal position that the women take with their use of henna and kohl—a position in which, using the same ingredients, they also put the victim. Passage and change of status. Keep in mind for a moment the recurrence of those elements that ensure passage for men—cutting their hair and nails, ablutions and prayer—and, for the women, ingredients that are "material" in essence, especially henna. Also keep in mind, last of all, that sacrifice and henna are often associated in other rites of passage (table 4).

Consequently, as it could be expected, the victim, as an intermediary and a symbol of the gift of oneself, is marked in two very different ways for women and for men (fig. 3). The men's way is sanctioned by the group which, on this occasion, is not distinct from the entire Muslim community. The women's way is not explicitly contradictory to the men's, nor is it even on the same level; but it differs from the first by its private character, beyond the sanction of the group. It is as if two parallel religions coexisted, the first calling for commemoration and prayer enacted by and for the word, and the

Table 4. Marginality and Its Operant Factors

Initial status	Rites	Operant factors	New statuses
Child	Circumcision	Henna/kohl	Boy
Bachelor/virgin	Marriage (sacrifice called *laḥlal*)	Henna/kohl	Married man/woman
Animal	Muslim sacrifice	Henna/kohl	Victim

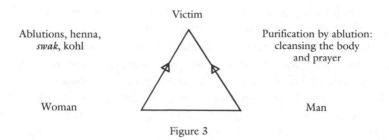

Figure 3

second, more or less silent, highlighting the efficacity of substances and physical results.

It is a rite of passage, then, prepared and executed by each of the two sexes; but in no way is it a definitive death, for the victim only moves from one life to another. The ingredients at work in the feminine ritual are evidence of the resurrection of both victim and sacrifiers in paradise. Henna and the other products form the metonymical signs of this place of purity par excellence. And these are also the same signs, in addition to a sacrifice, that one sees as operators of marriage and thus, of the foundation of the household.

But this is only the first step of an exchange that, surrounding the violence of the acts of immolation, takes on an even more spectacular appearance. It may be recalled that the animal is given a mixture of henna, salt, and barley "to drink," and then it is immediately slaughtered and some of the blood is collected as it spurts from the wound. The men slaughter; the women prepare the materials forced into the victim's muzzle and hold the ladle under the still-living victim's throat to collect the foaming blood.

Barley, the first grain to be cultivated, is here as well as throughout Morocco the object of religious respect. A feminine plant *(tumzin)*, yet its cultivation, from sowing to storing the grain by way of plowing, harvesting, threshing, and winnowing, is under male control. Only the spring weeding is undertaken by the women. But that is about all, and women are prohibited from entering the threshing floor when, in the summer heat, the men and animals tread upon the sheaves to separate the grain from the chaff. From this standpoint it is possible on a sexual level to contrast barley and sheep (the flock in general) on the one hand, and grass and the cow, on the other. Any observer will note that women, cows, and fowl are inseparable, while men take care of the barley, the "flock" *(lebhaym),* and the mule.

The main annual crop, barley is also the basic food stuff. It is the plant that feeds. All the rest is only an accompaniment. All the rest is there only so that "one can eat the bread." And it is right at this stage that men turn the barley over to women. As a plant, it belongs to men. As a grain, ready to be transformed into bread, the women take over, just as they take charge of the victim once the public ritual to prepare its immolation has ended.

Seen from this angle, the presence of barley sheds light on the use of henna. Henna is a blessed plant, which prepares the young couple about to marry and above all the woman. With the sacrifice of an animal henna makes possible a union that violates the central prohibition concerning sexuality. The immolation of an animal, a mark of the festival here as elsewhere, is called *lahlal,* from an Arabic word that literally means what is licit. Henna, in this lifting of the prohibition, shares both the conditions of the foundation of the household and reproduction.[15]

But while barley as a food is "naturally" associated with salt, the conjunction of the two with henna in a single ritual recipe seems paradoxical at the very least. But is this really food? It is doubtful, for while the animal swallows it, it would be absurd to claim that the officiants wish to feed it. In their own words, it is at most a matter of "drinking," for they make the animal drink *(n'sharrab lbhimet);* and above all, there is little sense in feeding an animal that one is about to kill at that very moment.

Thus it has to be admitted that the victim does not eat the mixture of salt, barley, and henna that the woman mixes for it and that this concoction is not food. Especially since henna, in practice as well as in thought, is not connected with fodder. If this is the case, the animal is not being offered a food product but three symbols of the human and the reproductive order: the food and the salt that puts the finishing touches on it, and the legitimate wife, of whom henna is both the sign and the adornment. Finally, salt is a metaphor for a woman's beauty; along with henna it completes her attractiveness, just as it heightens the taste of barley when it is eaten. The two finishing touches are simultaneously given in the same symbolic gesture. As an example of ritual action at work, this strange association once again recalls the working of dreams. It is a nonmeal presented in the form of a meal and food whose composition is absurd. For one can only point to the extravagance of this so-called act of eating, of the word used to refer to it, and the "deceit" of the rite/dream that retains of the act of eating only swallowing, to raise to the height of consuming a sacrament the ingestion and digestion that define the object and mechanics of eating.

From this standpoint, henna and/or kohl is to the human couple what salt is to the pairing of water and barley; the first is a preparation for sexual

consummation, the second for the consumption of food. But this prepara-
tory role is not all that they share; the fact that both are associated with
procedures for lifting prohibitions (concerning sexuality) and combatting
spirits indicates the presence of a quality that purifies and makes passages
easier. Salt can be compared to henna because it provides one of the principal metaphors for women's sexual attractiveness.[16] The bond between the
victim, the couple, and the kitchen is spectacularly conveyed by this act of
drinking and pseudo-eating. And in this way the victim is at the center of a
relationship of union and commensality that provides the basis for the domestic group. That the agent for this is a woman takes on its full meaning
once the men's actions are examined. But for a moment let us continue with
the women.

When the blood spurts from the wound that has just been opened by the
man's knife, the women collect a ladleful or its equivalent in a bowl. This
blood is dried and kept in a piece of cloth. It is hung with the gall bladder
(carefully removed when the carcass is gutted) on the kitchen wall or from
the ceiling, over the hearth. The pool of blood spread on the ground is
sprinkled with salt.[17]

The women's acts here still reflect a bond shadowed by powers of conjur-
ation. In fact, the victim has drunk materials from the home. In exchange it
provides two problematic substances that are nonetheless protective and
beneficial. The sacrifiers daub themselves with blood and use it along with
the bile as a protection and transmitter of blessings; also, they apply both
substances to certain wounds to heal them; occasionally they burn a blood
clot[18] to ward off the harmful effects arising from contact with spirits.

Islamic law forbids the consumption of blood; here as elsewhere, respect
for this prohibition is absolute. Outside this festival, blood is collected only
in a few other sacrifices involving both divination and trances. But in all
cases blood is inseparably linked with life, or seen as its double: it attracts
djinns (jnun) who drink it. Salt drives them away and banishes the misfortunes that their presence could provoke. Some sacrifices, on the other
hand, are carried out to appease them. Locally, in the sanctuary of Sidi
Shamharush, the king who reigns over all these terrifying beings, victims
are constantly immolated in order to procure a divinatory trance, to heal
sickness, or to conciliate the powers of the earth at the beginning of the
agricultural cycle (tighersi n'l'ada).[19] Finally, human blood is the principal
substance utilized in the witchcraft that threatens the lives of men and particularly children.[20]

The overall ethnographic context reflects the impurity and danger of blood, which one must always and at all costs discard. Paradoxically, in some cases, notably that of the canonical Muslim sacrifice, it is as if this rule must be contradicted by making the closest possible contact with the blood, while purifying the part that touches the ground. But this paradox is only apparent, for the blood of the victim has been mastered by prayer and the formulas uttered before the immolation.[21] Thus there is no danger in collecting it; quite the contrary, its presence can only be beneficial. This is no longer the case the moment it touches the ground, the abode of uncontrollable chthonic creatures who make haste to quench their thirst.

In any event, something from the impure flood that attracts the powers of misfortune is kept to cure sicknesses and protect the household. Through it a new identification of the sacrifiers and the victim is effected, but this time it moves in the opposite direction, for now it is the victim who, through the women, is brought closer to the group that offers it to the divinity. One can see in this gift of blood a rite of protection and a way to approach the sources of good, which is but one of a series of markers that includes the use of salt, the practice of all forms of ablution, fumigations, the wearing of amulets, the chanting of sacred texts, the repetition of the names of God, and so on. In this whole, a sexual division of labor assigns to the woman, among other things, the use of salt and blood, in the same way that prior to the immolation it assigned to the woman the task of offering the victim a false meal composed of grain, henna, salt, and water. The type of purification carried out by this feminine office utilizes substances that imply that the impurity is above all physical contamination. In this way, the sacrifice traces the contours of a women's religion based on manipulating and struggling against spirits. It is the gift of a life to God; one will easily agree with Evans-Pritchard on this point. But whatever the sacrifiers' intentions and inclinations, which are all that counts for Evans-Pritchard, the experience that I have just described outlines in one stroke the ideal and sanctified framework in which men and women perform actions that, because of their social positions—which are also religious positions and positionings with respect to an axis of values—receive greater or less public recognition.

Marcel Detienne emphasizes this focus on the social relationship in his study of Greek sacrifice, in which he analyzes not only the typical steps leading to the immolation of the victim but also the entire process, including carving the carcass and the ways in which it is distributed, cooked, and consumed. Unlike Hubert and Mauss, who reduce the rite exactly to the three-stage process of a rite of passage and to a dual goal of sacralization/

desacralization, Marcel Detienne rightly shows how this type of analysis leads to the prejudice that postulates Christian sacrifice as both the exemplary sacrifice and the final step in an evolution.

In the case of the Greeks, the presence of the god is evoked both by the sharing of the carcass and by the ways it is eaten, since this is how its immortality and distance from men are affirmed. Second, it is through the distribution of the meat among men that men divide themselves into groups by political categories. And lastly, it is in the debate about food that the attitude toward blood sacrifice becomes most clear, where the internal tensions of the city are revealed—in a compromise with its values or a rejection of the ethics that it embodies in the form of a collective sacrifier.[22]

From the outset Muslim sacrifice undertakes these determinations of ritual activities that underscore sociological boundaries and roots them, as will be seen, in a mythology of the birth of civilization as an ideal Abrahamic community. The dialogue between the sexes in the home continues around the carcass, once it has been skinned and emptied. Roasting is the task of the men. Cooking and boiling are the task of the women. The former take on this activity as they would an *initium,* thereby opening the cycle of consumption. The latter collaborate with this before they set about cooking, on the hearth, the pieces that the men cut up and deliver each day. The roasting is not done on the hearth, but over charcoal coals in a brazier or oven. Grilling on the brazier is especially reserved for the viscera. Not all: just the liver, heart, and lungs. These last, as well as part of the liver, are cut into little pieces and wrapped in caul to make *bulfaf.* The rest is likewise cut up in the same fashion, but cooked unwrapped; this is *kwah.* All the rest of the offal, including the head, fall in the domain of the kitchen and therefore the women.

Roasting, furthermore, is everywhere a man's business, even outside the festival: this is the way to prepare viscera that have been purchased or obtained because an animal has been slaughtered. The roasted carcass bought at the market *(shwa)* is also the man's affair. On the other hand, women cook any meat that is purchased raw. But while cooking on the hearth is an exclusively feminine job, grilling the viscera leads to a visible and openly admitted cooperation between the sexes, because the women go back and forth to the brazier, bringing the men what is ready for eating and putting what needs to be cooked on the grill.

Let us return to the overall context to examine, in light of other relationships, the ritual action that culminates around the immolation. There is nothing unusual about mixing barley and salt. The addition of water results in the basic ingredients for daily bread. Women's work par excellence. But what about henna? One has to admit that its association with barley and salt in the same recipe is, to say the very least, surprising. What the woman makes the victim swallow is not what she fixes for her husband. In his case the boundaries are quite clear between the preparation of bread and the readying of the body that the use of henna signifies. For in addition to its prophylactic properties, this plant is used to care for the body and hair. It perfumes them, and from this fact its erotic function is quite clear.[23]

But henna is like salt in that both of them chase away evil spirits; and metaphorically salt, like henna in reality, makes women desirable. Nonetheless, the association of these two substances together with barley is completely outside the ordinary. This grain is certainly the most sacred of all, and for that reason is the object of respect that verges on veneration;[24] but it has no use in any bodily preparations, cures, or as a deterrent against evil spirits, while for salt and henna these are principal roles.

However, the paradox of this association—barley, salt, and henna—is only apparent, for henna is to women what salt is to bread. A paradisaical substance, henna is also a beauty product that promotes a favorable conjunction between man and woman. Salt is the finishing touch for food. Food and reproduction are thus found to be associated in this act that at first sight, by bringing together barley and salt on the one hand, and barley and henna on the other, struck us as a paradox. It can be seen that the conjunction that is at the basis of these two ingredients leads to conjugal life and to commensality. So a special combination that joins commensality and the life of the couple is taken by the victim, which, through the offices of the woman, gives its blood and bile to the household.

The four substances in the first gift are frequently ordinary gifts. The regular gift of food theoretically obliges one to offer only food in exchange. This is not at all the case in the exchange between the victim and the woman. She offers the gift of ornament while the victim provides a substance (blood) that it is forbidden to eat. These two elements suggest a communication centered on different terms than the ones that define the circulation of edible products. The henna drunk by the animal, like the black powder (kohl) that adorns its eyes, refers to the gift of the body at the heart of the sacralized institution of marriage.

Now, what is the man supposed to give in the matrimonial exchange? Food, clothing, and a victim to sacrifice. In exchange for this gift, he expects to receive a woman who is adorned and ready for him. And just as there is no marriage without a sacrificial victim whose blood and flesh are offered, in theory there can be no union without the bride's virginity offered for bloody defloration. The blood of the sanctified and immolated animal—prepared according to the canonical model—corresponds to the blood of the virgin given to her partner at the end of a process sacralized by ritual and law.

The marriage sacrifice bears the name of *ḥlal,* generally translated as "licit" and opposed to *ḥram* ("illicit"). It will be noted that *ḥaram* and "sacred" are intimately linked; what is sacred is *ḥaram,* that is, respected and forbidden. It will also be noted that *ḥlal* comes from the root *ḥl,* which means "to open, undo," etc. In any case, and even admitting that the relationship between the meaning of a root and the conscious or unconscious reference of the signifier is not entirely clear, it is evident that access to permissible sexuality cannot take place without a sacrifice.

The gift of food and the marriage gift, two methods of exchange on which the social order is founded, are thus intimately entwined in the same gesture.

However, it is still not clear why, in the sacrifice, both gestures are made by the woman. To answer this question, first of all one must reconsider the ingredients of the gift. Then it is necessary to relocate this act in the overall process. This amounts to viewing it in light of the other ritual acts, the ones that, precisely, are never the business of women, which are forbidden to them by either law or custom.

What the woman gives the victim, we have seen, is part food, part adornment. What food? The food over which she normally exercises control. It is not the barley of the fields, nor the barley of the threshing floor that she gives. Even if she wished to do so, she would be unable to touch it. Except for the labor of weeding, barley is the exclusive province of men, from plowing to winnowing. And when the men and animals sweat over the trodden barley, the woman prepares the man's food and timidly approaches these places to offer it to him. In fact she is forbidden to cross the perimeters of the threshing floor *(anrar).* So she offers the victim the grain from the house: the grain that she changes into food that is mixed with the other ingredients to make bread. We have already resolved the paradox of the gift of henna that accompanies this offer of food. Here it will be noted, to further highlight this solution, that both food and adornment are linked by the fact that the ingredients and the activity they inspire and transform belong to the domain of women. It must be recalled however, that in the marriage, the man must provide the food and the sacrifice to receive the virgin and her blood, the status of a married man, a companion, and children. He gives to receive her; but she takes the food and gives him children, and she receives the victim's blood to give him her own. Sociologically, however, her blood will not be recognized, since it is through the blood of the father that the couple's offspring will be classified and identified.

In the sacrificial ritual she alone, without her husband, makes this gift, as if she were giving both food and ornament. If the latter is normally the woman's province, along with the gift of a body, of virginal blood, it is strange that adornment is briefly combined with food in one single feminine act.

This issue can be resolved by examining the sexual division of ritual labor. Men and women must prepare for the sacrifice by performing a series of purification rites. The immolation takes place on the tenth day of the last month of the year. The preceding month is particularly holy: rigorous ablutions, fasts, and sexual abstinence mark the life of pious Muslims. Some days, especially the ninth day of the month of the sacrifice, are times for more strict observance than others. This is the famous day of 'Arafat, during which, in Mecca, the pilgrims leave the city for Mount 'Arafat. Earlier they have carried out all the other rites, including the circumambulation of the *ka'ba,* the sanctuary sheltering the black stone and whose construction is attributed to Abraham. On that day, then, the pilgrims leave Mecca for Mount 'Arafat and stand before it for a prayer beginning at about two in the afternoon and lasting until sunset. Thus they have observed almost all the rites of "sacralization" *(ihram),* which they will conclude the following morning with the sacrifice. On that day, the tenth of the month, they will go to Mina, throw seven stones at an ancient stone monument *(rajm),* and then offer a victim. It is only after the sacrifice that the pilgrim can leave the state of *ihram*—in other words, only then may he cut his hair, shed his pilgrim's garb, and so on.[25]

In the village as in Mecca, one must move about in a state of sacrality. It is a consecrated man who must carry out the immolation. And it is in that state that the men and women of the village sacrifice. However, as we have noted, some acts are reserved for men. The prayers and hearing the sermon that follows it, the collective meal, and settling the Koranic master's fees are their exclusive province. Above all, the decisive act that slits the throat[26] of the victim turned toward Mecca is theirs alone. When they are unable to carry it out, a son, relative, or another man will carry out the task. In all cases, even when it is not a matter of a sacrifice, women are not allowed to slit the animal's throat. Furthermore, the sacrifier must be a married man, the head of the household. And if possible, it is good if there is a victim for each married man in an extended family living under the same roof.

In other words, the father has the responsibility and the duty to renew the act of Abraham each year. The sermon that he hears while at prayer explicitly states that it is an obligation and involves the whole community. What has been immolated is offered to God, like the son of Abraham and the blessed ram that was his substitute. The formula pronounced immediately before the animal's throat is slit—"In the name Allah, the merciful, the compassionate, Allah is the most great"—sheds light on the victim's status. These words must be uttered at the hunt before shooting and in a holy war before one offers oneself as a martyr in the act of defending the Muslim community. To kill or to offer oneself, in this context and from this standpoint, are equivalent. And in the strictest sense, only meat that has been sacrificed can be licitly consumed. But one could also say that the second part of the formula pronounced by the sacrifier introduces an equivalence between the sacrificial victim and the soldier who has fallen in the line of a sacred duty. In both cases, the community offers itself as a collective sacrifier.

The Rite and the Myth

Sense and Nonsense about the Sacrifice

10

Thus, the masculine, Abrahamic *mimesis,* the only phase of the process recognized by the community, overshadows the feminine gift. The woman's act has no public existence. A community of sacrifiers is defined by a sacrificial victim, and it seems that this process ought to follow the contours isolating and limiting each household. In fact, community and victim borrow from one another and are identical. The father's blood, like that of the victim, is sociologically identified as a domestic and patriarchal unit and identifies this unit as a sacrificing entity. On this point, my analysis is akin to that of Walter Burkert, without his evolutionism or the biological "foundations" of his interactionist functionalism.[1]

This process of definition, carried out exclusively by the victim's and the father's blood, on the one hand establishes the parallel and the kinship between the two and on the other hand offers a contrast to the gift of the virgin's blood, which makes her a victim, devoid of any capacity to transmit her own lineage. In other words, only two mediating factors are active in the entire group: the sacrificial victim and the martyr. The first operates between the group and God; the second between God and the Muslim community. These terms function on two levels that can be called, following Lévi-Strauss's usage in this respect, the religious code and the warrior code. One can see that the relationships between the aspects that respectively define them are equivalent. Thus the sacrificial victim is to the father of the family what the martyr is to the Muslim community. If the martyr is offered up in place of the sacrificial victim, if he is but a martyr in a community of martyrs, then the sacrificial victim is offered up in place of the father. The model can be refined, and one can distinguish in the social code a familial, domestic, and paternal code defined by the sum of the relations between it and the various family members, a sexual code defining the series of relations posited by the difference of sexes in the family, and so forth. However, at this point there would be little advantage in drawing up an exhaustive table of these codes, for they will naturally emerge as the analysis proceeds. Let us simply conclude that the gift, which preserves the public community, masks (and in some ways hides) the physical reproduction that is made possible by the woman's gift of food to the man just before the immolation and her gift of a son by which she reproduces the group. Since this second gift results from marital ties, it is not surprising that the woman, at a moment in the ritual process, gathers into her hands in one gesture the gifts of food and cosmetics as a sign of the sexual offering.

In ritual, one of these codes governs, on the domestic level, the father's place as head of the family with respect to the other family members. In the sacrifice, he has the lead at the climax of the action: he slits the animal's throat. The myth of Abraham sheds additional light on this matter. Let us compare the lesson drawn from the acts of the Patriarch with what the analysis of the rite has already brought to light.

In the area where I observed the feast, people know a version of the tale, universally told throughout the Muslim world, of Ismail's sacrifice by his father Abraham. Every year the imams recall the Patriarch's deed in their sermons or in the course of pious conversations with the villagers. Many of them have heard the story sung by wandering "praise singers" (maddah) at the marketplace or in the public squares of the town. In their repertoire, the exemplary obedience of the ancestor of the Semites holds a place next to the lives and miracles of the prophets, the deeds of the great conquerors, the highly exact descriptions of the apocalypse, and evocations of what befalls one the evening one is placed in the tomb. . . . A schoolmaster gave this account of the action:

> In a dream, Sidna Ibrahim—salvation be his!—found himself being ordered to immolate his own son so as to be nearer to God. To do this, he takes the boy aside on the pretext of looking for firewood for the house, and he tells him of God's order. The son submits, telling his father to sharpen the knife with care to make his death easier. But when God's prophet touches his son with the knife, his action has no effect, and the angel immediately appears with a ram [sent] from Paradise. After the sacrifice, the Patriarch goes off to found Mecca, which is the mother of cities.

This narrative, which oral tradition has borrowed from written sources, summarizes "facts" recorded in more luxuriant detail in the works devoted to the "tales of the prophets" (qaṣaṣ al'anbiya'): edifying literature belonging to a genre that has its masters and its classics. One of these, al-Tha'labi (d. early fifth century A.H./eleventh century A.D.) is the author of a work highly esteemed by the educated residents of the Ait Mizane villages.[2]

Many episodes in the written accounts do not figure in the oral tradition. It fails to mention Abraham's comings and goings between his own land— al-Sham—where Sarah, Isaac's mother, is found, and Mecca, where he establishes Hagar, the mother of Ismail; or his mount, none other than the fabled Buraq, later ridden by the Prophet of Islam; or his fruitless attempts to cut the throat of his son, miraculously protected by copper armor; or even the extraordinary biography of the ram, which according to some sources goes all the way back to Habil, the son of Adam. The interested reader may refer to al-Tha'labi's text. This author also provides a concurrent tale, supported by some of the early Islamic authorities, according to which—and on this point it agrees with Hebrew tradition—the son destined to be immolated would not be Ismail but Isaac, not the son of Hagar but the son of Sarah. Above all, al-Tha'labi's learned account places the foundation of Mecca and the Temple *(al-Bayt),* which according to the local version occurs after the sacrifice, as an independent episode that appears right after the Flood.

Whatever the differences between the local and the learned versions, they both present Abraham as a founding hero of civilization. The establishment of Hagar and her son in what will become Mecca provokes the appearance of water and the first human settlement. Indeed, the building of the temple completes the "creation" that is eternal Islam. Oral accounts, although more terse, give equal stress to the foundation of the "mother of cities." The "error" in the oral account in comparison to the scholarly version is not totally off the mark, and the decisive deed that is the sacrifice, which brings about both culture and the law, occupies the center of both narratives.[3]

Abraham submits to God, and Ismail to his father. A double submission and renunciation: one gives up his son, the other his life. Thus the two face the trial of death and through it win the founding contract of the city of men, which is that of God. The act initiating society and culture is thus accomplished in the most dramatic way imaginable, in a tragedy that, like any other, derives its mechanisms from a renunciation imposed by a supra-human force and ending with death.

Like any tragic act, the son's immolation by his father's hand, when judged by human standards, is ambiguous, incomprehensible. For on the one hand, God orders a human sacrifice, and on the other, the victim is a son begotten by an old and "plaintive" father, a child born in answer to his father's prayer and, more to the point, who is supposed to succeed him in perpetuating the religion.[4] Furthermore, the motivating factor in the immolation scenario is based on a goal that is ultimately revealed to be a deception. This lie serves to reverse ordinary social roles: the father takes the place of the mother and sets off to look for firewood. If one accepts the existence of this deceit and this reversal, is there a way to resolve the "inconsistency" in a text claiming to be a testimony and sign of truth?

First, it will be remarked that God orders Abraham to sacrifice his successor in the person of his son. A more serious action cannot be imagined, if one recalls that the goal of the household is the generation of sons, worthy extensions of the father. Lacking a male heir, Abraham is the end of his own agnatic line. For, in the logic of Arab-Muslim tradition, Ismail is the oldest son; furthermore, he is the child God gave to Abraham first when the old man begged him to grant him a spiritual descendant. Under these conditions, the sacrifice of Ismail puts an end to the lineage and leaves Abraham in the same situation as his wife, who also is incapable of prolonging her own family lineage, since in this system she is condemned to reproduce only that of her husband. It should not be surprising that the patriarch sees to collecting the firewood, since by the sacrifice of his own heir he already occupies a position approaching and congruent to that of his wife.

By sacrificing his son, the father is thus sacrificing himself as a father, a martyr to the contract of extreme proximity to God; and, at the same time, a martyr of the civilized community based on this submission. From this point of view, a double substitution can be seen in the myth: the son and the animal are both substitutes for the father. And death as a return to God and sacrifice for the continuation of the group (the foundation of Mecca) both find their meaning behind the horrible mask of the father's murder of the son.

In the overt content of the myth, the son is saved. Perhaps this is the most ambiguous point. Why is he saved? Undoubtedly, so that he can follow his father. In an oracular image laden with multiple keys, in fact it is the father who is saved, since the son is his substitute. But what does Abraham do right after the animal is substituted (which on the surface saves the son and on a deeper level saves the father)? He founds the city. Thus we are confronted with a continuity that requires its own disappearance for there to be a successor. It is not a true murder, as the Freudian myth claims, but a quasi-murder, heavy with suspense, averted in the nick of time by a miracle that transforms it into a socially regulated succession whose method is not further described in the myth, doubtless because it would add nothing more to the fundamental story.

Taking an abominable detour, in which God directs the murder of the son, the father's closest kin, the myth returns to the definition of the domestic unit that we have already encountered in the division of ritual labor. There we have seen that the sacrificial action defines the domestic unit in terms of the relationship of the group to its head, in the same way that the sacrificial victim defines the group as a sacrifying group. But the relation between this myth and the rite, which explains it in the eyes of the believers, is not obvious.

Of course, the exegesis is based on an extreme concept of sacrifice and a venerable tradition, the observance of which instantly condemns any stray thoughts about questioning them as a sacrilege; but, in addition to the fact that this is no way to explain the murder of the son, such an extreme renunciation can only take place or be represented through self-destruction. Christianity makes use of the divinization of the son to represent the father's self-sacrifice. Thus the myth kept in Muslim memory violates the ordinary norms, as well as the super-norms of extreme and extraordinary sacrifice. In that way it moves away from the rite, which is already differentiated from it, as we have seen, because the head of the domestic group is identified with the sacrificed victim. In this way, myth and rite are separated by much more than a simple divergence; from the victim's standpoint, the myth turns the rite upside down. Like some dreams, it works by presenting an inverted image of the victim.

Midway between the public evocation of the myth of Abraham and the immolation, which if not performed in public at least is universal, are the "women's customs," which in comparison to the masculine rites have something clandestine about them. Men are ambivalent toward these practices. They are careful not to forbid them and in some cases actually encourage them with a whole series of acts denoting their consent. But at the same time they claim to see them only as "women's customs," to which they need pay no attention. And while they sometimes happen to criticize them, the accommodation they display toward them is real nonetheless. For several years, from 1981 to 1984, I was able to observe a number of sacrifices. Only the young men being educated in town, in the state schools and universities that preach Islamic reform, categorically attempt to forbid the women to take part in preparing the victim. In a case I observed, the son stepped between his mother and the animal, thereby preventing her from carrying out her preparations. But whether prohibition or accommodation is admitted or not, the role women take is something very private with respect to the public meaning that tradition assigns to the sacrifice; and like the rest of the ritual acts performed by women, it often slips almost spontaneously into the event.

This is certainly the case when some of the victim's blood is gathered and grains of salt are thrown on the rest. The immolation is quick, for the blade must be very sharp and the movement sure, strong, and fast. The victim "must not suffer." It is set on its side facing east,[5] and a man assists the sacrificer by completely immobilizing it before the fatal blow. When the blood spurts from the animal's slit throat, the sacrifier's wife rushes forward to collect a ladleful.[6] She dips her index finger in it and draws a red dot on her forehead above her nose. The other women do the same thing. Some men and women dip their bare heels in the blood, which immediately soaks into the ground. The victim has already been released; it struggles for a moment, the death rattle sounding. When at last it lies still, it is dragged far from the pool of blood. The wound is washed; the neck is cut to remove the head from the body, and the dismemberment of the carcass begins. The sacrifier's wife quickly throws a handful of salt on the spot where the sacrifice took place.

The victim's blood is impregnated with *baraka:*[7] charisma, blessing, and supernatural power emanating from God and capable of becoming active in things, living beings, and persons. So, for example, the saints are endowed with *baraka.* But an offering to the saint takes on this quality as well, and an offering in the form of any kind of food is imbued with a sacredness that it communicates to those who eat it, a sacredness endowing it with a real power. For example, it can heal certain sicknesses and draw dangerous spirits away. The same is true of the victim's blood. The dried blood will be burned so that its smoke will ward off sickness. Along with bile, it is one of the parts of the animal endowed with curative properties. However, bile is exclusively used for wounds while blood, in the form of smoke, will be used more for sicknesses attributed to spirits. As for the salt thrown on the pool of blood left after the immolation, it is a matter of local knowledge that it drives away the harmful spirits, the djinns.[8] The Ait Mizane rarely offer any explanation for the custom of dipping their heels in the blood and the women's use of it to mark their forehead. The second practice is never explained, while local belief maintains that no matter how cold the winter, feet dipped in the blood never chap.

The immolation definitively hands the victim over to God. However, no one would ever claim that the flesh eaten by the household also goes to the Creator! Something else returns to him. There is in fact no clear local exegesis concerning this point, but everyone knows that the victim's soul goes to paradise, where it will join the souls of the good believers. And there is no relationship between the soul and the blood. The latter goes to the djinns while the former makes its way to the abode of the angels.

Having come to this point, let us examine these two pairs of associated terms: souls/blood, blood/djinn. The association of each one with blood is clearly expressed both in the sacrificial context and outside of it. But in the sacrifice it is explicit. Every year all the villagers of the valley gather after the harvests in the sanctuary of Sidi Shamharush, on the banks of the river and close to a spring.

The site is a half day's walk from the highest peak in the Atlas, Toubkal, where the waters originate. A huge feast is held, which attracts the crowd from the neighboring valleys and the big towns. The central rite carried out by the group consists in sacrificing a cow or bull in honor of Sidi Shamharush, "sultan of the *jnun*" (djinns) and patron saint of the valley. All the immolations occur in the same place, where the blood soaks into the ground, "drunk by Sidi Shamharush, who wants only blood." [9]

As we have seen, up to the moment of the immolation the sacrificial process defines and highlights the contours of the domestic unit. It also stresses the conditions for its continuity: the production of a son. But this cannot take place without the necessary intermediary of a woman, who is thus interposed between agnatic kin. How is she brought into this reproduction? By the double sacrifice that gives her the blood of a victim, in exchange for which, as a true sacrificial victim herself, she gives up her blood so that the father may continue his line. Once she is established in the house, she gives the victim (a substitute for the father) a blend of food and cosmetics associated with erotic life: two terms of physical reproduction. In turn she receives the blood. This exchange makes her the mistress and necessary intermediary between the world of dangerous spirits, those who haunt the darkness, and the world of men: the priests of God and of the angels. Every household has two priesthoods: that of the woman officiating in the relation between the human order and the dangerous and powerful supernatural order; that of the man officiating in the relationship between the human order and the powerful and beneficent supernatural order. Nevertheless, all depends upon the power of men, who initiate every ritual action. And while the men's office is recognized and valued, that of the women must in theory be disavowed, even though, like the women, everyone knows that it is impossible to live peacefully without reconciling, even neutralizing, the infernal powers. This is one of the principal sources of male ambivalence concerning these practices, especially since at certain times men become priests of cults, which are made to humanized beings with generally saintly characteristics, beings whose appearance is either left vague or, in some cases, explicitly described in terms of a chthonic being or djinn, as in the case of Sidi Shamharush.

Whether women took this role unbidden or were forced into it against their will by men, the relationship with the spirits in the sacrifice is the woman's realm, and she must face all its dangers; but these provide her with fearsome powers and weapons. Every man lives alongside a woman, and he is only able to avoid her dangerous power if she consents to protect him from it. Hence, this relationship of strength sanctioned by the sacrifice in which the man claims for himself alone the initiative for all, the relationship with God and the community of believers. While the woman, relegated to the exchange of food and blood, nonetheless handles dangerous powers, as the shadowy and terrifying mistress of reproduction. At the end of this process of exchange that she has undertaken with the victim, the victim gives her its excrement, which has been sacralized by the same masculine act of immolation. Once the animal has been cut apart and cleaned, its digestive tract is emptied. The woman carries off the excrement and spreads it in the stable, thereby moving from the reproduction of men to the reproduction of animals. The meaning and function of such a role and the discourse to which it gives rise are obvious; male ambivalence with respect to the woman's activity is particularly illumined by this ritual division of labor and the series of related terms by which her task is defined vis-à-vis that of her husband.

In any case, the woman's relation to the living victim, to its blood, excrement, and carcass, stops here. Unlike the immolation, the dismembering and cleaning of the carcass are not exclusively the province of the head of the house. His sons, married or single, take charge of the dead victim, and they do not leave it until it is readied for carving. It is extremely unusual, on the very day of the sacrifice, to carve the animal's flesh. On the first day only the viscera, internal organs, head, and feet are eaten. There again, we have seen, cooking styles are apportioned between men and women. The consumption of the viscera is directed by the men. The woman may be present, but her role is of a servant, not the chef. The tea ceremony that accompanies it is the men's domain. The woman cooks the rest in the kitchen, on the domestic hearth. This represents a succession and opposition of roasted and boiled that is singularly close to the one revealed by Marcel Detienne in the culinary and alimentary codes of Greek sacrifice.

The alternation and succession of roasted and boiled puts the woman on the side of the boiled, of the forces of nature, of Demeter, and thus also of the growth and renewal of edible plants (grains).[10] This place is likewise defined in the Hesiodic myth of the sacrifice in which, if J.-P. Vernant is to be believed, cooking is one of the three marks of the human condition, the others being marriage and agriculture. In the confrontation between Zeus and Prometheus, the smoke from the sacrificial victim goes back to the gods, once and for all separated from men who, if they are to feed themselves, must make use of perishable products (cooked meat). The woman— by marriage—and plants—by agriculture—become signs of finitude that are nonetheless indispensable to the reproduction of the human order.[11] These conclusions overlap and confirm those drawn from the study of the myths and rites of Adonis. Women are classified among categories denoting what is low, rotten, or flesh, and because of that position they are differentiated from those who do not reproduce themselves (men/female lovers of the Adoniades), who are always positioned on the side of the high, the dry, smoke, aromatics, and roasting.[12] In the Ait Mizane sacrificial process, agriculture and marriage appear in the two metonymies of the barley and henna that are forced into the victim's muzzle.

Like Greek sacrifice, Muslim ritual does not reflect the group but rather organizes it, so to speak, along the set of axioms set out in the relationship between God and man; in so doing it legitimizes these axioms, which then become the rule of the community engaged in the world of daily reality. Unlike Greek sacrifice, Muslim ritual is less sensitive to the debates that stir the city and is completely oriented toward domestic unity, as well as the moral and political community that Islam sees as transcendant. Furthermore, perhaps here "city" or "debate" cannot have the meanings understood and practiced by the Greeks; and as a consequence it would not be at all surprising if the Muslim ritual immolation of a victim appears as the sign and result of conformity.

In any event, the spiritualist and structuralist viewpoints propounded by Evans-Pritchard and Lévi-Strauss, respectively, inadequately reflect the full spectrum of the Muslim ceremony. Indeed, the first perspective, based on a dubious typology, reduces sacrifice to individual communication with God motivated by a feeling of culpability and its corollary, the need for expiation and redemption. The second states that this ritual is nothing but a meaningless discourse addressed to an absent term, initiating a connection that is quickly broken.

When in the late 1950s Claude Lévi-Strauss again challenged the theory of reflection in the analysis of myths, he addressed his objections to functionalist sociology, a view that by then had already lost ground, particularly in the study of ritual and religion. On the subject of sacrifice, Evans-Pritchard accused Hubert and Mauss of succumbing to what he called Durkheim's sociological "metaphysics,"[13] and, basing his arguments on what he claimed was the autonomy of the spiritual, he criticized the Durkheimians for dissolving the religious object when what was required first of all was to recognize its specificity. This objection undoubtedly takes aim at historical materialism as well.

For these two trailblazers of anthropology, ritual first of all must be approached as an act of communication, a view that is not foreign to the ideas of Mauss. But for Evans-Pritchard, this communication must be understood as a gift of the self to God via the intermediary of the metaphor that is the sacrificial victim. This leaves us far from regulated contact with the sacred, which heals the group and reveals to each conscience the transcendence that the Durkheimians identify with society itself.

Instead, all the symbolism converges in the link between man and an invisible and transcendent being, which is situated beyond any social relationship. This viewpoint excludes the notion of latent function, guilty in the symbolists' eyes of reducing the religious to what it is not and, furthermore, impossible to prove because it permits no empirical tests. Rather, the theological context that justifies the act of immolation and the preparation preceding it offers Evans-Pritchard observable signs of the identity between victim and sacrifier[14] and of the gift to God, from which the notions of contract and exchange are absent.

It is entirely possible to accept Evans-Pritchard when he speaks of metaphysics and evokes Durkheim's hypothesis according to which God would be nothing but a symbol for society. And one can only agree with him that a theory of gift and countergift insufficiently accounts for the relationship implied by sacrifice. As for Muslim ritual, it seems to substitute a victim for the sacrifier, in the manner of the Nuer ceremony that Evans-Pritchard places at the center of this people's religious practice.

Here the similarities end, however, for in the case of the Ait Mizane it is difficult to determine whether the ritual is a personal or collective act. It is personal in the sense that each one acts for himself, and collective in the sense that the whole Muslim community simultaneously performs it in an identical manner. Furthermore, the ritual marks and assures a transition and once again founds, as the basis for the law, the civilization that is identified with this community. Thus, it is as confirmatory as it is expiatory.

Now at last the typology on which Evans-Pritchard built his theory of sacrifice crumbles. For let it be recalled that the only sacrifice he considers to be religious is a personal, expiatory sacrifice; he excludes confirmatory sacrifice, which for him belongs to the domain of the festival.[15]

Not only does Muslim sacrifice involve the two types, but its expiatory character remains, shall we say, general; it is not undertaken as a response to any particular sin or misfortune. And the same is true of the pilgrimage that accompanies it for those who sacrifice in the city holy to Islam. On the contrary, other sacrifices expiate a number of individual sins. And there is more, for although the annual immolation of a victim is not one of the canonical obligations but only figures on the list of practices close to each Muslim's heart, anyone failing to undertake it would in some way be placing himself outside God's kingdom, and in this case, outside the village community that is its replica. Our ritual, then, follows the common prayer and initial and solemn sacrifice that must first be carried out by the head of the Muslim state, a repetition of the founding deed of Abraham, the chief and spiritual guide of a people devoted to God. In short, it would be impossible to see in it, as Evans-Pritchard saw in the case of the Nuer, something pertaining to the individual that could be clearly contrasted with something else that pertained to the collective.

Evans-Pritchard, then, arbitrarily sets apart confirmatory sacrifices, retaining only the expiatory rituals that confirm his personal vision of the religious. Such a limitation results in another singularity: the description of a practice in its theological context alone. Indeed, unlike the functionalists and the structuralists, he does not permit the investigation of meanings outside this context, as if religious practice took place in a world where theology reigns uncontested and constantly occupies people's thoughts and colors their actions.

On the basis of these good resolutions, Evans-Pritchard constructs a theology of the Nuer in which it will never be known whether any one of its parts, as reconstructed, was apparent to the mind of even a single Nuer. Oddly, the religion attributed to this people naturally devolves around concepts of God, error, and sin, and practices of sacrifice as expiation! And while Evans-Pritchard himself recognizes that the notions he uses to interpret the Nilotic ritual remain "implicit" in the actors' minds, he acts as if his construction postulates no unconscious elements. Thus presented, Nuer religion owes something of its theological consistency to the phenomenological systematization of Evans-Pritchard's mind.[16]

With this negation of the sociological context and the real actions of the people within it, made possible by the distinction between expiatory and confirmatory sacrifices, and in a ritual environment reduced to theology alone, from which even the play of symbols is banished, Evans-Pritchard easily arrives at the Christian figure, the exemplar of the sacrifice. Now at last all questions about the relationship between sacrifice and society vanish, and its ties with culture in the broad sense of the term are obscured. As we have seen, deprived of this relationship Muslim ritual loses much of its meaning, since in its functional classifications it serves to establish a truly regularized foundation of the community. It is impossible to subtract the actors' role in the mimetic drama from this symbolic efficacity. Between this belief, the source of human action, and its relative impact, openly acknowledged as the group's needs for physical continuity, lies the work of the symbolic as the condition and effect of structural tensions.

Evans-Pritchard is interested in the Nuer case with its theology, which he claims is specific—but only to arrive at a theory that obscures this specificity. Discussing the same example, Lévi-Strauss notes that there is a difference between the sacrifice and the totemic meal, a difference that however coexists with a general functioning belonging to each one, since the principle that governs them is universal. The relationships of opposition and complementarity noted by the human mind traverse all the levels of the real (which thereby become codes) and give rise to a cognitive organization of human experience, which analysis reveals in myth and rite.[17]

Diachrony and synchrony form one of those pairs of opposing and complementary terms. The totemic meal serves to reconcile them, for what Durkheim wrongly takes to be sacrifice is only a comparison between differences—systematic and general in the savage mind—that reasserts the persistence of two distinct and formally similar series in an unchanging organization, despite the disorders introduced by history. And, breaking with his predecessors (Radcliffe-Brown, notably), Lévi-Strauss finds these differences not in the concrete characteristics assigned by each culture to classified beings and things, but through a kind of introspection of the common and universal experience of mind as it is manifested among human beings despite their cultural and geographical distances. In this manner one arrives at a general epistemological orientation and status of sacrifice as it contrasts with totemism:

Sacrifice turns to comparison as a means of effacing differences and in order to establish contiguity; the so-called totemic meals institute contiguity, but only with a view to making possible a comparison, the anticipated result of which is to confirm differences.

The two systems are therefore opposed by their orientation, metonymical in one case and metaphorical in the other. But this anti-symmetry leaves them still on the same plane, when in fact they are on different levels from the epistemological point of view.[18]

Developing this contrast between sacrifice and totemism, Lévi-Strauss maintains that the former functions as a particular and meaningless discourse while the latter appears as a code. In addition to the fact that it is unclear why totemism would be unable to move from its status as *langue* to a discursive functioning and *parole* in ritual action itself, it appears difficult to justify the opposition between sacrifice and totemism. For if it can be admitted that on a gnoseological level totemic categories depend on a code, it is impossible to justify a vision that claims that the process of ritual action removes this code's extra weight. That is to say, precisely at the point where it becomes the manipulation of concrete symbols.

A discussion of the contrasting terms that Lévi-Strauss believes that he has established further highlights the inconsistency of his opposition. Indeed, he seems to contradict himself from one statement to the next. For if, as he thinks, sacrifice performs a comparison to erase differences and establish contiguity, while totemism establishes contiguity with a view to a comparison that confirms differences, it is impossible to avoid the conclusion that each one forms a particular discourse. And is it not the case that in the heart of the Australian rite one finds this same double movement of controlled contiguity with the totemic being and separation (taboo/consummation) that for Lévi-Strauss, who on this point remains faithful to Hubert and Mauss, animates sacrifice? At the very least, the question remains open, and there is no absolutely determining reason to accept the arguments of the founder of structuralist anthropology on this point.

The problems with such an interpretation all arise from the same bias, which views communication as the primary goal of human action but describes specific examples of human communication as simple logical and cognitive operations and then, inside this interpretative system, establishes two particular incidences of communication (sacrificial and totemic meal) as if they belong to two different systems (*langue* and *parole*); this amounts to placing two actions that are identical in form and type on two different epistemological levels. Undoubtedly, this error is the result of the scant attention paid to actual ritual action and the wish to make an absolute distinction between sacrifice and totemism, even if it entails violating the principles of a nonetheless legitimate critique of positivist prejudice. If there is no clear distinction between an action that causes objective results and a ritual action—for the good reason that the former is subjective in terms of its principle and centrifugal in terms of its consequences, while the latter appears to the actor as a contribution to the natural objective order—how can Lévi-Strauss support, in the name of this reasonable principle, his argument that sacrifice is a meaningless discourse because it connects two terms, one of which has no existence? This position cannot be defended without voiding the sacrificial act of all its subjective value and its orientation that, for the actor, has an indisputable existence and, for the anthropologist, has an objectivity as observable as that of any material technique.

For this whole demonstration claims that ritual is a logical solution to the unsolvable dilemma of time. Indeed, some societies explain themselves to themselves by means of history ("hot" societies) while others accomplish this by means of myth and rite, which are false historical discourses, for they belong to the present—or rather, they wish to deny the changes caused, notably, by demographic evolution and affecting groups. Etiological myths are false etiological myths, for they describe only the present. Rites display pure diachrony (the ancestral accession) in synchrony. Therefore they are the reconciliation of diachrony and synchrony in a system where, despite the famous formal correlation of the two series, natural and cultural, history introduces disturbances that must be (symbolically) eliminated.[19]

Meanwhile, sacrifice is forgotten. Would it be too closely tied to so-called "hot" societies? This idea has all the more force because Lévi-Strauss sets sacrifice up as a specific *parole* in opposition to totemism, which he describes, it will be recalled, as *langue*. Now our immolated victim, among the Ait Mizane as well as throughout the Muslim world, shows that in "hot" societies sacrifice carries on a diachrony within a synchrony. It is a commemoration, which relativizes—from this standpoint, of course—the typology of societies suggested by the "savage" mind. Such a convergence between the sacrifice and the *Intichiuma* not only weakens the opposition that Lévi-Strauss believes to have seen between these rites, but for us also shows that his theory risks impoverishing the meaning of them both. Analysis of Muslim sacrifice points to other ways: in particular because it is the commemoration of a first act that reveals man's proximity to God; the mimesis of a founding deed that opens not onto the logical resolution of the relationship between the ideal and history, but precisely onto the very contradictions of this world. Here, strictly speaking, no contiguity marks difference, but instead, too great a difference is the foundation for the law, in a paradoxical manifestation of God in his horrible commandment that the son must be murdered. Lévi-Strauss seems to have followed Hubert and

Mauss's footsteps, without foreseeing the problems that their formalism would cause in his own analysis.

The fact remains that men must live through this unhappy time, touched by grace but constantly rebellious against God. The passage of time is marked in this way: sacrifice and the masquerade after it occupy an intermediary position between the past and what is soon to be the present. It is the anticipation of history, one could say, that is set in motion by sacrifice itself, since the gravity of the entire day of the immolation that marks the commemoration is followed by joyous feasting and the exchange of food in living social relations that are once again legitimized by the ritual. The joy reaches its paroxysm in Bilmawn's escapades, where one finds the same need for a mythical foundation for an earthly destiny impervious to all logic, even that of salvation!

The Masks and Their Forays

Marginality, Hyperdefinition, and
the Revenge of the Son

11

My analysis of the masquerade will concentrate first on its internal components, interpreting them in relation to one another and then seeing how particular elements of the context illuminates them. To complete the task, the value of each element so isolated or associated will be compared to the features revealed by my study of the sacrifice. For, it bears repeating, no matter what differences—in the matter of sources, history, and inspiration—separate this Muslim ritual from the masquerade, to consider each in isolation leads to the errors and prejudices of my predecessors.[1] And, of course, striking similarities connect Bilmawn with the Saturnalia and Lupercalia of ancient Rome, and even more with the bull of the Bouphonia, sacrificed and dramatically brought back to life to be hitched to the plow.[2] But not only is it doubtful that it will ever be possible to establish a sure historical link between them, even if such a thing exists; this discovery would contribute nothing to the meaning or function that the masquerade holds for the participants today.

Like the sacrifice, the masquerade takes place at the end of each Muslim year. It brings to a close a time imbued with the sacred that lasts approximately forty days including the pilgrimage and sacrifice as well as the ceremonies of the 'Ashura. The Muslim calendar contains four identical periods corresponding to the four quarters of the year. Each marks a transition, moving from the end of one quarter to the beginning of a new one. This rhythm, it will probably be guessed, is different from that of the seasons. Locally, the Muslim calendar is not well known. But its importance is vital for the villagers. It is a "learned" calendar that enumerates the principal feasts, notably the sacrifice. Therefore one of the functions of the master of the Koranic school *(fqih)* consists in computing this calendar. In the two villages where it was possible to take a survey, there were barely two or three people who could list the twelve months of the lunar year. The old Julian calendar is of widespread use and indicates the principal phases of agricultural life. The peasants call it the agricultural calendar (*filaḥi*) and distinguish it from a third calendar that divides time into "periods" of thirteen days called *manazils* (mansions) based on the positions of the sun. This is the old scholarly zodiacal calendar, which indicates favorable and unfavorable times for practical activities (agricultural and others) as well as auspicious and inauspicious times for a broad range of human activities: it also describes the great transitions—particularly the summer solstice and the beginning of spring—which are signaled by intense ritual activity.[3]

The masquerade follows the sacrifice. It thus has a place in the Muslim calendar, and therein lies the first problem that must be noted. There is a tension around this computation of time, but also a tension at the heart of religious life and feeling. For nothing seems to tie the masquerade to the sacrifice, and the guardians of Muslim orthodoxy insist far more than the anthropologists of colonial days—and with such vehemence!—on what they perceive as the absolute need to separate them. Hence the conflict between the producers of Bilmawn and the specialists of Islamic knowledge that stir the village community into a debate on the subject with the partisans of a purified Islam.[4] Such controversies agitate society as a whole and project the scene onto the national destiny and far beyond it. The types of Islam forbidden by the "educated" and "refined" classes or the partisans of reform are not confined to urban areas; here as well, almost all these various groups (legalistic, fraternal, rationalist, etc.) oppose the masquerade and desire to banish it along with all other "vestiges of paganism." The first matter for conflict, then, lies in the fact that a festival that is seen as pagan occurs in the Muslim calendar. Even worse, it takes place at the same time as the orthodox sacrifice, overturning its rules as well as the standards of daily life. From this standpoint, it is now possible to note the weakness of certain formal correlations dear to the structuralists, especially as developed by Edmund Leach. The inversion carried out by the festival, by all evidence, is not simply a response to temporal inversion. Social issues lie at the heart of these formal contradictions. I return to this point later.

Cutting across local and global societies, the questions and challenges raised by the masquerade are furthermore anchored in the group's material survival. The relationship that the myth establishes between the ripening of corn on the one hand and the action leading to the characters' metamorphosis on the other suggests a relationship between the masquerade and the agricultural cycle, especially since Bilmawn's "visions" are always linked to this developmental stage in the cultivation. Everything, then, indicates the probable adoption, by the Muslim calendar, of an older feast, which perhaps had closer ties to the seasons and agricultural rhythms. Examples of analogous phenomena abound.[5] But if this seems likely in our case, no direct proof supports it. And it would be impossible to maintain, in a Frazerian perspective, Doutté's and Laoust's ideas about a rite celebrating the death and resurrection of a vegetation god.

However, one cannot deny, as Westermarck did, all relationship with agriculture.[6] The masquerade takes place at the end of the Muslim year and consequently cannot be pinned down to a fixed season or agricultural activity. But the invocation for a favorable year, repeated constantly throughout the masque and the procession, is obviously a wish for a rainy and bountiful new year. While it does not stand alone, the peasants' concern with a successful agricultural year nevertheless is preeminent and is equally present in the scenes of plowing and harvesting that are discussed further on.

In this context, the prayer addressed to God for a good year makes the conjunction of the Muslim feast and the masquerade all the more surprising, particularly since God will be invoked in a sacrilegious rite in which the Koran is parodied in a comic satire that includes the Creator's authentic words!

The ritual action of this yearly transition can be divided along the natural pauses in the action, which somewhat mitigates the arbitrariness of this first step of the analysis. Four "bundles" of actions can be isolated, first of all because the actors themselves distinguish them. Taken as a whole the action has no name, nor do any of the bundles, except that the entire process is referred to a "Bilmawn." First, a lengthy period of preparation takes place in the *takhurbisht:* this bundle will be called "offstage action." Then a procession through the village streets, accompanied by singing and dancing and punctuated by the obligatory search and visit to each house, forms the second bundle, the "tournament of masks." It serves as a kind of general category, for the third and fourth bundles occur within it, interrupting it at specific times. The scene for these two bundles is the central square of the village. First there is a performance of farming and traditional activities: marriage and the agricultural work of the yearly cycle. This bundle will be called "works and days," for convenience' sake and as a reminder of the Hesiodic inspiration so near to the themes that this "street theater" plays out one by one. Last, the fourth bundle consists of a performance of the events that have attracted attention and set tongues wagging during the previous year or even before. Again, for convenience' sake these scenes will henceforth be grouped together under the rubric of "revue," because of the striking resemblance they bear to this phenomenon.

The action offstage begins when the young men enter the *takhurbisht;* the humor is joyous, marked by boisterous joking. It ends when Bilmawn, followed by his troupe, bursts into the streets in a whirlwind of noise, violence, and obscenities. In the beginning all the participants have been plunged into a veritable "darkroom" and then brought out into the light; in the meantime everyone has been transformed. Bilmawn, the slave, and the Jews are born from this mutation, as well as the musicians and dancers, since before they entered the *takhubisht* the youths did not play these roles.

Such a radical transformation alters the initial identity of everyone who takes part. For Bilmawn the change is profound, for his new identity is the result of completely annihilating his old one: he takes off all his clothes, wears the skins of the sacrificed animals directly on his own skin, and disappears into the ashes of the hearth. This last act bears a strong resemblance to death, followed by resurrection and a violent resurgence into the world. The same scenario awaits the other characters, although it is somewhat attenuated; their new faces have something about them of everyday, visible reality, while Bilmawn's has no connection with anything in this world. Indeed the slave and Jews are transformed by simple tricks of costume and make-up and belong to familiar classes of men. The actor who has become Bilmawn, on the contrary, has left the human order. Among invisible beings he has the distinction that the only thing known of him in everyday life is his name. But, projected beyond the perceptible world of men, he nonetheless provides a benchmark for them, followed very closely in this by the slave. For it should be recalled that they both lose the power of speech; and whereas this lack is not at all surprising in the slave and does not exclude him from the human community, in Bilmawn this quality is the final touch and is a sign of his nonhumanity.

Bilmawn is to the human order what the slave and Jew are the community: the Other. He is otherness. But he is a radical otherness, while the slave and Jew represent specific cases in the universal classification of men. From this hybrid being, set as the extreme outer limit, stretches the continuum that reaches all the way to the human community par excellence, the village. Is it possible to be more precise about this limit, which is also the limit of the mind? It hardly seems feasible, for Bilmawn belongs to no known order or class: a two-footed animal, deprived of speech and uttering cries that link him to no other species, male or female . . . Above all, each time one characteristic predominates, a host of others emerge that keep one un-

decided. Is Bilmawn female? Yes, but he has only one breast in the middle
of his chest. Is he a man? Yes, judging from the testicles that can be seen
during his ludicrous dance, but a phallus dangles over his posterior from
the height of his sternum. Therefore he is irremediably lacking a fixed character, while the other actors are remarkable for what could be called their
social hyperidentification. Bilmawn's lack of definition brings one face to
face with four terms: Bilmawn, monster, slave, Jew. The first is invisible, the
second appears on stage, the third can be identified by his black color and
legal status, and the fourth is held to be legally inferior not only for social
and juridical reasons, like the third, but also because of religious and political factors that have become ethnic characteristics in the eyes of all. Their
participation in the same game serves not only to bare legal, religious, ethnic, and other differences. It is also a revelation of their being as it is instituted through their relationship with the invisible and in comparison to a
fifth term, one that is absent from the stage but very active in this classification: the free Muslim, who stands for the image of the community
itself. Because this community has attained through sacrifice the highest
form of sacrality, Bilmawn is able to leave his chthonic abode to invade
all of space disguised as a horny monster. The median terms mentioned
earlier now lie between him—this invisible, chthonic power—and
God, the invisible celestial power. This configuration is summarized in
table 5.

   The classes that have just appeared, as already mentioned, form a continuum linking and separating the Jew, the slave, and Bilmawn as one limit and
God as the other. But this series establishes the same type of relationship
between young and old, for the masquerade, it will be recalled, is theoretically the exclusive province of young men, whether married or single. The
stages of the series leading from Bilmawn to the free Muslim so close to God
apply to the condition of the young men. Once these characters have introduced the referents shown in table 5 and established an ontological and a
value scale, like all symbols they can no longer be seen solely in terms of
their habitual referent (the condition of slave, Jew, etc.). In other words, the
spectacle as a whole, which will be examined shortly, does not specifically
deal with monsters, Jews, or slaves, although it sometimes happens that the
initial referent for each term may coincide with its new symbolic referents.
In this way the young men, the principal actors of the drama, would be to
the heads of household as Jews are to Muslims, slaves to free men, or monsters to all categories, considering their indefinite position in relation to
that of the status of a head of a household. This is one of the central themes

Table 5. Position of the Characters Evoked by the Scene

1	2	3	4	5	6
Bilmawn as name	Monster	Jew	Slave	Free Muslim	God as name
Absence of status	Ambiguity, blending of statuses and traits	Hyperdefinition via recognized status and series of characteristics			
Invisible power					Invisible power
←					→
Negative		Axis of values and definitions of Being			Positive

of the sacrifice, and all these parallels will be confirmed by the analysis of the performances enacted in the village square.

It is understandable why this classificatory mise-en-scène issues from the darkness of the *takhurbisht*. It is a place where the dead are washed, where the baths and latrines are found. In short, it is a place where corpses are cleansed of their impurities to meet God, in the same way that the living prepare themselves with their ablutions to meet him in prayer. Leaving the *takhurbisht,* the first go to the cemetery, the others to the *talmqsurt,*[7] which is the exact opposite of the other place. One faces east and the other west, black with soot and dark. One receives purified men in prayer, the other focuses their impurities. When we recall that a true death followed by a resurrection gives rise to this being who propels the whole masquerade, it will be admitted that Bilmawn guides his troupe through the world of the living, not the world of the dead or the beyond. Such wandering fits well with the extraordinary nature of the character and his myth and singularly evokes what he leaves in his wake, the stuff of which literary plots are customarily made. Here the deception underlying the drama finds the logic with which it causes the village's transformation, after the young men have been transformed into actors. The illusion operates as if the visible and invisible cannot be distinguished, as if the second can manifest itself in broad daylight in the form of the first without confronting the exigencies of realism. The ritual action, which puts death and resurrection onstage, makes it possible for the invisible to go out into village streets that are now a stage. Once again, just as on the eve of the sacrifice, everyone complies with a rule based on a mythical past and the knowledge that a being dwelling at the outer edge, beyond the human order, has instituted it, a being that the village group seems to recognize as an ambiguous entity. Although everyone rejects him, they also fear him and look forward to his coming. People whose houses he has "forgotten" to visit will seek out the troupe and beg them to pay them a call.

Every village has its Bilmawn, and the value that the group attaches to its monster is seen in cases in which two groups, perceiving themselves as distinct entities and inhabiting the same village, "dress" two Bilmawin. This is what happens in Timezguida n'Oumalou. One of Bilmawn's functions is to run with the "bad luck" and deposit it at the edge of the neighboring village. This is the *ballush* race in which the *bilmawin* of neighboring rival groups try to be the first to arrive at the perimeter. This explains the paradox that not only are the band's most shocking behaviors tolerated, but they are desired and imposed on all by the community itself, in the houses, public squares, and the streets.

Again, the children are chased away from these places, just as they were from the preparations underway in the *takhurbisht*. Married men are also excluded from the village. Some of them play an important role in the preparation as "technical people" who ready the skins and make the masks: Bilmawn's goat's head and the Jews' masks. In fact, their role is to supervise the game so that it does not go too far. Most of the recently married men are there and make sure that the man in the skins is one of their own, more reasonable than the bachelors by the very fact that he is married. Their imposition on the proceedings is expressed and accompanied by a certain tension between the single men and the *iferkhan*.[8]

The mature men (those who count), the heads of households, are excluded; so the young men, unmarried girls, and married women remain on the scene. After Bilmawn's first round of visits, only the last can simply watch, while the "young people"—men and women—must play a role in Bilmawn. Let us begin by analyzing this first tour, for the actions and deeds of the man in the skins and his companions during the procession are basically a rehearsal for it.

The street taken by Bilmawn must be deserted, empty of the heads of household and the children, who are sent away to the village limits; husbands cannot be present. The rule has it that if perchance a husband falls into the hands of the company, all his secrets, particularly of a sexual nature, will be shouted aloud by the Jews. Away from the village, these men find themselves in the situation of having to perform tasks that the sexual division of labor ordinarily assigns to women: following the cow into the meadows, cutting the grass, and gathering the evening's firewood are some of the women's jobs that the men must undertake, since the women must stay in the house to welcome Bilmawn. A double inversion of the rule, since outside the men act like women while at home—inside—the women act like men, receiving Bilmawn accompanied by men who have hypertrophied sexual organs. It is true that the central character could not be more ambiguous, and the slave and the Jews, because of their status, cannot lay claim to all the characteristics of the men chased from the village. Nonetheless, they can exhibit their male organs and proffer obscenities to the women. As for the children, in theory they are frightened by Bilmawn. One of the variants of the myth that I present after the analysis of the rite explicitly reports that the monster specifically appears only after dark to ask the women for food to avoid frightening the children. On this point the rite, like the sacrifice, stands in contrast to the myth, for here Bilmawn makes his appearance in broad daylight.

But more importantly, despite the contrasting discourses that the rite and myth seem to carry on about one another concerning this last point, contact with women takes place in the absence of children and men, thus fulfilling conditions very close to the modes of contact described by the myth. And it could probably be postulated that the equivalence of Bilmawn's two actions—that described by the myth and the one occurring during the rite—matches the equivalence of these two statements: "I can only show myself to women in the discretion provided by the night"/"I can only show myself to women in the discretion offered by a village devoid of children and men"—especially because while the myth mentions the children's absence, it has nothing at all to say about the men. Bilmawn rises out of the darkness of the chthonic world of the *takhurbisht* (in a cloud of ash from the hearth that is evidence of his origin) and sets off to ask the women for his food. He travels through many places before he enters the house but moves about under circumstances comparable to night and in the exclusive presence of women, since children and men are outside the village.

This makes it clear that there cannot be any spectators outside; the women are indoors to greet the visitors and are consequently playing a role; the young men are attacked and marked with ash and identified with this supernatural band; they are called on to take part in the dancing and singing and to draw the young women in—by force, if need be. The noise accompanying the appearance of the man in the skins strikingly resembles the disturbance aroused by the intrusion of a wild animal into an inhabited area. He raises a ruckus and is repulsed and attacked wherever he goes. But the slave constantly defends him by fending off all comers, and the Jews beat everyone who approaches him and pelt them with ash; this is the way he enters the house.

In the sacrifice, the myth and the rite seem to be using an apparent opposition to develop two identical discourses. This technique is not unusual in certain types of humor, in which the very insistence upon a refusal is proof of ardent desire; but it is also, as noted earlier, a common oneiric device. The same type of relationship is found between the myth of Bilmawn and the masquerade, concerning exactly the same complex of social relations. In the sacrifice, it occurs between the father and the son, where the mother, present on the mythic level in the dialogue, is absent from the action and present at the ritual level, but covertly—two ways of being present that are extremely close to one another. In the masquerade, it occurs between the heads of household who monopolize the decision-making and the young; the former disappear to give up their houses, leaving their doors wide open and their wives to the latter. If one wishes to make a case that the generation run out of the village represents the fathers and the one that chases them the sons, it is the sons who sacrifice their fathers, and not the other way around, as was the case in the overt text of the Abrahamic myth. And when these young men enter the houses, which they take over along with the women inside, it is they, not their fathers, who trace the outlines of the domestic unit in the masquerade, and so now they play the role that, in the sacrifice, was taken by their fathers. This observation can be put another way by saying that the father is to the son in the sacrifice what the son is to the father in the masquerade.

Thus, in the shadow of a monstrous being—since unlike the Jews, the slave, the male and female dancers, he is beyond all classification—the young men take possession of the women and the houses. However, the rule stated by the sacrifice positing the father as the unifying and dominant term of the domestic unit is not completely overturned. Such a total inversion would result in the mother taking power. The rule is violated, however.

Moreover, this transgression only reaffirms in everyone's eyes the connivence among slave, Jews, and Bilmawn, on the one hand, and between Bilmawn and the women, on the other. The sacrifice has already displayed this predilection of feminine religion for chthonic "divinities" and its rites involving blood as well as other parts of the victim, efficacious in the relationship with the djinns and healing—two terms, furthermore, that are intimately linked. The law of the sons makes it possible to replay, in the home, the commerce with the invisible powers (of the earth, darkness, and blackness) in its three aspects of contact, therapeutic use, and expulsion.

Women and nursing children submit to Bilmawn's touch for protection and healing, in intimate contact in the heart of the house; and once this gift has been received, the women respond with a gift in exchange. Once this has been accepted, the company must leave the premises. But in fact, as is fitting, three gifts, moving in three directions, are exchanged: food to be eaten on the spot/blessing and healing/countergift of food to be eaten elsewhere (among the young). A gift of fecundity is offered in the midst of a web of sexualized and obscene repartee, in exchange for a gift of basic foodstuffs: grains, eggs, meat. On the one hand is raw food in which the role of women blends with that of men; on the other are foods that the women cook and control. And perhaps also the symbolic gift of sex, if one notes that here the egg is popularly associated with feminine sexuality. There is nothing surprising about this last detail, for by means of a whole series of approaches and pleasant exchanges, the women give themselves to Bilmawn.

The violation of the home by the troupe of the man with the skins is equivalent to the "rape" of the woman, mistress of the interior space, by this monster. Her accommodation to these singular guests and the very need for this encounter with the representatives of the chthonic world places her, as is the case in the sacrifice, on the side of danger and the threatening powers of darkness, but also on the side of the transgression made clear by a "copulation" that takes place outside the accepted rules of sexual commerce. Is this an unavoidable, necessary "prostitution," consubstantial with the normal order that conceals it? Its link with fecundity and healing and the fact that the same troupe introduces her (and at the same time the *baraka*) into the home are sufficient evidence, especially since the rest of the ritual reveals a means of escaping this contradictory fate that men find unbearable.

But let us first look at the myth of Bilmawn, for in addition to the fact that it is desirable at this time, after some of its elements have been integrated into the analysis of the masquerade, to construct a view of the whole, this myth places the sacrilegious rape at the center of a primordial event of which the masquerade is the enacted record. Like the sacrifice, the masquerade is a mimesis finding its origin and justification in a primordial event. The myths of Bilmawn and Abraham present a clear etiology.

Two men approach a sanctuary. Women are staying in this sacred place. The men enter, rape the women, and are transformed into the beings known as Bilmawn. They live outside the community, in the forest. The action takes place at the time when the corn is ripening. The version recorded by Doutté indicates that these beings come to the village only at night to ask for food, because they do not wish to frighten the children.

The two Ait Mizane versions, as well as Doutté's, contain a tale and commentary. The narrative breaks off with the metamorphosis and exclusion from the human group. The habits of the beings that are the result of this mutation are depicted in the commentary. The plot is well knit, its logic perfect: transgression followed by punishment. Occurring in a sacred place, the misdeed begins a cycle of new life in an unknown world, far from the humanized space.

This progression can be compared to the order of the masquerade. Here, Bilmawn leaves the *takhurbisht* to visit the women, while in the myth the men rape the women. The masquerade has the women giving themselves to Bilmawn in the house. In the myth, the men rape the women in the sanctuary. In the rite, the men undergo a transformation before they receive the women's gift. In the myth, men in their natural form seize the gift, and their metamorphosis is the result. In the masquerade, the men transform themselves to receive an erotic gift that is willingly offered; in the myth they take the women by force. Once again, the full range of the contrast is evident: myth and rite propose two opposing discourses—except for the detail of the house, which in the local culture is not the opposite of the sanctuary but contiguous to it. The relationship between house and sanctuary represents an affinity in their meaning: sacred like it and, in theory, inviolable. The sanctuary contains the social group and its values. The house shelters the honor and harmony of the domestic group, whose foundation rests on the same values that the sanctuary embodies and guarantees. Once again, despite two apparently contradictory surface texts, myth and rite seem to comment on each other and join together. The unholy violation of the sanctuary and the conquest of the women are at the origin of social norms that take shape as they are transgressed. If one considers the logic of eliminating the fathers (or the father, which is what the central episode of the procession illustrates) along with the mythical rape, the actual rape played out in the masquerade, and the transgression of the rules of home and sanctuary (that is, the violent conquest of the women and the sanctuary at the expense of the generation of their fathers) have their place in the same consistent whole. A logic that is inescapable as long as women assume the roles that are theirs in the reproduction of the domestic unit, i.e., in the maintenance of the lineage of agnates and the order of men. Hence, women are constantly vilified and ranged among the sinister powers; they are seen as beset by uncontrollable sexual impulses that dishonor men in their roles of husband, father, and brother or as guardians of patriarchal morality. Yet it is impossible to do without women, even though the utopia of a world without females endlessly haunts the contradictory world of men. A look at the procession, among other things, sheds light on this last detail and makes it possible to pinpoint the identity of the characters and the meaning of their actions. Table 6 distinguishes the principal units of ritual action that form this tournament of masks (the second bundle of the masquerade).

Affinities among these units make it possible to regroup them. Thus, sections 1 and 2 list actions that open the public spectacle and start a day "that is not like other days" because of the tumult, noise, and racing about of this "demon" (the *'afrit* that has burst out of the darkness). It is possible to speak of a change in temporality. For, it should be recalled, Bilmawn appears at night to the women so that he does not frighten the children. Next are the actions grouped under section 3, marked by the appearance of the chorus, which agrees to dance and sing around Bilmawn, and the recalcitrant young people who are pursued. The brawl will be ongoing, and a category that refuses to join this strange company will make its presence known by its attacks on the Jews and Bilmawn. Immediately after this episode come the escapades listed under headings 4–8, where all the agents of the confusion are in the house. Here the situation is parallel to that in the myth, where disorder in the sanctuary is created by the presence of men who have denied their quality as Muslims by raping women; these agents of disorder then find themselves all engaged in the act of giving food, the countergift of healing and blessing in the midst of obscenity, and the parody of the invocation to God: the inversion of the ordinary situations of gifts and blessings. But it is a partial inversion, since the gift and countergift do not change directions. Hence one can group together the actions listed under numbers 8–10, which bring the visit to the women and the house to a close and begin a new race through the street in which the same episodes are replayed with many improvisations on obscene themes like the ones listed under headings 11–12.

The procession is interrupted when the crowd arrives at the central square; it gives way to the series of episodes called "works and days" and the "revue," and then once again it runs through the village. However, for reasons of clarity I will examine the procession before considering the other actions.

As reconstructed here, the proceedings have both high and low moments. The festival has, if one can accept the expression, its ups and downs.

Table 6. Units of Action of the Procession: Succession of Ritual Units of Action

1	2	3
Exit of the slave pursuing the children in an atmosphere of noise, violence, and darkness The children flout the slave	Bilmawn bursts out of the *takhurbisht* like a demon (*'afrit*) in a cloud of ashes Pursues everybody; the Jews follow him Atmosphere of noise, violence, and obscenities The Jews strike and receive blows	Brawls between Jews and young men The Jews cover them with ashes; obscenities are exchanged The young are constantly called "sons of whores" The women are constantly treated like whores Group singing and dancing around Bilmawn and his companions

4	5	6
The slave enters the first house on the outskirts of town The Jews call out to the women with obscenities Bilmawn pursues and strikes; the Jews do likewise	The slave stirs everything up Rifles through the house and goes out to stand guard by the door In front of the house the rabbi offers a recipe for fertility (ingredients ground up and mixed that must be sat upon after the customary fumigations). . .	Bilmawn goes into the house followed by the Jews, who call out to the mistress of the house and question her about her sexual life and her husband's prowess The women go along with the game

7	8	9
The women serve the Jews a meal	The Jews ask for and demand gifts: flour, eggs, and the bone of the hind foot are offered	Bilmawn gets ready to leave Touches the women with his hooves Touches an infant presented to him on the doorstep

10	11	12
Parody of invocation to God for the prosperity of the house (parody of the *fatiḥa*)	New race: the slave chases the children and young people, Bilmawn runs to a new house, the Jews exchange blows with the young and order that everybody do *aḥwash* (that they organize the dance)	On a terrace, scene of Jews coupling

And nowhere can anything in it be found that resembles the ongoing exaltation and frenzy which, according to Durkheim, produce an alteration in consciousness.[9] On the contrary, bursts of exaltation follow periods of "depression" during which the dancing stops, the dancers look around for places to sit down or even leave the scene, and young and sometimes even married adults approach one another without the nervousness dictated by the rules. These times of quasi-rest are brought on by fatigue, even by the demoralization of the principal actors themselves, until a funny or violent incident once again unleashes the attacks and counterattacks, the insults and pursuits, and incites the Jews to order the music to start up again.

This is the overall pattern of the procession, and it is precisely by means of these peaks of excitement, these ups, that the creativity or violence, or most commonly, a combination of the two, is unleashed. Such is the case in the following exchange with the women in which the rabbi starts playing a peddler, doubling as a sorcerer-healer. The articles he proposes? Frog skin, hedgehog's prick, and pieces of the washed sheepskin used for a prayer rug (*haydura*).

The recipe? All these products must be mixed together and ground up. Then one burns it for its smoke "after taking off your pants. And it is recommended that you sit down on what's left . . ."! The crowd of women cries out, hoots with laughter, shouts, and displays enough pleasure that the actors are inspired to come up with other gems.

The reader will find this pact between women and sinister powers, healing and sorcery, familiar. The rabbi and the women are the protagonists. The traditional division of labor between Muslims and Jews is fully exploited here; similarly, the special competence attributed to the Jews in matters of the "occult sciences" is implied. A comparison of table 5 (p. 145) with table 7 makes it clear that the terms located between Bilmawn and the free Muslim can be replaced by youths and women.

Women on the one hand, Jew and slave on the other partake of related although not identical status. In all three cases, social and juridical restrictions limit their freedom of movement. This is so when Islamic law and traditions are applied with rigor. And if women share with the Jews a connection with what is impure and dangerous, the same is true for the slave in the specific sense accorded him in this drama: originally a black, whose color and possible confraternal and cultural associations are more or less tolerated.[10] The young, people repeatedly told me, for their part are "like goats. They run all over and don't stay in one place." They truly form their own club, between children and the heads of household, "betwixt and between," to use Victor Turner's famous phrase. It is not at all surprising that

Table 7. Equivalent Categories Labeling Terms 2–5 of Table 5

1	2	3	4	5	6
Bilmawn as name	Youths	Women		Free Muslim	God as name
Absence of status	Ambiguity, blending of statuses and traits	Hyperdefinition via recognized status and series of characteristics			Absence of status
Invisible power					Invisible power
←					→
Negative					Positive

they appear in the guise of a monster that they celebrate with so much zest after the sacrifice. Finally, the Muslim, the term absent from the scene, as already mentioned, is not only an indispensable mental and imaginative category in the continuum presented in these tables. In fact, he is active behind the scenes, even if he does not occupy center stage. During the feast, it will be recalled, the young people outside the circle of dancers are constantly harassed to join in with the others. This is the pretext for the ongoing battle pitting them against the Jews. Their refusal to join such a company surely indicates the presence of a term in which it is unacceptable to be compared to the others. The free Muslim tolerates the impure characters who move about onstage, he stands between them and God, at the pole of the ontological and valorizing scale.

But this is not the only message we can read in the association of Jew and woman in the procession and in this scene, especially. For the rabbi's funny, obscene orders obviously concern a fecundity that is procured by means of ingredients and techniques in which medicine and sorcery are blended. Reproduction and sorcery again situate women in this commerce with demonical, dangerous, and at the same time necessary powers. Henceforth they also find themselves, as it were linked to the chain identified earlier that leads to Bilmawn.

Woman is infernal, just like the powers she worships. But ever so necessary. For without her, how would reproduction take place? One possible solution would be for men to reproduce among themselves. And indeed, publicly proclaiming that women are prostitutes and sorceresses allied with the powers of evil, the drama is in a sense forced to indicate a solution. First, the elements of the contradiction must be emphasized before analyzing this outcome: woman is the threatening Other, a menace that weighs first of all upon physical integrity. She can heal but she also can sap one's strength, causing sexual incapacities among others. She masters the male sex through sorcery. Second, she is a menace to honor, for her sexual obsession makes her available to all men. She threatens all one's goods, squandering them in her business with the peddler. She must constantly be reminded of her defects and tightly controlled. But one must be circumspect, for although she trades an inordinate amount with the peddler, she also brings life to the circuit of fecundity. It will be recalled that women offer Bilmawn's companions flour and eggs—and that in the first house they are often given a part of the sacrificed animal's large intestine stuffed with eggs and flour called Bilmawn's churn, or Bilmawn's Sabbath, which is offered in this way to the Jews surrounding Bilmawn.

All these symbols of reproduction and abundance given to Bilmawn elicit in return the gift of blessings and *baraka* that he brings to the household. If one notes that during the first visit he also receives the animal's scapula, used for divination, it becomes apparent that this exchange between him and the woman, on the threshold of a new year, is a foreshadowing of anticipated prosperity. Hence men's ambivalence with respect to the two partners and their diabolical commerce, which nevertheless are indispensable to maintain fecundity.

Attributing to women a sexual obsession that is his at least by the fact that it gnaws at him alone, a man must at once resign himself to this female intermediary in order to obtain his successors. In other words, she is the one who provides the males, those very same men who must reproduce the group in the integrity of its values and identity. Hence the extraordinary dilemma: this recourse to woman, so scandalous according to patriarchal norms and yet impossible to avoid. Hence the mass of ambivalent images portraying her, in which healing and danger are mixed; a two-faced image that reflects to the ambiguity of Bilmawn, the Jew, and the slave. Sexual behavior is ambiguous as well, since these young men, representing their whole generation and disguised as Jews, conquer the women but also the men of their own age whom they push around, subjecting them to their authority as if they were women and with whom they often pantomime sexual intercourse. Offstage, in the *takhurbisht,* we noted the Jews' recurring pursuit of the young men as sexual objects. This type of scene, as well as the violence that accompanies it, will be repeated, to force the unwilling to submit to the rule of the game. Thus it should not be surprising that at certain high moments the ritual coupling between men is played openly and with admitted delight. The scene of sodomy between the Jews on the rooftops described earlier derives its meaning from this form of dodging—at the outer limits of symbolism—the obligatory recourse to women, especially because the contradictions treated in this way are given their most extreme treatment in the scenes called "works and days," which now must be examined more closely.

On Indetermination and the Deceptions
of a Second Founding Drama

12

In Imi-n'Tassaft, where I observed the spectacle, the episodes of the works and days as well as other scenes were partly censored by young men educated at modern schools or who had returned from Europe with new ideas, which in their minds were incompatible with "this shame." Consequently I utilized observations undertaken in the village of Timezguida n'Oumalou to complete my description and shed light on the actions seen in the first village.

This explains the fact that in the following tables (8–11), which summarize the entire spectacle and divide it into smaller units, the marriage scene is missing, even though it figured in the description in chapter 6. Here my intention is to focus the analysis first on what I was able to watch in Imi-n'Tassaft, to reconstruct it as a process, and to refer to data reported from other villages only to complete my analysis.

It must also be emphasized that this censorship results in the elimination of a female character that elsewhere is played by a man. In Imi-n'Tassaft the censors' puritanism apparently could not accommodate such a travesty. Hence, Bilmawn's transformation into a woman (tables 8.3 and 10) to meet the needs of the game. As a result, it is necessary to distinguish this disguise from the metamorphoses that normally are part of the script: Bilmawn as the blacksmith's bellows, an anvil, and a milk cow (tables 8.3 and 9.6, regrouped in 8.3).

When these transformations are in keeping with the logic of the character, in spite of everything else, the traits Bilmawn adopts to play the female role will be found in our discussion of the women. It is pointless to return to it now, as my examination of the procession has already furnished many details on the subject. However, it should be noted here that the qualities attributed to the female sex are brought to their height, and a woman's squandering of her man's goods, of which this character is guilty, is repeated

157

Table 8. Units of Preparing the Plow: *Succession of Units of Ritual Action*

1		2		3
The slave looks for the plow; goes into a house and comes out with it on his shoulder	The plowshare sharpened like the penis cleaves the soil as the penis cleaves the woman	Sharpening the blade; he will split it! he'll split it; he's got to split it! (Table 11.5) Sharpen the blade (Table 10.2) The *khammas* excites the animal with the stick put in its anus (Table 11.1–5)	Bilmawn's transformations	Bilmawn transformed into the smith's bellows fans the fire. Bilmawn = anvil (Table 10.4) Bilmawn = milchcow (Table 11.2–5) Bilmawn = woman available to all

4	5	6
The rabbi heats the iron	The blade is sharpened on the anvil: between Bilmawn's thighs, to cries of "May you grow large and may you prosper!"	The Jews urinate on the iron to cool it

Table 9. Units of Plowing

1	2	3
The slave, then the Jews pursue a young man to make him take the role of the *khammas* (they throw ashes on his head)	A young man forced to play the *khammas*	The Jews sow the ashes

4	5	6
The *khammas* plows and strikes with his stick the animal pulling the plow; they stir it up by placing a stick in its anus	Suddenly the *khammas* pivots the plow on its base; making a circle just above the ground, the handle mows down Jews and the slave	Bilmawn Tamugayt (the cow) gets away. He is brought back by force.

in a striking way (table 10.1–2). Henceforth this trait is referred to as the Pandora syndrome.

The performance normally begins or ends with scene in which "she" is united with the man. This is the case in other villages when censorship is absent. The spectacle opens with a marriage followed by plowing the fields. And if the woman plays the part when the suitors request her hand in marriage, appearing flighty and concerned only with the size of her future hus-

Table 10. Units of the Harvest and Harvesters' Meal

1	2	3	4
Rabbi, now the boss, oversees harvesters	Bilmawn becomes a woman and fixes harvesters' meal	*Bilmawn changed into a woman; Pandora's syndrome/Ruins the food; receives the phalluses* — Slave supervises; when he moves off, one of the Jews comes to have intercourse with Bilmawn-woman. (1) (3) (4) (5) (9) (11) (12)	The slave surprises the Jew and beats him

5	6	7	8
He moves off and another Jew comes to have sex with Bilmawn-woman	Beating is repeated, but this time the slave replaces the Jew on top of Bilmawn-woman	The rabbi catches them; beating and general confusion	Bilmawn-woman finishes fixing the meal; the harvesters wait with the rabbi-boss.

9	10	11
Bilmawn-woman watches over the couscous on the fire and puts on her make-up	The Jews constantly make sexual advances to her	The rabbi waits for the meal with the harvesters

12	13	14
Bilmawn-woman sets off with the dinner on her head	While walking, Bilmawn-woman trips over a stone and spills the food on the ground	Bilmawn-woman takes off, pursued by the hungry harvesters, who shout, "Where's our dinner, whore! Where's our dinner, daughter of a whore!"

band's penis, the suitors hardly appear in a favorable light either. In other words, this is no dramatization of the contrast between virtue and vice. The men are incapable of moderating their desire, and the father of the family, manipulated by the mother as she takes over the important decisions (choice of the penis), is ridiculous. Moreover, the relationship between Bilmawn-woman and the men (table 11.2–4, etc.) confirms their laxity and total lack of vigilance. And their search for a young woman, which goes on forever, reaches scandalous proportions when they are no longer even able to satisfy her because of their advancing age!

Viewed along with what the procession has dramatized, the scene por-

Table 11. Units of Paying the Fieldhands

	1	2	3
Workers' revolt/Rabbi tries to stockpile the goods and receives the phalluses	The rabbi sits down on his stick and farts loudly (Table 10.5) Table 10.3 Receives sexual triad and sperm from the workers (Table 10.4) Receives sexual insults	Rabbi discusses their pay with the fieldhands	Workers overcome — He calls on them one by one to dress them: each has an obscene name Workers heatedly discuss their pay Workers answer to ridiculous, obscene names and accept the clothes given by the rabbi

4	5	6
Utters the number 3 and he is offered 3 + milk (penis, testicles, and sperm) with an obscene gesture of the fist	Exchange of insults between rabbi and fieldhands; insults repeated by the crowd of young people surrounding the scene Confusion and laughter	Troupe races about; repeat of the *aḥwash* and procession.

trays the foundations of domestic life as the complete opposite of the foundation created by the sacrifice. However, it should be recalled that there as well, even on such a pure and solemn occasion, cooperation between the sexes retains its full ambiguity.

In any case, harnessing oneself to married life and leading one's team out to plow constitute the two decisive acts that bound the indeterminate state of youth and place young men, on the moral and political level, in service to the community. Integrating life and the masquerade that turns it upside down into Muslim temporality, they will assist their fathers, public sacrifiers in the mode of Abraham, while their wives will be satisfied with these private and half-sacrilegious exchanges with the victim. While the young men wait, they must put all their energy into physical labor and remain suspended between adolescence and the status of an independent head of a household, which they will only truly achieve with their father's death.

Thanks to this ambiguous creature, this undetermined state puts them in a position to produce a civilization bearing the very signs displayed by the myth of Abraham (domestic group, agriculture, worship).[1] Yet these scenes are disorderly and erratic, as the action speeds up under the direction of a hero who is indissolubly both sacred and sacrilegious. Hence the inversions and disorders: plowing the threshing ground instead of the field; planting ashes, which are a substance of the beyond and the result of decomposition, instead of living seed; parodying a prayer, the "Jews' prayer"; tempering the blade of the plow with an impure liquid (urine) while all those who take part in the plowing must on the contrary seek to attract *baraka;* and these hundreds of obscene gestures and words so far from the seriousness of everyday activities—which also have been modified, since the procession excludes the village heads of household and makes them carry out certain feminine tasks.

All these inversions, beginning with the one that the masquerade makes of the sacrifice, bring to mind events of the same type occurring in a variety of ceremonies by so-called nonliterate societies as well as in the European festivals known as carnivals and charivaris. Like many others, our festival presents a rite of passage, and like them as well, it takes us from gravity and serious attitudes to licentious joy and play. Late in the preceding century, Frazer saw contrasted in this succession the juxtaposition of pain and joy accompanying the death and resurrection of a vegetation god. Thus ancient religion would regularly renew nature, with the murder and reappearance of this hero. The idea found its followers, ready to assign this role to Bilmawn. I have already stressed the inconsistencies of such an interpretation (see chap. 1), and, following Leach on this point, I will seek the meaning of the festival in the terms that combine within it. But is it possible to reduce these terms to the formal correlation between two binary oppositions posited by Leach?

Leach finds an oscillation in Greek mythology between two contrary principles accompanied by a third, which comes and goes and unites them. Myths combine these principles in an interplay of terms, thereby conceptualizing time in its two qualities of irreversibility and return.[2] It can be understood how this back-and-forth movement would animate those myths and rituals linked to transition. At work in the festival, this shifting is the foundation on which the inversion is based. Chronos is not a wheat spirit, and his feast is not the celebration of seasonal renewal. Here the disguises and violations of ordinary rules are a response to the inversion of time in a rite of passage that marks the two opposing directions of time as duration: time that ends and time that begins. From that point on, it is imperative that there be a liminal space, one that transforms the beings that occupy it, intermediary beings fully engaged in their transformation. These include both the sacrificial victim and the characters of the carnival. Among the latter as well, the breaking of ordinary rules corresponds to this interval which is outside of time.[3]

But if this binary plot is generalized in the Carnival and festivals of pre-industrial Europe, it has been noted, with increasing insistence, that social and cultural splinterings and struggles are nonetheless enmeshed in it.[4] Beyond the conceptual oppositions, these celebrations represent "a sort of comprehensive and poetic description of society," in the words of one historian, and the tensions that are literally played out can lead to violence and civil war.[5]

Viewed in this light, it is possible to compare the Carnival to our masquerade, which utilizes inversion and constructs a comic spectacle on the basis of works and days. It takes the consequences of a reproductive hierarchy, which regulates access to the erotic, to the prestige of procreation, and to power, to their height. Then, by the same mechanism, it pillories innovation in daily life. This is a function of censorship akin to what may be observed in attacks using the boisterous mockery of the charivari.[6]

Most importantly, applying Leach's view of the carnival to this masquerade leads to the risk of seeing nothing more than this seductive formal correlation, which fails to question the identities of the disguised figures. Bilmawn, the Jews, and the slave are performed by young Berber-speaking Muslims, and their performances say something specific that differentiates them from the characters of the carnivals. The differences associated with the identities of the masked figures, far from signifying only a relationship to temporal inversion—which in itself has nothing specific about it—provide the meaning of the festival as it has just been revealed through analysis.

Moreover, the inversion here is partial and, as has been recently noted of the African ceremonies, it is based on differences rather than on logical contradictions.[7] And the rules and objects taken from the sacrifice are also crucial in creating the effects of Bilmawn's act. With these contrasting elements creating a kind of interference, or static, the dynamic of the entire festival reveals the back-and-forth motion between two scenes whose central characters, both inhabitants of liminal space, are not without connections to each other. The resulting ambiguity sets up the action as *ludus,* charade, and puzzle, but forbids one to take it as a purely intellectual game.

There is ambiguity here, indeed, but not anti-structure in Victor Turner's sense of the word. For to raise the objection (as he has done against structuralism) that the rite mixes up established categories of thought and action in order to express what is continuous and in motion, is first of all to take the theory of structure for what it is not. An example of this can be found in the relationships between terms governing social institutions and organizations, such as the definition of roles and statuses that he proposes. And for it to be possible to oppose Bergsonian continuity and movement[8] to Lévi-Straussian structure, the former two would have to be seen at work in myths and rites. Instead, Turner (and it is understandable!) is content to identify them with being[9] and, in a purely theoretical move, to place them in opposition to roles. Applied to a case such as the one discussed here, this opposition immediately comes apart, for it would lead us to close our eyes to the fact—which my analysis amply illustrates—that the masquerade and sacrifice function, on the contrary, by and for the hyperdefinition of normative and social positions that guarantee the status quo.

The pageant of the masked figures is on a quest for a second foundation for civilization and its roles (with respect to those provided by the sacrifice). The principle of this foundation—come to life in the guise of Bilmawn—is ambiguous but indispensable: an agent of disorder, yet necessary to the reproduction of the human order itself, present in the dream and abominable murder of the son decided on by Abraham but rejected in the outcome of the myth. If one accepts the dramatization of this principle—in the character of Bilmawn—then his metamorphoses, which make it possible to work the earth and to bring it fertility by the plow and seed, take on meaning. His overall character puts him in the company of figures of creative ambiguity to which other mythologies attribute an iniatory role.[10]

As reorganized in tables 8–11, most of what occurs in the bundle of episodes called "works and days" can be summarized in five key statements:

1. The plowshare, hot and pointed like a penis, cleaves the soil as the penis cleaves the woman;
2. Bilmawn can be transformed and take on varied identities: tool (bellows and anvil), female animal (a milk cow and not a bull), woman;
3. This woman gives herself to everyone and, in her flightiness (putting on makeup while preparing the meal), destroys what her husband has accumulated (rabbi-field boss, etc.), Pandora's syndrome;
4. The rabbi-boss accumulates the harvests and rules the workers;
5. The rabbi-boss receives from them the sexual "threesome," insults, and the stick in his anus.

However, some units do not fit these headings. These are episodes that are postulated by the scenario, "technical" acts. Whatever the incommodities of too fine a distinction between technique and ritual (recently stressed by a number of scholars), the search for the plow, for example (table 8.1), differs from the acts that follow as the construction of a mosque differs from a prayer. There is reason to state that the first act is essentially technical, the second essentially ritual. It is vain to say that the law of cause and effect operates in them both; the effect of ritual action seems less differentiated from the subject than an object (mosque), no matter how strong the bond between perception and subjectivity. In any event, the search for a plow is not played, it is instrumental. The recruiting of the *khammas* (table 9.1), another action that is not listed, is more complex: on the one hand, it gives rise to comic exchanges between the Jews and the boy they pursue to force him to take the role, and on the other, the pursuers use ashes to mark their victim (table 9.1–2). In addition to its use as seed, ash is constantly employed by the Jews in their systematic (and sometimes violent) attempt to do everything possible—while the procession is underway—to ensure that everyone plays a part in this drama where the invisible comes into view. The deserted village, it bears repeating, and the crowd of recalcitrant participants covered with ash serve to create this *artificial night* in which Bilmawn appears; because everyone is an actor, there can be no spectators. It is as if these units were there solely to formulate a sixth statement: "What happens here is unreasonable and could not really take place in broad daylight." Seen from this standpoint, these units offer information only about the status of the drama, its true connection with the invisible world, and the comic traces, already discussed, which call for the spectacle to be produced in broad daylight and at the same time claim that it is shrouded in night. Such business is confirmed, in the usual comic fashion, by this other unclassified unit in which the *khammas* mows down the whole troupe (table 9.5). These elements are what moves the action along, the veritable perpetrators of dramatic illusion.

Strictly speaking, statement 2 (table 12) should be listed with the themes of the play and among these dramatic elements, particularly since some of its components can be included in other groups and indeed are found in our listings (table 8; all the units listed in table 10.3). Consequently, one is in fact confronted with two types of action: those which say something about the life and conditions of men and beasts, and those which carry out the dramatic deception. Statement 2 is a reflection of this indetermination which gives rise to the slippages and metamorphoses situated, it must be stressed, in mythical times. These statements are reformulated in table 12.

One can see in all these elements the equivalent of this work of distortion, which not only covers up a hidden meaning but makes it possible for the message to escape censorship, that Freud unearthed in the functioning

Table 12. Two Types of Statements

Statements of the First Type: *Statements describing the condition of living beings (esp. men and women)*	Statements of the Second Type: *Statements governing the dramatic deception*
1. The heated and sharpened plowshare opens the ground as the heated and erect penis opens the woman	1. The ashes and the recruiting of the *khammas* recall the conditions of the game
2. Bilmawn is changed into implements and into a woman who gives herself to everyone (Pandora's syndrome)	2. Bilmawn's transformations recall the conditions of the game: a mythical time of indetermination
3. The rabbi-boss (= the man) accumulates his harvests and exercises authority over his workers	
4. The rabbi-boss (= the man) receives the masculine sexual triad from them, as well as insults and a stick in his anus	

of dreams. Undoubtedly, statements of the second type function in this way, thus making it possible for the scandalous words of the unseemly beings to be heard, especially since the drama, like a dream, is presented as a jumble, a hopelessly mixed up montage of ordinary, commonsense actions and statements and others that at first glance are absurd.

Just because a statement operates to further the dramatic action does not mean that it is incapable of conveying meaning. This quality of meaningfulness is shared by statements of both types. Meanwhile indetermination— the condition for transformation—is found at the basis of agriculture and industry: in other words, at the origin of civilized life. And within this framework human existence continues, bounded by servitude and labor, the fertility of the soil and that of women, the wound men trace upon the soil and the female body; the submission of this body and the threats it poses; the ambivalences about domination, obedience, and revolt. All statements of the first type can be summed up in this small number of tensions.

The reader will have recognized that Bilmawn is that ambiguous character—quite common in a number of cultures—of the founding hero, a venerable but comic figure, contradictory and set apart from men by his actions that so often are ferocious, bloody, and unclassifiable. What matters here is that he acts as a kind of limit that, with the aid of simple equivalences, defines the condition of the members of the society: workers submit to the boss as a woman submits to a man; workers oppose their boss and try to weaken him, just as a woman tries to weaken a man; other men attempt to threaten the boss's honor and prestige, just as the woman ruins her husband by giving herself to everyone; the young are to the "old" what the Jews are to the Muslims (on this last statement, see the analysis of the preparations and the procession); and so on. All these "facts" are primordial and perhaps unchangeable, for they define a way of life sanctified by tradition and by the heroes who wield the apparently contradictory power of mixing up all classifications and, simultaneously, making possible smelting and agriculture, obscenity and reproduction, dishonor and the continuity of the group's cherished values, that is, its being.

In these aspects, then, the foundation story underlying the masquerade is identical to that of the sacrifice. But while the sacrifice puts impurity and sacrilege in a shameful light and makes high claims for purity, the masquerade insists on the duality of the concrete by using terms and relationships (Bilmawn, Jews, slave, woman, workers, *khammas*) that in everyday life are evidence of otherness and social conflict. They deny the strictures of purity that the sacrifice attempts to impose (despite the feminine ritual that accompanies it and timidly challenges it) and expose the law of the real to the light of day. The constant threat of the duality, perhaps most exemplary of all, represented by the male–female relationship in this patriarchal society overshadows all other dualities and, so to speak, colors the whole. For people faced with such an omnipresent contradiction in their everyday life, it is not surprising that from time to time the utopian fantasy of male reproduction, revealed in the analysis of the procession (table 6.5), would flash like lightning.

The drama brings to life not only ongoing realities, the tensions that reflect the dynamics of a structure in the concrete sense I have given to the word. In the actors' descriptions, certain traits already reveal which specific categories take the initiative and which react: the young go off to conquer women and houses, to the detriment of the "old men," in a move partaking of both a rite of initiation and a challenge. The stakes are another marginal category with respect to the group norm: women. A certain complicity between the two categories ensues. It is not at all surprising to see the older men keep some means of control over the process: some of them prepare the masquerade and "supervise" it, so to speak, thanks to their technical skills (preparing the skins and dressing Bilmawn). And when the choice of the actor who must wear the skins is discussed, they incline toward a young married man.[11] In this manner social conflicts continue within Bilmawn's play itself; historical tensions between groups surround its very preparation.

This can be seen in the conflict, which over the past several years has

become more intense, between "reformers" set on abolishing "this paganism" and partisans of tradition firmly attached to Bilmawn. In fact, this debate has become generalized, concerning much more than the man dressed
in the skins; for it pits the purists, who wish to banish everything that for
them does not strictly pertain to the "authentic Islam," against the other
believers, who are faithful to a traditional Islam and do not wish to change
any of their customs. For the second group, there is no clear demarcation
between Islamic and non-Islamic practices. Indeed, they act with the con-
viction that everything they do, they do as Muslims. Concerning Bilmawn,
the traditionalist's Islam clashes violently with the reformer's Islam, thus
echoing a debate active in all Muslim countries. In this way, a local conflict
of ideas connects with global, even universal concerns.

Whether open or latent, local or generalized, the conflicts played out by
Bilmawn utilize the terms available to this particular, localized culture, just
as other festivals celebrated in other societies bring structural contradictions to life, making use of events in a completely natural way. Bilmawn
shows his sensitivity to heated conflicts especially in certain incidents that
sometimes occur in the middle of the procession as well as in the bundle
called the revue. Like the marriage, the revue was censored from the repertoire at Imi-n'Tassaft. Once again the observations conducted in Timezguida
n'Oumalou served to complete the picture. On the other hand, the violent
incident that broke out in the first village, where the son of the *moqaddem*[12]
of the neighboring group was beaten, indicates that tensions between villages combine with oppositions between social and political categories.

This sensitivity to the everyday emerges in the "revue," as can be seen in
these two sketches performed in Timezguida n'Oumalou:

An old man rides his ass in the sun. On this occasion Bilmawn changes
into a donkey stallion, just as for the plowing he changed into a cow. The
donkey is as old as its master. Halfway up a hill, the animal comes to a halt.
The master urges it on; the animal does not budge. The master loses his
temper and strikes the animal. The ass lies down on the ground, inert. En-
raged, the master sits on his mount and complains. Judging by the words of
the local commentators, the donkey and its master are known in the village.
The man is miserable, and his misfortunes are so numerous that they become funny.

A notable who is well known in the village keeps a hotel highly esteemed
by mountaineers and tourists. Eminently respectable because of his relative
social success, his piety, and his title of *hajj* (he made the pilgrimage to
Mecca), the moment a group of foreign women arrives, his behavior under-

goes a radical change. Beaming with delight, he immediately sheds all evidence of his respectability. He rushes out to the vehicle to open the doors, fawns obsequiously, and begins speaking another language. That evening, his friendliness goes beyond all bounds, for he takes to dancing with his guests and exchanging with them smiles of erotic complicity.

The business of the old man and his tired and disobedient mount and the portrait of a pious old fellow dancing with foreign women are depictions of everyday life that are neither more nor less realistic or symbolic than the admirable picaresque evocations that Spanish writers raised to the dignity of a universal art. The same spirit of caricature and self-directed irony dominates these two scenes, the second of which also provides a commentary on tradition and innovation.

In these two cases, as in the masquerade, acts and gestures that overturn everyday norms are found (a mount refusing to carry out its usual function, piety/licence, etc.). But as always, the inversion is a partial one, for the donkey does not ride the master, and the satirized dance does not involve any village women. Furthermore, in this last scene, the innovation shows contact with otherness in the person of the foreigner. In the masquerade, the Other is presented in the monstrous face of Bilmawn and in turn takes on the faces of slaves, Jews, and women.

Notes

Introduction

1. "Das Römische Karneval ist ein Fest, Das dem Volke eigentlich nicht gegeben wird, sondern das sich das Volk selbst gibt" (Goethe, *Das Römische Karneval in Italienische Reise,* Goethes Werke 9 [Munich: Hamburger Ausgabe (1978), 484]).

2. The *'id-Lekbir:* literally, Great Festival—the *'id Umeqqur* or *tafaska, tfaska* (Berber). A number of French authors transcribe it as *Aïd el-Kebir.*

3. *Bujlud:* (Arabic), "the man with the skins"; *Bilmawn, Bu-Islikhen* (Berber, the Shilha and Tamazigh dialects, respectively). One also finds the Arabic *Bubtayn,* or even *Sba'Bubtayn,* "the lion with the skins." Finally, one also sometimes hears the term *Herrma.* Edmond Doutté, who transcribed it as *Héréma,* thinks that this word comes from the Arabic root *HRM,* which means "to grow old"; hence *Herrma* "the decrepit one." But one could also think of Hermes. On Doutté, cf. chap. 1, nn. 19–20, below. *Bilmawn:* pronounced like "Brown" or the German "Braun" (transcribed *Bilmaun* for the French reader). The plural is transcribed as *Dilmuwin.* Other Berber and Arabic words are transcribed according to the system indicated in the foreword.

4. The Muslim calendar is a lunar one and reflects a discrepancy of thirteen days with respect to the Gregorian calendar. However, locally, just as throughout all of peasant Morocco, Berbers and Arabs use the Julian calendar (*filahi*) to refer to the months and seasons of the agricultural cycle and the ceremonies associated with them. Other "climatic" and ritual periods are recorded in the zodiacal calendar, accessible only to certain learned specialists, particularly Koranic schoolmasters. In addition, it is quite common for the Ait Mizane (and they are not the only ones) to be unable to name the months of the Islamic calendar, except for the sacred months. However, they are well informed about the agricultural calendar.

5. Clifford Geertz, "Thick Description: Toward an Interpretive Theory of Culture," in *The Interpretation of Culture* (New York: Basic Books, 1973), esp. 6–10; idem, "From a Native's Point of View: On the Nature of Anthropological Understanding," in *Local Knowledge* (New York: Basic Books, 1983), 55–70, esp. 57–58.

6. The undertaking that gives rise to *structure* as it has just been described is empirical and inductive. It was first inspired by Radcliffe-Brown. Unlike him, however, I call "organization" everything that he calls "structures" and "institutions," reserving the term "structure" for the relationships induced from the relations between the components of a social organization. On these points, see A. R. Radcliffe-Brown, *Method in Social Anthropology* (Chicago: University of Chicago Press, 1959), 168–70, 176–77, and especially for an example of induction of structure, idem, "The Comparative Method in Social Anthropology," in *The Journal of the Royal Anthropological Institute* 81 (1951[1952]): 18–19, 20–22.

In my discussion this structure does not preclude action strategies, as referred to in Pierre Bourdieu's reflections on the margin for maneuvering in time that play allows in the midst of structures that are nonetheless very restrictive, e.g., those which govern the riposte to a challenge in a lineal social organization; see Pierre Bourdieu, *Esquisse d'une théorie de la pratique* (Geneva: Libraire Droz, 1972) 26, 31–32, and idem, *Le sens pratique* (Paris: Editions de Minuit, 1980), 178–79.

Between structure and action are the perceptions and ways of doing of the actors—heirs of an education and a history—that Bourdieu calls *habitus.* The relationship between the life situation and the habitus creates a structure of action and gives it a logic and motivation that are differentiated from the explicit and conscious perception and motivation of the actor (Bourdieu, *Esquisse,* 92, 94–96, 102, and 163, where the author discusses the application of the concept of habitus to ritual action).

Like any action in and over time, ritual action reacts to a perception of the present and future by means of habitual (ritual) actions, and according to a logic that pertains to schemes acquired in practice whose "generative formula" is found in the relationship between the sexes (in the Algerian case studied by Bourdieu); see *Le sens pratique,* 362, 366–67, 347–48, and 411f.

However, in the case of the Ait Mizane, the practical function—essentially linked to the cycle of production and reproduction—that Bourdieu assigns to ritual (cf. *Le sens pratique,* 351, 374, 376–77) does not appear in the foreground. And if it does exist, it coexists with a discourse that this society seems to carry on about itself. A discourse that presents cultural norms and concepts more or less completely by transgressing them. It seems possible, starting from the immanent and practical schemes, in Bourdieu's sense of the term, to find one's way back to some observable norms and symbols that define culture in the sense that Geertz gives to these words. Cf. in particular, C. Geertz, "Thick Description" and "From a Native's Point of View," as well as his "Deep Play: Notes on the Balinese Cockfight," in *The Interpretation of Cultures* (New York: Basic Books, 1972). This book is an attempt to move in the same direction, without postulating that culture has any specific coherence; this ambivalence with respect to cultural norms will be apparent throughout my description and interpretation of the festival.

1. Colonial Anthropology on the Sacrifice and the Masquerade

1. Leon L'Africain, *Description de l'Afrique,* trans. Épaulard (Paris: Adrien-Maisonneuve, 1956), 1:213.

An early twentieth-century Moroccan writer also quotes a memorandum attributed to a qadi who condemns the masquerades practiced in Marrakech on the occasion of the 'Ashura festival. This document, now lost, would have been written at the beginning of the nineteenth century, since, according to our author, it was addressed to the sultan Mouly Slimane. It condemns the festival in strong words and depicts some characteristics bearing a close resemblance to details described by twentieth-century ethnographers: men dressed as women, Muslims dressed as Jews, the "imitation of people known from such and such a tribe or town," and the wearing of masks.

The actors accompany themselves on musical instruments and take goods without the consent of their owners, who "give to protect their honor and avoid blows and insults. . . ." On all these points, consult the biographical dictionary of Mohamed b. Lhaj Mustafa Bujandar (in Arabic, *al-Ightibaṭ bi-tarajimi a'lam ar-ribaṭ*), ed. with notes by Abdelkrim Kriem (Rabat, 1987), 183–84.

It should not be surprising that the condemnation of the masquerades occurred at this time. In the beginning of the nineteenth century, the central power of Morocco attempted a religious reform which, in the words of its promoters, aimed to purify Islam of all kinds of practices that were deemed unorthodox. This awareness of a certain form of Islam went beyond the borders of Morocco and was marked by repercussions throughout the East as a result of the direct intervention of European forces. On this reform in Morocco, see J. Brignon et al., *Histoire du Maroc* (Paris: Hatier, 1967), 267–69.

2. As the rest of this chapter discusses only the most important treatments of the question, other works that may be consulted include:

A. For Morocco: René Basset, *Textes berbères du Maroc. Parler des Ait Sadden* (Paris: Geuthner, 1963), 13 and n. 3; the Ait Sadden or Beni Sadden are located to the east of Fez a short distance outside the town. Alfred Bel likens Bujlud to the sultan of Tolba and adopts the same viewpoint as Laoust concerning the interpretation of the masquerades: see his "Coup d'oeil sur l'islam en Berbérie," *Revue de l'histoire des religions* 75 (1917): 53–124. On the festival of the sultan of Tolba, Pierre de Cenival, "La légende du juif Ibn Mech'al et la fête du sultan des Tolba à Fes," *Hesperis* 5 (1925): 137–218; and in Marrakech, Doutté, "La khotba burlesque de la fête des tolba à Marrakech au Maroc," in *Recueil de mémoires et de textes,* 14e Congrès des orientalistes (Algiers: Jourdan, 1905), 197–219; and Wattier, "Le carnaval à Marrakech," *France-Maroc* (15 July 1919), 3–8. Finally, I myself attended travesties and processions in 1969–70 on the occasion of the feast of the sacrifice and the 'Ashura in the Ouarzazate region. On this region, see as well G.-H. Bousquet and J. Peltier, "Carnaval de l'Achoura à Ouarzazate (Maroc)," *Revue africaine* 92 (1948): 185–86.

B. For other countries and regions of North Africa: see Charles Monchicourt, "La fête de l'Achoura," *Revue tunisienne* 17 (1910): 278–301; Desparmet, "Notes sur les mascarades chez les indigènes à Blida," *Revue africaine* 52 (1908): 265–71; W. Marçais and A. Guiga, *Textes arabes de Takrouna* (Paris: Leroux, 1925), 1:347–52; H. Marchand, "Masques carnavalesques et carnaval en Kabylie," *4e Congrès de la Fédération des sociétés savantes de l'Afrique du Nord* (Rabat, 1938; Algiers, 1939), 805–14. On the festivals and masquerades in Libya and notably the 'Ashura, see G. Cerbella and M. Ageli, "Interpretazione storico-ethnologica di un rito islamo-cristiano," *Libia* 1, no. 2 (April–June 1953), and E. Rossi, "Appunti su feste e costumanze religiose dei musulmani di Tripoli," *Annali dell'istituto universitario orientale di Napoli,* n.s. 3 (1949): 179–86; and von Moltzan, "Reise in den Regenschaften Tunis und Tripolis" (Leipzig, 1870), 3:88–92.

On the subject of Egypt, documents seem even rarer than for Libya; on the phallic masquerades and comedies, see Ahmed Amine, *Dictionnaire des coutumes et traditions égyptiennes* (Cairo, 1953), 288 (in Arabic, *Qamus al-'adat wa at-taqalid al miṣriya*); and Ahmed Chafiq, *Mémoires sur un demi-siècle* (Cairo, 1934 [1935?]), 1:78 (in Arabic, dated 1352 A.H., *Mudhakkirati fi nisfi qarn*).

On the other hand, certain scenic themes and techniques in the masquerades find parallels in the Egyptian and Turkish shadow theaters; on this point see Metin And,

Karagöz: Turkish Shadow Theatre (Ankara: Dost Yagiulari, 1975), esp. 10, 30–32, 39–40, 52–69; this type of theater was also known in the Maghreb and notably in Algeria until 1843, when it was forbidden by the French because it criticized their occupation of the country (And, *Karagöz*, 70); and Mohieddine Bachetarzi, *Mémoires, 1919–1939* (Algiers: SNED, 1968), 424. On this theater in the Maghreb, see also Dr. A. Bernard, *L'Algérie qui s'en va* (Paris, 1887), 66–67; M. Quedenfeldt, "Das Türkische Schattenspiel im Maghreb," *Ausland* 63 (1890); 904–8, 921–26; and W. Hoenerback, *Das nordafrikanische Schattentheater* (Mainz, 1959), 43–44.

3. On all these festivals, see the articles in the *Encyclopedia of Islam* (Leiden: Brill, 1913–34; 2d ed., 1960–), s.vv.

4. Auguste Mouliéras, *Le Maroc inconnu: Etude géographique et sociologique* (Paris: Challamel, 1899), 2 vols. His description of the "Carnival" among the Jbala, 2:608–14; his description of the same festival in the Rif (Temsamane), 1:102–11. Although Mouliéras's work should be viewed with caution, since his information was provided by an itinerant "dervish" far from the region involved, in Oran, after twenty-four years of absence (!), there is no major reason for suspecting his description of this region, which closely matches descriptions I obtained in 1973. On his work see P. Shinar, *Islam maghrébin contemporain,* annotated bibliography (Paris: CNRS, 1983), 232.

5. Mouliéras, *Maroc inconnu,* 2:613.

6. Ibid., 611.

7. Ba-Shikh, Old Man Papa, the Chief, the Master: the multiple meanings of this word indicate the dignities and positions that contrast with his role.

8. For these details, Mouliéras, *Maroc inconnu,* 2:609.

9. Ibid., 610–11.

10. Ibid., 611.

11. Ibid., 612–13.

12. When there is no water, Muslims may perform their ablutions using a smooth stone chosen for that purpose.

13. E. Westermarck, *Ritual and Belief in Morocco* (London: Macmillan 1926; repr. New York: University Books, 1968), 2:134–47; idem, "The Popular Ritual of the Great Feast in Morocco," *Folklore* 22 (1912): 131–82.

14. Mouliéras, *Maroc inconnu,* 2:608–14; on the spectacle as a copy of the Saturnalia, ibid., 614.

15. Westermarck, *Ritual and Belief,* 2:149; the same remark is repeated in Westermarc, *Pagan Survivals in Mohammedan Civilisation* (London: Macmillan, 1933), 160.

16. E. Aubin, *Le Maroc d'aujourd'hui* (Paris: Armand Colin, 1907). Visit to Morocco in 1902–1903 (see preface, p. 1): on games and scenes of the 'Ashura, 287–88; S. Biarnay, *Notes d'ethnographie et de linguistique nord-africaines* (Paris: Publications de l'Institut des Hautes Etudes africaines, 1924).

17. E. Doutté, *Magie et religion en Afrique du Nord* (Algiers: A. Jourdan, 1908), 507 and n. 1; on Bu Hamara, see Aubin, *Le Maroc d'aujourd'hui,* chap. 8; M. Moudden, "Bou Hmara," stenciled typescript, Faculté des lettres et sciences humaines (Rabat, 1982).

18. Aubin, *Le Maroc d'aujourd'hui.*

19. Doutté, *Magie et religion,* 507. *'Achoura ('Ashura):* Feast of the Muslim New Year; see *Encyclopedia of Islam. Mechouar (meshwar):* exterior courtyard of the sultan's palace, where delegations of the people would come either to pay homage to the sovereign or to make their complaints. Also the place where certain great feasts where held that the sovereign attended. *Qadi:* Muslim religious judge.

20. Doutté, *Marrakech* (Paris, 1905), 270–321, 370–421.

21. E. Laoust, *Mots et choses berbères* (Paris: A. Challamel, 1920); cf. esp. on the feasts and games, 104–5, 191–93, 204–24, 308–50, 371–432; idem, "Noms et cérémonies des feux de joie chez les Berbères du Haut et de l'Anti-Atlas," published in three parts in *Hesperis* 1 (1921): 3–66, 253–316, 387–420 (henceforth "Noms et cérémonies").

22. On these characters, see Laoust, "Noms et cérémonies," esp. 19–20, 29–33, 412–16.

23. Laoust, "Noms et cérémonies," 261–64; 262, nn. 1–5. Laoust points out that *Builmawn, Bilmawn* comes from *ilm* "skin," *Bubtayn* from the Arabic *btana* "skin"; *bu-isliyen* from *asly* "skin"; *tagesduft,* etymology uncertain. *Igherm, tighermt:* Berber for fortified village, fortified castle inhabited by a lineage, or even a communal fortified storehouse.

24. Laoust, "Noms et cérémonies," 269–73, 275–78, and esp. 292–94.

25. Westermarck, *Ritual and Belief.* This author has devoted many articles and books to Morocco: *Marriage Ceremony in Morocco* (London: Curzon, 1914); *Wit and Wisdom in Morocco* (London: Routledge, 1930); and finally, *Pagan Survivals in Mohammedan Civilisation* (London: Macmillan, 1933).

26. Westermarck, *Ritual and Belief,* 2:134–47, 147–48; idem, *Pagan Survivals,* 158. Earlier he had discussed the Feast of Sacrifices and the masquerade in "The Popular Ritual of the Great Feast"; see n. 13 above. *Baraka:* benediction, grace, charisma; on this notion cf. Westermarck, *Ritual and Belief,* vol. 1, chap. 1; E. Gellner, *Saints of the Atlas* (London: Weidenfeld and Nicholson, 1969), chap. 1; V. Crappanzano, *The Hamadsha: A Study in Moroccan Ethnopsychiatry* (Berkeley and Los Angeles: University of California Press, 1973), 48–49, 73–74; R. Jamous, *Honneur et Baraka: Les structures sociales traditionnelles dans le Rif* (Paris: Maison des sciences de l'homme, 1981); and cf. the article "Baraka," in the *Encyclopedia of Islam.* On all these points, see Westermarck, *Pagan Survivals,* 158, and idem, *Ritual and Belief,* 2:147.

27. See the works published in the collection "Villes et tribus du Maroc" (Paris: Leroux, 1915–30, and Champion, 1931–32), and the two journals *Archives marocaines* (1915–20) and *Archives marocaines* (Paris, 1904–36).

28. Concerning the works of colonial historians, see A. Laroui, *The History of the Maghrib,* trans. Ralph Manheim (Princton: Princeton University Press, 1977); Marcel Ben Hammou, *L'histoire antique de l'Afrique du Nord* (Paris: Maspero, 1970); as well as Mohamed Sahli, *Décoloniser l'histoire* (Paris: Maspero, 1967); Germain Ayache, *Etudes d'histoire marocaine* (Rabat: SMER, 1979; 2d ed., 1983).

29. Doutté, *Magie et religion,* 453, esp. 459, 473, 477. Doutté's whole description is an effort to find there the characteristic stages of ritual as described by Hubert and Mauss; cf. as well 461.

30. "It would be impossible to construct a theory of sacrifice based on orthodox

Muslim sacrifice" (ibid., 458). In the following pages, Doutté describes this orthodox sacrifice, always citing some of its differences and similarities with other sacrifices: on spirits and djinns, marabouts, etc., cf. 459f.

31. Ibid., 468–69, 597, 601–2.

32. Ibid., 469–73, 486.

33. Ibid., typology of North African sacrifices, 477f.

34. Cf. all of chapter 11 on the extremely varied representations and personifications.

35. Doutté, *Magie et religion,* 512–19.

36. We know that the data on which Frazer based his discussion of the subject were later found to be questionable.

37. Doutté, *Magie et religion,* 515, 518–22.

38. Ibid., 525, 528–29, 533.

39. Laoust, "Noms et cérémonies," 254.

40. *Mots et choses berbères,* 320–21. On ritual murder and sexuality, cf. 193, 218–24, 308–14, 330–35.

41. Laoust, "Noms et cérémonies," 226.

42. Ibid., 264–75. On the route of the ram-god into Muslim sacrifice by way of Christian Easter, based among other things on the gloss of the word *tfaska* (name given in Berber to the Muslim sacrificial feast), likened to *pessah* and the French *pâques* "Easter," 269–70. This is the course taken by Laoust's imagination at the end of his interpretative attempt: "We can now return to Bujlud. We have wanted to prove that the masquerade in which he figures is not juxtaposed with the Aïd el-Kebir by simple whim; that it comes after the sacrifice of a ram and that this ram was a god; that the victim, or *tafaska* of the Muslim feast, perhaps perpetuates, across the ages, the memory of the old Libyan god Amaron, who after known vicissitudes is gradually assimilated into Baal-Hammon, to become the African Saturn under Roman domination, later on to blend with the paschal lamb when Christianity flourished. After so many apostasies, the meaning of these diverse consecrations could have changed many times; but if the gods are dead, if the beliefs have disappeared, the rites have survived" (ibid., 276–77).

43. Ibid., 277–78.

44. Cf. esp. the ceremonies described in "Noms et cérémonies," 20–23; on the ceremonies in which real couplings take place, although they are symbolic because the boys, according to Laoust, do not threaten the girls' virginity, cf. ibid., 38. These are the same ceremonies already described in *Mots et choses berbères,* 191–93 and 218–24, but for which—as is often the case—Laoust does not cite the sources of his information.

45. A. Bel, see note 2, above.

46. Westermarck, *Ritual and Belief,* 2:151.

47. Ibid., 151–52.

48. Ibid., 153–57, and idem, "Popular Ritual."

49. Westermarck, *Ritual and Belief,* 2:154.

50. On the concept of substratum, A. Laroui, *Les origines sociales et culturelles du nationalisme marocain* (Paris: Maspero, 1977), 168–70.

51. Westermarck, *Ritual and Belief,* 149; on all these points, see as well idem, *Pagan Survivals,* chap. 6.

52. Marie-Rose Rabaté, "La Mascarade de l'Aïd el-Kebir à Ouirgane (Haut Atlas)," *Objets et mondes* 7 (1967): 182.

53. Ibid.

2. Human Action in Its Environment

1. *Assif* (Berber): "torrent, river." Equivalent to the Arabic *wad.* This description draws from several works published on the High Atlas, particularly J. Dresch, *Recherches sur l'évolution du relief dans le massif central du Grand Atlas* (Tours: Arrault, 1941), 258f.; idem, *Documents sur les genres de vie de montagne dans le Grand Atlas,* Institut des Hautes Etudes marocaines no. 225 (Tours: Arrault, 1941), and J. Dresch and J. De Lepiney, *Le Massif du Toubkal: Guide alpin de la montagne marocaine* (Rabat: Office chériffien du tourisme, 1942); J. Despois and R. Raynal, *Géographie de l'Afrique du Nord-Ouest* (Paris: Payot, 1967), chap. 5, "Le Sud Atlantique et les pays chleuh," (340–58); D. Noin, "La neige au Maroc," *Notes marocaines* 15 (1961): 5–11; and J. A. Miller, *Imlil: Moroccan Mountain Community in Change* (Boulder, Colo.: Westview, 1984).

2. Miller, *Imlil,* 44, on temperatures and rainfall.

3. Data for the Ait Mizane are still unavailable, but for the neighboring valley of Azzaden, to the west, a survey made in 1976 revealed a shortage of barley above fifty percent (A. Hammoudi, "La vallée d'Azzaden, contribution à la sociologie du Haut Atlas," Doctoral thesis, 3e cycle, Paris III, 1977, 213).

4. A barley porridge is also eaten. A Moroccan author in the eighteenth century describes it as a typical dish of the Berber lands of the Upper Atlas. In those days it was probably made from sorghum; on these points, see B. Rosenberger, "Cultures complémentaires et nourritures de substitution au Maroc (15e–18e siècle)," *Annales, Economies, Sociétés, Civilisations* 3–4 (May–August 1980): 477, 487–88.

5. To avoid the risk of theft and arguments, dates of the corn harvest, like that of walnuts, are most often decided in common by the village council.

6. Miller, *Imlil,* 75.

7. Based on a survey I conducted with the collaboration of M. Mahdi and H. Rachik, *Enquêtes sur la composition et le fonctionnement des foyers chez les Rheraya* (Rabat: Institut agronomique et vétérinaire Hassan II, 1982), currently being analyzed.

8. Miller, *Imlil,* p. 25.

9. *Bilmawin* (plural of *Bilmawn*). On the ceremony at Timezguida n'Oumalou, see chap. 6, below.

10. Hammoudi et al., *Enquêtes.* Of the seven cases in which the *takat* is confined to one household unit, two had no land and thus were identified neither with property nor with crops.

11. Quarrels and lawsuits are presented to the gathered group, who attempt to resolve them with the use of collective sacrifices and meals, the best known of which is the *ma'ruf* (customs organized in honor of local saints). Fines are publicly an-

nounced, without naming the guilty party. On the *ma'ruf,* see Hassan Jouad and B. Lortat-Jacob, *La saison des fêtes dans le Haut Atlas* (Paris: Seuil, 1978); and Hassan Rachik, "Les repas sacrificiels: Essai sur le rituel d'un tribu du Haut Atlas," thesis, Faculté de Droit (Casablanca, 1986), 130f., 154, 175–77. I have personally observed disputes and such announcements at a large *ma'ruf* given by the Ait Mizane.

12. The Sus: in the south of the Upper Atlas and between the Dra and the Atlantic with, today, the town of Agadir as a large urban center. The man clothed in skins of Imlil is sometimes called Bilmawn of the Sus (Bilmawn n'Sus).

13. See, in the context of the Seksawa, the discussion of local and great history in J. Berque, *Structures sociales du Haut Atlas* (Paris: PUF, 1956), 94, and the postface to the new ed. (1982); on the shift back and forth between absolute chief and communal management, ibid., 91. On the council of elders *(jma't),* R. Montagne, *Les Berbères et le Makhzen dans le Sud du Maroc* (Paris: Alcan, 1930), 178, 180, 220; Berque, *Structures sociales,* 323, 325–27, 374; and R. Bidwell, *Morocco under Colonial Rule* (London: F. Cass, 1973), 283. The Treaty of the Protectorate was signed in Fez in 1912, but the region under discussion here was not taken over until around 1927.

14. On the organization of the modern state in rural areas, R. Leveau, *Le Fellah marocain défenseur du trône,* new expanded ed. (Paris: Presses de la Fondation nationale des sciences politiques, 1985), 29f. and chap. 3. The family of notables under discussion furnishes the *sheikh* or (Berber) *amghar.* On the attributions of the *sheikh* and (on a lower echelon) the *moqaddem* in the administration of the rural areas, ibid., chap. 3. The functioning of customary pasture agreements among tribes can be seen locally in the use of the great pastureland in the Oukaïmedan; see J. Gilles, A. Hammoudi, and M. Mohamed, "Oukaimedene, Morocco: A High Moroccan Agdal," *Proceedings of the Conference on Common Property Resource Management* (Washington, D.C.: National Academy Press, 1986), 281f. *Mussem* of varying importance reunite the former confederation and attract participants from different areas, including the towns: Moulay Brahim near Asni and Sidi Fares on one of the tributaries of the Rheraya *wad.* Lastly, Sidi Shamharush, at the foot of the Toubkal, is organized by the Ait Mizane and attracts many pilgrims from the mountains as well as the plain and the towns. On Sidi Chamharouch, see below, chaps. 9–10, and Rachik, "Les repas sacrificiels," 70, 94.

15. Miller, *Imlil,* 44. Over half the volume of the Ait Mizane river flows between March and May, and a tenth of the whole between July and September.

16. On Sidi Shamharush and its feast, see Rachik, "Les repas sacrificiels," 70, 137. H. Rachik drew my attention to this division between the young, of which I was unaware when I wrote the first draft of this work. On the criterion that the father must die before the married man finally, after being only a *afrukh,* moves to the status of *argaz* "adult man"; ibid., 193. On the sacrifice of the *mussem* and the distribution of the leftovers to the young married couples, classed as *iferkhan,* ibid., 191–93.

17. Customary sacrifice. Collective sacrifice carried out in the sanctuary of Sidi Shamharush in the upper valley. Also held in the vicinity of local holy men, preferably next to one of the springs in the rest of the valley. *Ma'ruf:* what is known, custom. The procedure of this feast is well known (n. 11 above). Disputes are more

or less arbitrated by the assembled group. There is also competition, as I have personally observed, between families and lineages, since the carcasses of sacrificed animals are carved up and auctioned off. A small part is saved for a collective meal for men and women separately. The pieces, imbued with *baraka*, are then sold at high prices, with the meat of course going to the one who pays the most. Very often this rivalry leads to harsh disputes that have no effect on the progress of the feast. Apparently such conflicts rarely lead to physical violence.

18. A survey I conducted in 1984 with the help of Mohamed Mahdi, Hassan Rachik, Rachida Rachik, Halima Oulmaati, and Naïma Zryouil. I am extremely grateful for their assistance.

19. Miller, *Imlil,* 33–34, and n. 7; see also J. Celérier, "L'Atlas et la circulation au Maroc," *Hesperis* 7 (1927): 475–78. *Swak:* bark of the walnut root. On its use, see chap. 9, n. 12, below.

20. J. A. Miller (*Imlil,* 37 and n. 17) estimated the number of tourists to be five thousand annually, based on observations made in 1974.

3. The Sacrifice

1. On *tfaska* and *tighersi,* cf. E. Laoust, *Mots et choses berbères* (Paris: A. Challamel, 1920); on *tighersi,* ibid., 324, 383, 432; and idem, "Les cérémonies des feux de joie chez les Berbères," *Hesperis* 1 (1921): 269–70, where the author provides a lengthy gloss of the word *tfaska,* which he likens to *pessah* (Judeo-Arabic *fsakh*) and the French *pâques.* I lack the competence to judge the value of such an etymology. However, as will be seen, it appears that the Feast of the Sacrifice has co-opted Bilmawn, who in some respects is linked to an agricultural cycle while the Muslim festival follows the lunar calendar. In other words, Bilmawn could have belonged to another cycle—a Christian one governed by the Roman calendar—that the Muslim festival has dislodged.

2. It must be recalled that these ablutions are a form of purification required before prayers. As a general rule the body is washed in a specific order: first the genitals, then the hands and arms, then the face, the nostrils, and ears, after which one wipes one's wet hands, joined at the fingertips over the top of one's head. Last one washes one's feet, being careful to pass the water and gently rub between the toes. Then, before standing up, for all this takes place while seated, one sprinkles a little water to the right and to the left.

Another indication of the distinction made between ablution and hygiene can be seen in cases where water is lacking: one rubs one's hands against a stone and then over the parts to be purified; or again one uses sand to make one's ablutions. The same thing occurs in the ritual cleansing after sexual intercourse *(ghasl-al janaba),* where bodily parts must be purified in a certain order.

3. *Takbir:* the act that consists of shouting, "God is the most great!" *(Allahu Akbar!).* This formula is repeated three times. Forming the first phrase of the call to prayer, it is also uttered before the sacrificial victim is slain, before bringing down game, and before entering battle in defense of a sacred cause (a holy war).

4. Sunna: the traditions related to the conduct of the Prophet and his decisions and edicts. For Muslims the Sunna is the second source of inspiration and law after

the Koran (*Encyclopedia of Islam,* s.v.). Hadith: traditions (sayings, judgments, deeds) attributed to the Prophet.

5. Muslim tradition records that Ibrahim leads Ismail and not Isaac to the sacrifice; however Muslim authors differ on this subject. On these points consult al-Tha'labi, Abu Ishaq Ahmad b. Mohamed b. Ibrahim al-Nisabury, *Qaṣaṣ al-'anbiya' al-musamma 'ara'is al-majalis* (Beirut, 1981, new ed.), 93f. The author (cited hereafter as al-Tha'labi), who died in 1035 (427 A.H.), is also a commentator on the Koran. His works are very well known. Cf. C. Brockelmann, *Geschichte der Arabischen Litteratur* (Leiden: Brill, 1936–42), 1:350.

6. *Shard:* literally, "that which is stipulated" (in this case, in the contract between the *fqih* and the village who employs him): from the Arabic *sharṭ,* which means "stipulation, condition."

7. *Fdur* in Berber, "breakfast." Here it is eaten quite late in the morning, because of the time needed for the prayer for the sacrifice: from the Arabic *ftur,* "breakfast, breaking one's fast."

8. *Ḥabus:* elsewhere called *waqf.* On these notions see the article "*Waqf*" in the *Encyclopedia of Islam.* Goods provided to religious institutions by benefactors who literally bring them to a stop (*waqf, ḥabus*) for their benefit. Very often, gifts in mortmain reverting to these institutions after the death of the last descendant in the male line of the one making up the *waqf.*

9. Feast of *fiṭr* that brings the month of Ramadan to a close, which breaks the fast and gives its name to the month after Ramadan.

10. Widespread practices in the Moroccan countryside. I personally have observed examples of them in the Haouz of Marrakech and in the High Atlas. Divination using these animal bones is an old technique known and practiced in Arab societies and apparently transmitted to Europe during the Middle Ages. On this last point, see Charles Burnett, "Arabic Divinatory Texts and Celtic Folklore: A Comment on the Theory and Practice of Scapulimancy in Western Europe," *Cambridge Medieval Celtic Studies* 6 (1983): 31–42.

11. As for example at the time of the Al Asnam earthquake (Algeria), where they were collected to aid the ill-fated town.

12. "Ait" is a word put before proper nouns to refer to all those who belong to a group; thus for example Ait Ahmed means those of Ahmed, the descendants of Ahmed, who is supposed to have given his name to a lineage, village, or tribe. But it can also simply mean the fact of belonging to a place, for example Ait Ugadir, the people from Ugadir, or Ait Mizane. It is interesting to note that the young men playing in the Bilmawn masquerade are referred to as Ait Bilmawn.

4. Narratives about Bilmawn: The Scenario

1. *Tamugayt* (Shilha): "cow." *Ismakh* (Shilha): "black, slave." The same semantic "convergence" is found in Moroccan Arabic dialect, where *'abd,* which also means slave, can, depending on the context, mean black as well. *Akhnif:* characteristic of some valleys of the western Upper Atlas and Siroua, this heavy black cape, which is no longer worn, is completely or partly made from goat hair. In some regions (Siroua and Tifnout), a spot on the back is decorated with motifs borrowed

from carpet weaving. In one or two areas this spot is red-orange. Here, *akhnif* means "burnoose."

2. *Ferrah* (Arabic): pottery vessel in which bread is baked; the part that has been set on the fire is covered with thick soot. *Akhurbish* (Shilha) or the feminine *takhurbisht:* in a mosque, the anteroom to the prayer room, where ablutions are performed. It is also the room in which water is heated for that purpose.

3. The entrance is made in the following order: Ismakh, Bilmawn, and last the Jews. *Lfateh* (Shilha, for the Arabic *fatiha,* or *fatha* in dialect): invocation and prayer to "close" a ritual. Here, the general meaning of an invocation to God.

4. *Jma't:* group gathered together, council in the sense of village council. On this institution and its activities and prerogatives, in addition to the works of Montagne and Berque cited above in chap. 2, n. 13, P. Pascon, "Désuétude de la jmaâ dans le Haouz de Marrakech," *Annales marocaines de sociologie,* Rabat, 1967; A. Hammoudi, "L'évolution de l'habitat dans la vallée du Dra," *Revue de géographie du Maroc* 18 (1970): 44; R. Jamous, *Honneur et Baraka: Les structures sociales traditionelles dans le Rif* (Paris: Maison des Sciences de l'homme, 1981), 35; Ali Amahan, *Abadou de Ghoujdama, Haut Atlas marocain: Étude sociolinguistique* (Paris: Geunther, 1983), 37–38, 40, 47 n. 20.

5. *Akhummas:* from the Arabic *khammas,* a man who works for a landowner in exchange for one fifth of the harvest (J. Berque, *Etudes d'histoire rurale maghrébine* [Tangiers: Editions internationales, 1938], 69–82).

6. Kohl, a black powder made from a base of ground antimony, used by women to blacken their eyes. See as well chap. 3, above, regarding kohl applied to the eyelids of the victim just before it is slaughtered.

7. In other words, by pushing each leg back and forth, as if to operate the traditional bellows at the forge. On that industry, see A. Paris and F. Ferrol, "L'industrie du fer chez les Berbère du Maroc," *Hesperis* 2 (1922): 339–45.

8. Just as one strikes the white-heated plowshare to sharpen it.

9. The character of Herrma appears in this description; cf. the descriptions of Doutté and Laoust in chap. 1, above. In the ceremony described in our two villages, the character of the old man seems to have disappeared. This old man, horny and impotent, is played by the rabbi, who never stops trying to copulate with Tamugayt. It will be noted that in other ceremonies (chap. 1, Mouliéras's description) there is a kind of synthesis in which the old man wears a billygoat's skin on his head. *Asays:* the central square in the village; *ahwash:* traditional group dance; cf. H. Jouad and B. Lortat Jacob, *La saison des fêtes dans le Haut Atlas* (Paris: Seuil, 1978).

10. Azzaden: the valley immediately to the west of that of the Ait Mizane. In 1975, during a visit to this valley, I was surprised and startled one evening by Bilmawn who was returning to the village after a day of wandering. The next day, in another village, Bilmawn was constantly routed from the village by people perched on the terraces who showered him with stones. Bilmawn ran after them all, especially the children and young people, whom he was sure to hit with his "shoes" every time he could get near them. *Kafur:* camphor.

11. Medical prescriptions(!): *ikhan n't fullust:* chickenshit; *ijbir n'ugru:* frog feathers; *izuran n'Oumadlou:* fog roots; *idarn n't fullust:* roasted [chicken] drumsticks. The woman answers: "Yes, o my [little] peddler; okay, o . . ."

12. Villages of the Ait Mizane valley; Imnan and Nfis are two contiguous valleys. Imnan: valley immediately to the east of that of the Ait Mizane. The river of the same name flows into the Assif Ait Mizane, near Asni. The Nfis wadi drains the valleys located west of that of the Ait Mizane, including Azzaden. It flows into the Marrakech plain and into the Tensift wadi.

13. Instrument used to sift ground wheat or barley to separate the flour from the bran.

14. Goudman, Udman: high valley on the south slope of the Upper Atlas, east of the high Tichka range.

15. *Iḥazzan* (Shilha) for *ḥazzan* (Arabic): "rabbi." *Ikhan:* human excrement. Here "shit" or "shitty rabbi." *Addikun:* I was unable to establish a gloss for this word. *Ḥakham* (Hebrew and Arabic): "judge." Penetration is mimed, of course. "Three plus *ṭuz* plus milk!"

16. *Ṭuz:* onomatopoetic word familiarly used to mean a fart, and here "milk" refers to sperm.

17. Here the narrator seems to be using the term Herrma to refer to the slave, which goes against the familiar usage that names the slave Ismakh, as we have just seen. Herrma has disappeared and is apparently confused with one or the other character.

18. A detail contradicting the first account, where it was said that the Jews are not covered with soot.

19. *Ṭolba:* here, people who have studied the Koran (and can teach it), and sometimes the rudiments of grammar and religious science. "Substitute for God on earth": term designating the king as head of the Muslim community (*"Khalifatu allahi fi al-'ard"*). *Jahiliya:* age of ignorance and paganism in Islamic tradition. It is the word the educated use to refer to the "age of paganism" that for them preceded Islam (it is "the age of ignorance"). By extension, it refers to all practices condemned as non-Islamic or harmful to Islam. "Whoever imitates a people then belongs to that people": catch phrase, found always among educated people but widespread enough in the common parlance to mean that those who imitate or copy other customs are excluded from the community and can only matter to the people whom they imitate.

5. Bilmawn Observed: His Preparation and Accession

1. Mohamed Mahdi, a sociologist from Rabat, who is preparing a study on the rituals connected with stockbreeding in the Rheraya Mountains and in Oukaimedan.

2. The preparation of charcoal is regulated by the technical forestry services, who supervise logging and oversee the protection of woodlands. Violations are punished by fines. But it is difficult to monitor a poorly traveled region with few roads.

3. A form of request by sacrifice once widespread in Morocco. Its efficacy lies in the mechanism and concept of *'ar* that it engages and which transforms a request into an obligation. On the notion and mechanism of *'ar,* E. Westermarck, *Ritual and Belief in Morocco* (London: Macmillan, 1926; repr. New York: University Books, 1968), 1:518–19; recently, R. Jamous, *Honneur et Baraka: Les structures sociales traditionnelles dans le Rif* (Paris: Maison des sciences de l'homme, 1981), 213–16,

and K. Brown, "The 'Curse' of Westermarck," *Acta Philosophica Fennica* 34 (1982): 219, 241f.

4. Only in theory, for I was able to observe cases in which men did not leave their houses. They were content to hide in an out-of-the-way room, their presence apparently sufficing to keep the game from going too far.

A similar case took place before my eyes. An old man passing by not far from the group was pulled over. After the "revelation" of a few details related to an amorous commerce he was supposed to have had with his own donkey, he was released. He escaped from the fate the others wished to impose on him only thanks to his own supplications and the surreptitious but energetic interference of his own children.

5. It will be recalled that this is the divination bone (see chap. 3).

6. This is a small stream that flows near Marrakech and into which the refuse and sewers of the old city drain. Thus the prayer slides into parody, with the inevitable sexual connotations.

7. Referred to as *ghunbaz* (marigold, *Tagetes hybrida*), these flowers are grown everywhere in the valleys on leftover patches of terrace. In addition to their ornamental use, they seem to be associated with love, music, and dance. For example, when the women of one village wish to invite a group of drummers known for their expertise to an *aḥwash*, they send them a bouquet of *ghunbaz* via a man they trust. In theory, the drummers cannot refuse such an invitation.

8. This thievery is not pushed too far, however. There is something of a rule that says that one demands and the owner is unable to refuse; but that one does not demand too much for fear of spoiling the game.

9. We were careful to keep our distance when the obscene remarks were addressed to the women. Since the rule claimed that no man should be present, I asked Mme Khadija Belaouinat to record some of these comments. As can be seen, she herself is the object of some of the invective. I heartily thank her for her collaboration. Mme Belaouinat and her husband, M. Abdellah Herzenni, a geographer and a sociologist, respectively, from the office of the Haouz in Marrakech, accompanied me during my observations in September 1982.

10. In the name of . . . God: parody that begins with the actual opening lines of an Islamic invocation, only to move into an absurd phrase that is perhaps a sexual allusion as well. *Sha'ba*: ravine. It becomes a rushing river during the rains. The Issil wadi: see above, n. 6. Name that denotes the idea of flowing (from the verb *issil*, "to flow"). Si Abdelkebir, Sidi Mohammed: two extremely common proper names. Here, preceded by *si* and *sidi*, "mister" and "your lordship." In this context they refer to the penis. Note the use of these two names, of venerable tradition, with his connotation!

11. The medical "prescription" is a parody of these magical recipes whose ingredients women purchase from the peddler, a familiar figure in all Moroccan villages. Women and merchants are always accomplices in the process that results in sorcery and magic, here a parody of healing and sexual attentions and perhaps fecundity. *Fasukh*: medicinal plant.

12. *Alla'b*: Arabic word with an extensive semantic field. From the verb "to play" (*l'ab*); "to play together, to play with something or to play an instrument, play a role," etc.

6. Bilmawn Observed: Street Theater

1. On this point, see chap. 4, n. 7.

2. Representative of the villages' central administration.

3. Sura 1; English translation by A. J. Arberry, *The Koran Interpreted* (New York, Macmillan, 1976), 29. I do not vouch for all the subtleties of the recitation.

4. Ḥwizzine, deformation of the proper name, Husine. The word formed in this way can be literally translated as "fuck the beauty."

5. "Uncover it," etc.: *'arri-n'duq,* in Arabic as it is played. 'Atiqa: a girl's name. It is an urban name, thus pretentious and ridiculous in this Berber-speaking, peasant context.

6. Aisha Qandisha: *jinniya* (feminine of *jin,* or djinn). She sometimes appears to those she wishes to attract in her woman's guise. Sometimes, too, she takes the form of an animal. Her sanctuary is located near a spring in the Zerhoun (in the Meknes region). This spring is found behind the sanctuary of Sidi Ali ben Hamdush, patron of the ecstatic brotherhood of the Ḥmadsha.

On Aisha Qandisha (or Kendisha), E. Westermarck, *Pagan Survivals in Mohammedan Civilisation* (London: Macmillan, 1933), 21–23; on "djinn," idem, *Ritual and Belief in Morocco* (London: Macmillan, 1926; repr. New York: University Books, 1968), 1:384f. On the patron of the Ḥmadsha, see V. Crappanzano, *The Hamadsha: A Study in Moroccan Ethnopsychiatry* (Berkeley and Los Angeles: University of California Press, 1973).

7. The girl's first name often changes. These are all Arabic and uncommon names that are incongruous in this context.

8. *Riḥane* (Arabic): "myrtle"; plant used in all sort of ritual activities. It is a holy plant, reputed along with some others to have come down from paradise. The root of the word places it in the same semantic field as *raḥa* (rest and peace).

9. "May God give it back to him!" A formula normally uttered when one has received a gift from someone else.

7. Local Exegesis

1. Educated in the old way and influenced, like this entire generation, by nationalism and ideas of Islamic reform inherited from salafism, which were very popular in Islamic universities under the French protectorate; on this point, see D. F. Eickelman, *Knowledge and Power in Morocco: The Education of a Twentieth-Century Notable* (Princeton, N.J.: Princeton University Press, 1985).

2. *Majus:* religion and beliefs of the magi; Babylonia and the Persian empire before Islamicization. *Jahiliya:* period of ignorance, thus a term used in Muslim tradition to refer to pre-Islamic times. Tradition: in this context, religion.

3. *Ḥorm:* sacred precincts.

4. *Ḥjab:* enclosure. From the Arabic verb *ḥjab* "to hide, remove from view."

5. This refers to a great tribe of Sus, in the south of the Upper Atlas. A small Isuktane tribe is found close to the Ait Mizane, to the northwest; but from all evidence the account is evoking the Sus, considered as the aboriginal tribe and the tribe

of origins. Also, the term denotes a large and powerful confederation of Sus tribes in the Jbel Siroua.

6. This is the version given Doutté by the qa'id Goundafi; on this chief, see R. Montagne, *Les Berbères et le Makhzen* (Paris: Alcan, 1930), 300f. and 326f.; L. Justinard, *Un grand chef berbère; Le caïd Goundafi* (Casablanca, 1951); Paul Pascon, *Le Haouz de Marrakech: Histoire sociale et structures agraires* (Tangiers, 1980), 1:342f.

Here is the account as Doutté gives it: near Moulay Brahim (a great regional saint), two individuals of the Gedmiwa want to abuse two children. The children hide in the *ḥorm* (holy precincts) of the saint, who transforms the aggressors into *bujlud* (Arabic for bilmawin), "fabled beings that the Shilha call *herrma*, i.e., 'were-wolves'; and they immediately go into the forest. One of them dies, but the other is still alive; at night he goes down into the villages and often knocks on the door of a house; he asks for food, and he adds, 'I cannot come during the day because I frighten the children; so I come at night.' If Tayeb assures us that one time he saw a bujlud in a cornfield, he could see directly only the two horns" (E. Doutté, *En tribu* [Paris: Geuthner, 1914], 86).

7. Mohammed Khair-Eddine, *Légende et vie d'Agoun'Chich* (Paris: Editions du Seuil, 1984), 45–47. I cite and discuss this author all the while recognizing that his striking text is not at all concerned—and this is understood—with sociological in-terpretation. Elsewhere the author evokes the masquerade in these terms: "The chil-dren had their own festival: 'Ima'ashars,' the equivalent of the Christian Mardi Gras. Genuine license was permitted them. They resorted to satire to express their discon-tent. The children would take off their usual clothes and deck themselves out in rags. They piled on necklaces made of snailshells and wore goatskin masks. The aim of this travesty was to frighten the girls and the credulous, all those who would see evil spirits appear everywhere in one form or another. Freed for a few days from their Koranic studies, these rascals would organize into rival bands and come into house-hold courtyards. They would make off with chickens and eggs that belonged to old deaf and blind women, but most often they would get themselves a good beating from the plucky scolds. That day the thefts were not punished by the law of the community; the victims took justice into their own hands when they caught the thief in the act. Generally one would avert these petty crimes by offering the youngsters a few bowls of barley or even a fowl. These bands were called 'Itrkiins,' which means Turks, the word of course making a derisive allusion to the misdeeds of the Turks who at the time were colonizing much of the African coast of the Mediterranean. This festival reached its climax with the appearance of Baqshish (the buffoon). Only the adults could see his act. Baqshish did a perfect imitation of the sexual act of the billy goat. With remarkable skill, in the blink of an eye he transformed a flap of his robe into a phallus, roared and noisily tossed off meaningful sounds while drooling. He didn't hesitate to hurl himself on the women who were watching."

This is the festival called "ima'shar," which is celebrated at the time of the 'Ashura, about thirty days after the sacrifice. In many regions like this one, in Taf-raout, the masquerade takes place during the 'Ashura rather than after the feast of the sacrifice. In this case, as in Tiznit, Bilmawn is reduced to one or two people dressed in goatskins who run through the village or town accompanied by a few youths who protect him. The company indulges in a few pranks that accompany an obligatory round of quests.

On Bilmawn and the Ima'shar festival, personal communication by M. A. Lakhsassi (professor at the Faculty of Letters in Rabat), whom I gratefully acknowledge for these valuable details gathered in the course of a lengthy interview that I do not discuss in these pages. The festival at Tiznit merits its own monograph.

8. Theoretical Approaches

1. 'Ashura festivals, celebrated in the beginning of Muḥarram, the first month of the Muslim year, which follows the month of the sacrifice. In rural and urban areas, the rites used to include nocturnal outings where the young women would sing the praises of the deeds of a character who had just died: *Baba 'Ashur.* Meanwhile the boys took part in games and, toward the end, joined in the well-known rhythms of the *ta'rija,* which went on for a good part of the night. Fires were lit, and the young men would jump over them. On the last day a visit to the dead would take place: in some regions the girls would hide a doll *(Baba 'Ashur)* in the tombs, which the boys took delight in unearthing. On the 'Ashura, see E. Laoust, "Noms et cérémonies des feux de joie chez les Berbères du Haut et de l'Anti-Atlas," *Hesperis* 1 (1921): 3–66, 253–316, 387–420.

2. M. Gluckman, *Rituals of Rebellion in South-East Africa* (Manchester: University of Manchester Press, 1956), 5–6; idem, *Custom and Conflict in Africa* (New York: Harper and Row, 1956; 2d ed., 1973), 115; idem, "The Role of the Sexes in Wiko Circumcision Ceremonies," in *Social Structure: Studies Presented to Radcliffe-Brown,* ed. Meyer Fortes (Oxford: Clarendon, 1949), 152–53, 160, 163f.

3. Hilda Kuper, "A Ritual of Kingship Among the Swazi," *Africa* 14 (1944): 232–39, 241–53; idem, *The Swazi: A South African Kingdom* (New York: Holt, Reinhart, and Winston, 1964). Gluckman, *Rituals of Rebellion,* 20f.; on the concept of catharsis taken in the Aristotelian sense of the term, ibid., 20.

4. R. Caillois, *L'homme et le sacré* (Paris: Gallimard, 1939; 2d ed., 1950), 42, 91, 106f., 113, 115, 117.

5. Ibid., 50, 62, 86–87, 91.

6. Ibid., 113–17, 123, 124–26. R. Caillois, *Man, Play, and Games,* trans. Meyer Barash (New York: Free Press, 1961), 131, 139–41.

7. Victor Turner, "Betwixt and Between: The Liminal Period in Rites de Passage," *Proceedings of the American Anthropological Society* (Seattle: University of Washington Press, 1964); repr. in idem, *The Forest of Symbols: Aspects of Ndembu Ritual* (Ithaca, N.Y.: Cornell University Press), chap. 4 and pp. 93–113; idem, *The Ritual Process: Structure and Anti-Structure* (Ithaca, N.Y.: Cornell University Press, 1977), 95–96, 131–32, 167–69; idem, "Liminality and the Performative Genres," in *Rite, Drama, Festival and Spectacle,* ed. J. MacAloon (Philadelphia: ISHI, 1984), 21.

8. T. D. Beidelman, "Swazi Royal Ritual," *Africa* 36 (1966): 373–75, 385, 398, and 401. Hilda Kuper, *An African Aristocracy: Rank among the Swazi* (Oxford: Oxford University Press, 1961), chap. 13, esp. 197–98, 207–8; and idem, *The Swazi:*

A South African Kingdom, 68–72. For a criticism of this symbolic interpretation, which insists on this duality of the character of the monarch in the rite, see Pierre Smith, "Aspects de l'organisation des rites," in *La fonction symbolique: Essais d'anthropologie,* ed. M. Izard and P. Smith (Paris: Gallimard, 1979), 158–59.

9. Notably in the analysis of the myths of Oedipus and Asdiwal, cf. Lévi-Strauss, *Structural Anthropology,* trans. Claire Jacobson and Brooke Grundfest Schoepf (New York: Basic Books, 1963), chap. 11, and *Structural Anthropology 2,* trans. Monique Layton (New York: Basic Books, 1976), chap. 9.

10. J.-P. Vernant, "At Man's Table: Hesiod's Foundation Myth of Sacrifice," in *The Cuisine of Sacrifice among the Greeks,* ed. M. Detienne and J.-P. Vernant, trans. Paula Wissing (Chicago: University of Chicago Press, 1989), esp. 36, 49–51, 69–70, and 73–74; idem, "Sacrifice in Greek Myths: 1 Prometheus," trans. Gerald Honigsblum, in *Mythologies,* ed. Yves Bonnefoy (Chicago: University of Chicago Press, 1991), 1:422–24; M. Detienne, "Culinary Practices and the Spirit of Sacrifice," in Detienne and Vernant, *The Cuisine of Sacrifice,* 6–8 and 13; M. Detienne, *Dionysos mis à mort* (Paris: Gallimard, 1977), 43–44.

Marcel Detienne stresses this notion of context and points out that it is Lévi-Strauss who introduces this new element in his analysis of the myth of Asdiwal (however, for Lévi-Strauss the ethnographic context is limited to pointing out the *levels of meaning* and the *semantic horizon* of the myth). On this notion, cf. M. Detienne, *Dionysos mis à mort,* 19 and 27–29.

11. Clifford Geertz, "Deep Play: Notes on the Balinese Cockfight," in idem, *The Interpretation of Cultures* (New York: Basic Books, 1973), 412–53.

12. Sigmund Freud, *The Interpretation of Dreams,* trans. James Strachey (New York: Basic Books, 1955), chap. 6.

9. Prayer and Preparation of the Victim

1. Orthodox Muslim practice requires this prayer of any Muslim participating in Friday prayers. In other words, he must be a free man, having attained puberty, who has a fixed abode. It is not obligatory for women, prepubescent males, travelers, and slaves.

2. The reverse order was recommended for the sacrifice in Mina on the occasion of the pilgrimage. Cf. A. Bel, "La fête des sacrifices en Berbérie," *Cinquantenaire de la faculté des lettres d'Alger* (Algiers, 1932), 97 and n. 2. On the attributes of the victim, consult the summary made by Sidi Khalil (trans. Perron).

3. Bel, "La fête des sacrifices," 98; also Godefroy Demonbynes, *Le pélerinage à la Mecque,* vol. 1 (1928), cited in A. Bel. Nor should the victim's breath have an unpleasant smell.

4. Sura 37; cf. as well the collections devoted to the "accounts" (*qaṣaṣ*) of the prophets, for example the well-known (including in our villages) al-Tha'labi, cited in chap. 3, n. 5.

5. Muslim tradition has it as Ismail. But views are not unanimous on this point, and some claim it is Isaac.

6. Different then from ordinary ablutions for prayer, which do not involve the whole body, and similar to the complete ablutions following sexual intercourse.

7. It is one of the blessed nights, among which are the 27th of Ramadan, the first of Shawal on the evening before the fast is broken, and the 15th of Sha'bane, the month before Ramadan.

8. It will be noted that these last rites also include closing the principal orifices of the body: ears, mouth, nose, etc. Organs of communications and exchange with the outside, nature, and for certain bodily discharges (excrement, mucus, etc.).

9. *'Umma:* Muslim community in the broad sense. See *Encyclopedia of Islam,* s.v.

10. Custom observed in other religious celebrations and widespread in rural Morocco. Westermarck observed it early in this century: "The Popular Ritual of the Great Feast in Morocco," *Folklore* 22 (1912): 137.

11. Muslim tradition attributes the change in route to the Prophet himself.

12. Said Boulifa, *Textes berbères en dialecte de l'Atlas marocain,* Ecole des lettres d'Alger no. 36 (Paris: Ernest Leroux, 1909), 139–40. *Kohel* (kohl), black powder made from crushed antimony that women put on their eyelids for festivals and celebrations. *Swak:* bark of the root of the walnut tree. Used by women to soothe lips and gums. This product gives a reddish saffron color.

13. On the uses of henna *(Lawsoniá inermis)* see W. Marçais and A. Guiga, *Textes arabes de Takrouna* (Paris: Leroux, 1925), 1:399 and n. 15; for the Marrakech region, Fr. Légey, *Essai de folklore marocain* (Paris: Geuthner, 1926); concerning marriage, the reader may consult the same work, as well as E. Laoust, "Le mariage chez les Berbères du Maroc," *Archives berbères* 1 (1915–16): 44–80. On marriage and its ingredients, Mme de Lens, "Un mariage à Meknès dans la petite bourgeoisie," *Revue du monde musulman* 35 (1917–18): 31–55, and E. Westermarck, *Marriage Ceremonies in Morocco* (London: Macmillan, 1914), esp. chaps. 3–4. Elsewhere this author stresses that henna is a preparation for the feast of the sacrifice: "An important preparation of the feast is the application of *ḥénna* to persons, animals, and dwellings. This colouring matter, produced from the leaves of the *Lawsonia inermis* or Egyptian privet, is considered to contain much *baraka;* hence it is not merely a favourite cosmetic among the women, but it is also frequently used as a means of protection against evil influences. Among all the country people with whose customs I am acquainted, whether Arabs or Berbers, the women paint their hands, and very commonly also their feet, with *ḥénna,* as a rule on the eve of the feast" ("The Popular Ritual of the Great Feast in Morocco," *Folklore* 22 [1912]: 132); on other uses of henna, ibid., 133, 141; on the use and association of henna, kohl, and *swak* on the eve of the feast, p. 134.

14. Some state that the ram sacrificed by Abraham had henna on its forehead and on one of its hooves.

15. From the standpoint of strict Islamic law, a marriage is rendered legitimate only by a document indicating the acceptance of the parties involved and specifying the sum of the dowry deposited by the man. In practice, marriages concluded according to this procedure were the exception until recently, especially in rural areas. Even now, in the Ait Mizane, as in many other rural regions of Morocco (Arabic- or Berber-speaking), marriages are ratified before witnesses—which can replace the written act—and by the feasts and rites that follow.

16. A beautiful woman is a "salty woman." As for the presence of salt in foods, it must be noted that there are many indications that one does not salt food merely for the taste; the recipes for propitiating or conciliating spirits used to ready a newly constructed house for its inhabitants have no salt. The chick peas and other cooked cereals thrown along the walls and at the entrance of the house are not salted. Salt is incompatible with the *masters* (spirits) of the place.

17. Collecting the victim's blood and using it for various purposes, notably divinatory and curative, is widespread in rural Morocco. On these customs as observed early in this century, E. Doutté, *Marrakech* (Paris: Comité du Maroc, 1905), 369; idem, "Figuig: Notes et impressions," excerpt from *Bulletin de la Société de géographie* (Paris, 1903), 198; idem, *Magie et religion dans l'Afrique du Nord,* (Algiers: A. Jourdan, 198), 469–70; Bel, "La fête des sacrifices en Berbérie," 109–10; and, on blood and the gall-bladder, Westermarck, "Popular Ritual," 148–49.

18. I was unable to observe these practices directly. But I received many reports of them in various villages, including the one where I observed the sacrifice, and from many inhabitants of both sexes. The woman makes a round spot of blood in the middle of her forehead. Men and women often dip their bare heels in the blood spilled on the ground to protect them from chapping and cracking in the winter cold.

19. "Customary sacrifice" (*l"ada,* pronounced *la'da*), practiced collectively shortly before plowing. On this sacrifice, see Hassan Rachik, "Les repas sacrificiels: Essai sur le rituel d'un tribu du Haut Atlas," thesis, Faculté de Droit, Casablanca (1986).

20. The blood of victims of a violent death.

21. "In the name of God, God is the most great!" Basic formula used to drive away Satan and all harmful spirits.

22. Marcel Detienne, "Culinary Practices and the Spirit of Sacrifice," in *The Cuisine of Sacrifice Among the Greeks,* ed. M. Detienne and J.-P Vernant, trans. Paula Wissing (Chicago: University of Chicago Press, 1989), 2–3, 4–5, 7–8, 13. On the ideas of Hubert and Mauss, ibid., 15–16.

23. A green plant that leaves a red stain. There is probably also a whole symbolism of colors that I was unable to study systematically on site. Green is associated with peace; it is also the color of Islam and the Prophet. Red enters into many associations with virility, blood, and strength.

24. Men take their shoes off when they enter the threshing floor (which is forbidden to women) and to enter storerooms or silos. Grains of barley, like bread, must be picked up when they are found on the ground, so that they are not stepped on, etc.

25. On the *hajj, Encyclopedia of Islam,* s.v.

26. "Slits the throat" is a convenient expression that needs further explanation. Here the means of slaughter practiced is the *dabh,* which consists, according to Muslim law, in slitting the animal's throat and carotid arteries with a well-honed knife.

10. The Rite and the Myth

1. Walter Burkert, *Homo Necans: The Anthropology of Ancient Greek Sacrificial Ritual and Myth,* trans. Peter Bing (Berkeley and Los Angeles: University of California Press, 1983), chap. 1, esp 73–78. Burkert's book was originally published in German in 1972.

2. Al-Tha'labi, cited in chap. 3, n. 5.

3. On all these points, see al-Tha'labi, 79–95. On the construction of the *ka'ba,* 85–91; on Abraham's dream and what followed, 91–94; the two versions, one involving Abraham and Isaac, the other Abraham and Ismail, 93–94.

Abraham, according to the same tradition, moved Hagar with her son Ismail to the settlement of Mecca and the "Temple" to avoid the quarrels between her and Sarah, who remained with Isaac and the patriarch in Sham. On this account, al-Tha'labi, 71–72. Such is the beginning of the foundation that later Abraham and Ismail will complete by building the "house of God" (the *ka'ba*). On Abraham's sacrifice, Koran, Sura 37; on the establishment of Abraham's descendants near the Temple, and the foundation of Islam, Sura 14; foundation of the Temple, Suras 2 and 22; on the pilgrimage and the sacrifice, Sura 22.

Sham: corresponds to the modern Syria–Palestine, with Jerusalem and Maqam Ibrahim as places of primary importance for Muslims, and later Damascus as the capital of the empire.

4. Koran, Sura 37, and al-Tha'labi, 81–82. According to the Syrian philosopher Sadeq Jalal al-'Azm, Abraham's sacrifice begins with a pseudo-tragedy, not a true one (like the Greek tragedy he compares it with), since in it the characters benefit from a happy ending. On this point, Sadeq Jalal-'Azm, *Critique de la pensée religieuse* (Beirut, 1982), 67–68, 76–78, and 81–82 (in Arabic, *Naqd al-fikr al-dini,* [Beirut: Dar al-tali'a, 1982]).

5. Pointed toward Mecca. It is false to claim, as A. Bel does, that the victim must suffer. He stresses a mistaken "theory" about prolonging the victim's suffering, to back up a "theory" of the victim as a scapegoat that must suffer for a long time before dying in order to show "that it indeed contains the sins with which it has been burdened" (A. Bel, "La fête des sacrifices en Berbérie," *Cinquantenaire de la Faculté des Lettres d'Alger* [Algiers, 1932], 108; see also 105).

6. A large wooden ladle used in the kitchen. Often used in the past in processions to bring rain, where it was dressed like a doll and called *tlghonja.* On this custom, cf. E. Laoust in "Noms et cérémonies des feux de joie chez les Berbères du Haut et de l'Anti-Atlas," *Hesperis* 1 (1921), and esp. *Mots et choses berbères* (Paris: A. Challamel, 1920), 204.

7. On *baraka,* see chap. 1, n. 26.

8. *Jnun:* plural of *jann* (djinns), which I translate here as "harmful spirits," are supernatural invisible beings. Islamic cosmology divides invisible supernatural beings into two categories: angels and djinns. Both are in the service of God. However, while angels are beings of paradise, pure and beneficial, djinns are created from fire and can afflict humans with sickness or other calamities. Popular wisdom has it that djinns, under certain conditions, "strike" humans. One must therefore act with caution to avoid provoking any blows. However, once they start to act, there are ways

to neutralize them. Magic and sorcery can put them to work for men. Local knowledge has it that salt and metal are particularly efficacious protection against the intervention of djinns. On djinns in Morocco, E. Westermarck, *Ritual and Belief in Morocco* (London: Macmillan, 1926, repr. New York: University Books, 1968), vol. 1, chap. 4, and *Pagan Survivals in Mohammedan Civilisation* (London: Macmillan, 1933), chap. 1.

9. Here blood and djinns are constantly associated, as throughout the rest of Morocco. As a result butcher shops and especially slaughterhouses are places especially frequented by djinns and, for this reason, dangerous. Furthermore, the blood of victims who have died by violence is a feared ingredient in sorcery fatal to children. This belief is universal among Moroccan women.

On Sidi Shamharush, besides H. Rachik, "Les repas sacrificiels: Essai sur le rituel d'un tribu du Haut Atlas," thesis, Faculté de Droit, Casablanca (1986), see E. Doutté, *En tribu* (Paris: Geuthner, 1914), 90.

10. Marcel Detienne, *The Gardens of Adonis: Spices in Greek Mythology,* trans. Janet Lloyd (Hassocks, England: Harvester, 1977), 111f., also 82.

11. J.-P. Vernant, in Marcel Detienne, *The Gardens of Adonis,* Introduction, v–vii; and J.-.P Vernant, "At Man's Table: Hesiod's Foundation Myth of Sacrifice," in *The Cuisine of Sacrifice among the Greeks,* ed. M. Detienne and J.-P. Vernant, trans. Paula Wissing (Chicago: University of Chicago Press, 1989), 36. On the three terms marriage/agriculture/boiled dishes and man as eater of perishable portions and the cooked, 17–49, 50–51, 69–70, and 67–71; sacrifice/agriculture/marriage, 73–74. On what goes back to the gods and men with respect to the sacrifice see also M. Detienne, *Dionysos mis à mort* (Paris: Gallimard, 1977), 43–44.

12. Detienne, *The Gardens of Adonis.*

13. E. E. Evans-Pritchard, "The Meaning of Sacrifice among the Nuer," *Journal of the Royal Anthropological Institute* 84 (1954): 28.

14. On the consecration and symbolic identification that it brings about, Evans-Pritchard writes, "I have not, it is true, heard Nuer say that this is what the laying on of hands means to them—it is our interpretation, what it means to us—but I have given reasons elsewhere, in describing Nuer acts of dedication and consecration and in discussing their symbolism and the role of cattle in their religion (Evans-Pritchard, 1953 a, b), for my conclusion that this meaning is *implicit* in their sacrifices" (28, emphasis added). The two articles quoted in this text as Evans-Pritchard 1953 a and b are: "Nuer Spear Symbolism," *Anthropological Quarterly* 26, no. 1 (1953): 1–19, and "The Sacrificial Role of Cattle among the Nuer," *Africa* 23 (1953): 181–98. All these discussions concerning the equivalents and substitutions lineage/spear/bull/victim/man are repeated and convincingly systematized by Evans-Pritchard in *Nuer Religion* (New York: Oxford University Press, 1956; 2d ed. 1974), 239–45ff. and 272. These ideas are summarized in Evans-Pritchard, "The Meaning of Sacrifice," 21.

On the symbolic substitution of the animal for the man in the sacrifice and the critique of Hubert and Mauss's theory of the gift, see Evans-Pritchard, "The Meaning of Sacrifice," 28 and also 25–27; and *Nuer Religion,* 279–81.

15. Evans-Pritchard, "The Meaning of Sacrifice," 25. On the subject of Hubert and Mauss's essay, Evans-Pritchard writes, "There is much of value in this essay, but

it is too abstract. This is partly due to the arguments being based on Brahmanic interpretations of Vedic Sacrifice, not on the living drama of sacrifice but on its rubrics, its stage directions. It is also partly due to treating sacrifice as a mechanical rite and without reference to religious thought and practice as a whole, without regard to what men conceive their nature and the nature of the gods to be. How fatal to compare Hebrew and Hindu sacrifices outside the contexts of these two religions which are so entirely different! Both weaknesses derive from the Durkheimian sociologistic metaphysic." On the distinction between the two types of sacrifice and consequences of the interpretation of sacrifice, see Evans-Pritchard, "The Meaning of Sacrifice," 21, 25, 28, 30f.; idem, *Nuer Religion,* 279–81, 284–85.

16. See this reconstruction in Evans-Pritchard, *Nuer Religion,* and above, n. 14.

17. See for example, Lévi-Strauss, "The Story of Asdiwal," *Structural Anthropology 2,* trans. Monique Layton (New York: Basic Books, 1976), 161f.; cf. as well *Totemism,* trans. Rodney Needham (Boston: Beacon, 1963), 89–91.

18. Lévi-Strauss, *The Savage Mind* (Chicago: University of Chicago Press, 1966), 227; cf. also *Totemism,* 3 and 29.

19. Lévi-Strauss, *The Savage Mind,* 231–32, 233, 236, 238–39.

11. The Masks and Their Forays

1. On this point, see chapter 1.

2. Concerning the association between Roman festival and Bilmawn: most authors seek the origin of the masquerade in various ancient Mediterranean, especially Roman, festivals. On this point, in addition to E. Laoust, "Noms et cérémonies des feux de joie chez les Berbères du Haut et de l'Anti-Atlas," *Hesperis* 1 (1921), and E. Doutté, *Magie et religion en Afrique du nord* (Algiers: A. Jourdan, 1908—see chap. 2, above), the reader should refer to E. Westermarck, *Ritual and Belief in Morocco* (London: Macmillan, 1926; repr. New York: University Books, 1968), 2:153–58; Jean Bayet, *Histoire politique et psychologique de la religion romaine* (Paris: Payot, 1956; 2d ed., 1969), 79. C. Geignebet, *Le carnival* (Paris: Payot, 1979), 19–21, rightly finds the same meaning in ancient rites and games as in those of the modern carnival. His whole book is made up of these comparisons, which we have declined to make here. On the Bouphonia, H. Hubert and M. Mauss, "Essai sur le sens et la fonction du sacrifice," *L'Année sociologique* 2 (1899): 68–69, and esp. 107; and recently, M. Detienne, *The Gardens of Adonis* (Hassocks, England: Harvester, 1977), 54–55.

3. On the computation of time and calendars, see E. Laoust, *Mots et choses berbères* (Paris: A. Challamel, 1920), chap. 6, as well as the other chapters devoted to agricultural labors. On solstice rites, Laoust, "Noms et cérémonies"; Westermarck, *Ritual and Belief,* vol. 2, Muslim calendar, chap. 13, solar calendar, chap. 15; and idem, "Midsummer Customs in Morocco," *Folklore* 16 (1905): 27–47. More recently, Ali Amahane, *Abadou, village des Ghoujdama* (Paris: Geuthner, 1983), chap. 3, and the charts, pp. 101–5.

4. On these battles between specialists on religious knowledge and worship, see P. Bourdieu, "Sur le pouvoir symbolique," *Annales, Economies, Sociétés, Civilisa-*

tions 3 (1977): 405–11; idem, "Genèse et fonction du champ religieux," *Revue française de sociologie* 12 (1971): 299f.; also idem, "Une interprétation de la théorie de la religion selon Max Weber," *Archives européennes de sociologie* 12 (1971): 3–21, and *Le sens pratique* (Paris: Editions de Minuit, 1980), chap. 7.

5. For the adoption of ancient calendars and events by the Christian calendar, see Geignebet, *Le Carnaval:* the adoption of calendars, 27–30, and further on, the assignment of Christian saints to places (probably) previously occupied by other mythological personalities, 63; Saint Anthony, chap. 5; for Saint Paul, etc. It will be noted that all these probable adoptions do not support the ongoing meanings that the author accords the ritual. Also J. Caro Baroja, *Le Carnaval* (Paris: Gallimard, 1979), 71 and 151f.; Peter Brown, *The Cult of the Saints: Its Rise and Function in Christianity* (Chicago: University of Chicago Press, 1981).

6. Westermarck, *Ritual and Belief,* chap. 3, and "The Popular Ritual of the Great Feast," *Folklore* 22 (1912): 178.

7. *Talmqsurt:* from the Arabic *maqsura,* prayer room; also *tamqsurt.*

8. As is the case in Imi-n'Tassaft (see chap. 4), as well as the notion of *afrukh* opposed to that of *'a'azri,* i.e., the newlyweds and bachelors.

9. E. Durkheim, *The Elementary Forms of the Religious Life,* trans. Joseph Ward Swain (London: Allen & Unwin, 1915), 210–15, 217–33; Durkheim comes back to this on 360 and in his conclusion (422). Elsewhere he speaks of a kind of delirium provoked by the rite (347–49, 375).

10. On the word and the origins of the black brotherhoods called Gnawa, see Delafosse, "Relations entre le Maroc et le Soudan à travers les âges," *Hesperis* 4 (1924): 155. On the brotherhood of the Gnawa in Marrakech, D. Jemma, "Les confréries noires et le rituel de la *derdeba* à Marrakech," *Libyca* 19 (1971): 243–50. For other countries of North Africa, E. Dermenghem, "Les confréries noires en Algérie," *Revue africaine* 97 (1953): 314–67, and A. J. N. Tremearne, *The Ban of the Bori: Demons and Demon Dancing in West and North Africa* (London: Heath, Cranton and Ousley, 1914).

12. A Second Founding Drama

1. Once the troupe has been formed, all the great moments of ordinary life are enacted: marriage, repairing the equipment and plowing, harvest, etc. In addition to the invocations and parodies of the Koran, sometimes there is also a "Jews' prayer" *(tazallit n'Udayen).* Here are the principal episodes of this prayer as they were observed by M. Mohamed Mahdi in 1985 in a village of the Imman (a neighboring valley to the Ait Mizane).

The troupe played and repeated the other scenes. Then a man suggests the prayer scene *(tazallit).* The actors, with the woman who has been given in marriage, form a line behind the imam, who is none other than the rabbi. So this is a "Muslim" prayer led by a Jew, and on top of that, the people pray facing west! The presence of a woman amidst the men also represents a serious infringement of the rule.

Care has been taken to place a stick behind the imam so that he may sit on it like a chair. People check to be sure that the stick is "well lodged" and begin with this invocation: "God behind him!" (*Allah urah!* an expression uttered out of context, of course, and which ordinarily means "Let's go, with God's help").

The recitation of the verses that normally accompany the prayer is performed as an unintelligible babble. The imam bows down, followed by the others who hurl themselves in all directions into the disorder. But incited by the rabbi, the group takes up the prayer again. This time one of the Jews, taking advantage of the fact that everyone is bent over, slips behind the imam, sodomizes him (symbolically), and takes off before the faithful can rise. The audience laughs.

But the imam acts as if nothing happened and starts reading from the Koran. The faithful are now seated, and they listen to this recitation of the holy text in a language never before heard. The masks turn their heads from side to side to show their appreciation of the chanting, and one of them takes advantage of that to kiss the girl.

The scene is repeated several times, after which the faithful, as they should, ask the imam questions concerning their religion:

Q: Can a woman pray with the men?

A: Of course she can; it is even necessary [which is contrary to Muslim practice, where mosques have a space reserved for women].

Q: Should she be in front or behind?

A: It's best if she's in front, for if she is next to you you can touch her; then *Abakku* [dialectal Arabic: "to make a hole," lit., the instrument that makes holes] gets up (has an erection), and you lose your ablutions [according to Muslim rule, one must repeat one's ablutions after any emissions considered polluting in a religious sense: semen is one of these].

After these questions and answers, the imam gets up to deliver his sermon in Berber. A piece of cardboard serves as a book, which he deciphers with great difficulty.

"Here . . . is a place where respect is lacking *(lhashma).* . . . Those who find themselves in the presence of their parents would do best to leave. . . . *Because here* we speak only of certain things. . . . *Yes, only of certain things that . . . take place at night.* . . . If a father finds himself in the presence of his son . . . , the son would do well to leave. . . . *No, it's the father who should leave!"* (Emphasis added, to link it with what has already been said on the one hand about night in the myth and the procession, and on the other about the expulsion of the fathers, who must leave the village).

2. Edmund Leach, *Rethinking Anthropology* (London: Athlone, 1961), 131.

3. Ibid., 136.

4. Mikhail Bakhtin, *Rabelais and His World,* trans. Helene Iswolsky (Cambridge: MIT Press, 1968), 7, 88–90. Also Natalie Z. Davis, "The Reasons of Misrule: Youth Groups and Charivaris in Sixteenth-Century France," *Past and Present* 50 (1970): 53–54, 63–64, 73–74; E. Le Roy Ladurie, *Carnival in Romans,* trans. Mary Feeney (New York: Brazilier, 1979), 307–9, where the author adopts Van Gennep's scheme.

5. Le Roy Ladurie, *Carnival in Romans,* 316.

6. Natalie Z. Davis, "Reasons of Misrule," 50–54.

7. Marc Augé, "Quand les signes s'inversent, à propos de quelques rites africains," *Communication* (1978): 28, 57, and esp. 61–62.

8. V. Turner, *The Ritual Process: Structure and Anti-Structure* (Ithaca, N.Y.: Cornell University Press, 1977), 110–11, 132.

9. Ibid., 96–97, 107–8, 127–28; *Revelation and Divination in N'dembu Ritual* (Ithaca, N.Y.: Cornell University Press, 1975), 27–28, 173–74, 177–78, 181–87; ibid., 185.

10. This is the well-known trickster figure. Cf. Paul Radin, *The Trickster: A Study in American Mythology* (New York: Schocken, 1972), esp. 22–40 and 124–41. Cf. as well, in the same work, K. Kerényi's suggestive comparisons with certain figures of Greek mythology (179f.).

11. In Timezguida n'Oumalou, M. Mohamed Mahdi was present at a lively discussion between two "specialists" who were preparing the skins, on the subject of whether one ought to succumb to the pressure of the young people and allow a young bachelor to wear the skins. They finally agreed that a young man wearing the skins is capable of doing "stupid things . . . no matter what . . . to put a married man in the skins brings some assurance that the game would not degenerate." There were also powwows and squabbles between young married men and bachelors. This reflects a tension among members of the same generation divided by marriage into two classes that could also, on occasion, come to conflict.

12. *Moqaddem:* agent of local authority in a village or a group of villages On the organization of the rural administration by the Moroccan state, see Rémy Leveau, *Le Fellah marocain soutien du trône* (Paris: Presses de la Fondation nationale des sciences politiques, 1976, new expanded ed., 1985), 48–49.

Index

Ablutions: in the absence of water, 172n.12; for the feast of sacrifice, 111, 112, 113, 116; before prayers, 177n.2

Abraham: Bilmawn compared to, 149; building of the *ka'ba*, 123, 188n.3; and the feast of sacrifice, 51, 110, 111, 124, 126–29, 163; founding of Mecca, 126, 127, 188n.3

Abstinence, 112, 113

Actors, 93–95.

Adrar, 40, 45

Aguir, 62

Ahwash, 61, 65, 72, 74, 78

A'isha Qandisha, 182n.6

Ait Abdallah, 39

Ait Ali, 39

Ait Mizane: and calendars, 169n.4; cathartic effect of the masquerade for, 100; chief of, 39; clan relations, 38–39; feast of sacrifice celebrated by, 4–5, 49; language of, 4; and Marrakech, 47; marriage customs, 186n.15; masquerade performed by, 5–6; poetic elan of, xi–xii; remoteness of, 47–48; youths' view of the masquerade, 92

Akhnif, 58, 178n.1

Akhummas, 59, 179n.5

Akhurbish. See Takhurbisht

Algeria, 15, 172n.2

Alla'b, 75, 181n.12

Année Sociologique, 16, 25, 26

Arabs, viii

Ardem, 65

Aqabli, 93

'Ashura, 1, 16, 19, 20, 30, 184n.1

Asraf, 85

Assif, 40, 175n.1

Assuqi, 93

Aubin, Eugène, 19, 20, 24

Azzaden, 61, 65, 66, 179n.10

Balinese cockfights, 104–5

Ballush, 81, 146

Baraka, 130, 149, 155

Barley, 116–17; barley porridge, 175n.4; cultivation in Imi-n'Tassaft, 35; for feeding

the sacrificial animal, 114; in the sacrifice, 120–21; sex roles in cultivation of, 37, 122

Ba-Shikh, 17, 18, 172n.7

Beidelman, T. O., 103

Bel, Alfred, 30, 171n.2, 188n.5

Berber carnival. *See* Masquerades

Berbers: Ait Abdallah and Ait Ali, 39; and Arabs in Morocco, viii; ceremonies studied by Laoust, 28–31; Isuktane, 91, 182n.5; marriage customs, 186n.15; original religion of, 9, 19, 25–26, 28, 29; pantheon of, 21; Rehamna, 20; Roman influences on, 30; Sektana, 23; social relations within the village, 41. *See also* Ait Mizane

Biarnay, S., 19, 24

Bile, 130

Bilmawn (Bujlud; Tanugayt): the actors who play, 93–95; and the agricultural cycle, 177; ambiguity of, 165; Bilmawn's Sabbath, 155; correlation with the local chief, 39; costume and character, 58–65, 69; driven into the forest, 43; etymology of the name, 173n.23; in the ima'shar festival, 183n.7; as *jnun,* 90; Koanic schoolmasters' views on, 88–90; Laoust's description of, 21–23; Lupercus compared to, 29; myths of, 91–92, 149–50, 183n.6; name variations, 169n.3; narratives about, 57–66; old men likened to, 46; old men's contribution to, 166; preparation and accession, 67–75; pulling the plow, 76–77, 86; role in the masquerade, 1, 21, 24, 30–31, 58–65, 71–87, 143–56; in sacrifice of the cow scene, 85; in second foundation of civilization, 163; skins obtained for, 55–56; in Timezguida n'Oumalou, 81, 146; transformation of identity of, 143–46, 157–59, 165; as vegetation god, 161; Westermarck on, 30–31; and women, 62, 72, 73, 78, 101, 147, 149, 150, 155; young Ait Mizane's views on, 92

Bilmawn's Sabbath (Bilmawn's churn), 155

Blood, 54, 118–19, 123, 130–31, 189n.9

Bourdieu, Pierre, 169n.6

195